Perspectives on Campus Tensions

PERSPECTIVES ON CAMPUS TENSIONS

PAPERS PREPARED FOR
THE SPECIAL COMMITTEE ON CAMPUS TENSIONS

EDITED BY DAVID C. NICHOLS

KENNETH E. BOULDING · WILLIAM M. BIRENBAUM
MARCUS G. RASKIN · PETER SCHRAG · KENNETH KENISTON
GWENDOLYN PATTON WOODS · EDWARD SCHWARTZ
DAVID A. KEENE · SEYMOUR MARTIN LIPSET · JUDSON JEROME
DOUGLAS F. DOWD · SAMUEL PROCTOR · CLARK KERR
LANDRUM R. BOLLING · STEVEN MULLER · HARRIS WOFFORD, JR.
J. L. ZWINGLE · RALPH D. HETZEL, JR.
MORTON A. RAUH · E. WILLIAM ZIEBARTH

AMERICAN COUNCIL ON EDUCATION · WASHINGTON, D. C.

© 1970 by American Council on Education
One Dupont Circle
Washington, D.C. 20036

Library of Congress Card No. 70-132059
ISBN 0-8268-1363-1
Printed in the United States of America

Contents

FOREWORD

IN THE AFTERMATH of widespread campus turmoil in the spring of 1969, the Board of Directors of the American Council on Education approved the establishment of a Special Committee on Campus Tensions. The Committee, chaired by Sol M. Linowitz, and composed of lay leaders and spokesmen from the main segments of the higher education community, undertook to study campus tensions and to assist institutions in finding remedies.

To provide a background of information and insight, the Committee invited a number of persons to write papers on their views of how to go about reducing campus tensions. Many of those papers appear in this volume.

It will be noted that the authors present a wide range of opinion, although all of them share a desire to find helpful solutions. My hope is that this book will be a useful and timely contribution to discussions about the resolution of the many issues troubling higher education.

Personally, and in behalf of the Council, I thank the authors for their contributions to this volume. I want also to express our gratitude to the officers and directors of the Mary Reynolds Babcock Foundation, who helped to support the work of the Committee.

LOGAN WILSON, *President*
American Council on Education

PREFACE

THE PAPERS in this volume were commissioned late in 1969 by the Special Committee on Campus Tensions. They provide valuable insights about current problems of higher education and, together with institutional case studies, interviews, and other sources of information, were of considerable value as background for the Committee's report, *Campus Tensions: Analysis and Recommendations,* published by the Council in April 1970. The quality of many of the contributed papers clearly merited their separate publication.

The first section of this book deals with the nature of the crisis in higher education while, in succeeding sections, the authors address the discontents of students, faculty, administrators, and trustees. The internal logic of this structure is the same as that of the Committee's report: that each constituency should be heard, in turn, and that individual cases should be received on their own merit. Insofar as it was possible to do so, the Committee consciously avoided making value judgments. The result is a report and companion set of papers that, if widely read and discussed, may help point the way toward reconciliation of students, faculty, administrators, and trustees.

DAVID C. NICHOLS

PART ONE

The New Situation

KENNETH E. BOULDING

Fundamental Considerations

IT IS NOT EASY to say how deep is the crisis in American higher education. Quantitatively, it may not seem very profound. There are disturbances on the campuses, especially the larger campuses, which make the headlines, get photographed, and annoy parents, alumni, and legislators. Once the demonstrators have gone home, however, and the students have cleared out of the buildings, a few administrators may change, a few faculty members may leave, but on the whole things continue much as they were. Classes are held, examinations given, grades posted, degrees awarded, research grants obtained, buildings built, faculties meet and argue, and so on. Certainly for 99 percent of the time things go on in the university much as they always did. Indeed, in spite of a severe worsening in the spring of 1970, the crisis seems to be less severe in the United States than in some other countries, for example, Japan, where major universities have been shut down for months, or in Burma, where higher education has virtually ceased, or in Cuba and China, where the universities are continually being disrupted by the demands of romantic socialist states. There are certainly no signs at the moment in the United States of any massive failure to transmit what might be called the ad-

» » « «

Kenneth E. Boulding is Professor of Economics, University of Colorado, and a Past President of the American Economic Association.

vanced segment of the culture from one generation to the next, which is, after all, the major function of higher education.

Qualitatively, however, the sense of malaise and even alarm is much greater than the statistics of class hours interrupted or buildings occupied would suggest. There is a feeling of the turn of the tide, a sense that a period is coming to an end and that the future may look increasingly different from the past. There is considerable doubt, also, whether the future will be better than the past, and if better, whether it may be even more difficult and challenging. The ancient legitimacies have been challenged and the traditional role structure called into question. Ancient legitimacies are hard to defend when their raison d'être is chiefly their antiquity, for the very attempt to defend them often calls them into greater question. The crisis of universities, therefore, is now as much a pervasive uncertainty and uneasiness about the future as it is any major breakdown in the system itself.

It may be useful, therefore, to look at some projections of various aspects of American society in the next ten to twenty years to see how universities may be affected.

Demographic Structure

A good deal of the current "youth problem" in this country (and elsewhere), and part of the reason for the difficulties of the universities, is the remarkable "bulge" in the birth rate, which began in 1946, extended through the fifties, began to decline in the sixties, and has now largely ended. The crude birth rate in the United States is currently the lowest ever recorded. Table 1 shows, from 1940, the total number of births and the fertility rate, that is, the number of children per thousand women of childbearing age, which is perhaps the more significant birth rate. The first really large cohort, born in 1947, has now graduated from college and is beginning to enter graduate school. The high proportion of young people in the population has made for high rates of unemployment among them (a reflection of age specificity in the labor market), and their great numbers have also, of course, filled the colleges and universities to bursting. The rise in the proportion of young people going to college, coupled with the increase in the proportion of young people in the population, is the major factor that has created a sense of pressure on higher education. If the behavior of rats under conditions of overcrowding is any indication, the sheer overcrowding of the campuses may be causing a considerable part of the unrest.

The end of the bulge, however, may mean that, by the end of the seventies, colleges and universities will face quite a different problem. The children born in 1961, when the decline in fertility began, will be entering college around 1978–79. The early eighties may well see an absolute decline in the number of college students and will certainly see a sharp decline in the rate of enrollment growth. Meanwhile, the output of Ph.D.'s and potential college teachers has been increasing; already the tight labor market in many fields is over and from now on we may run into an increasingly serious problem of unemployment among aspiring college teachers.

TABLE 1: *Fertility and Births in the United States, 1940–68*

Year	Fertility Rate (Births per 1,000 Women of Childbearing Age)	Live Births (in 1,000's)	Year	Fertility Rate (Births per 1,000 Women of Childbearing Age)	Live Births (in 1,000's)
1940	79.9	2,559	1954	118.1	4,078
1941	83.4	2,703	1955	118.5	4,104
1942	91.5	2,989	1956	121.2	4,218
1943	94.3	3,104	1957	122.91	4,308
1944	88.8	2,939	1958	120.2	4,255
1945	85.9	2,858	1959	120.2	4,295
1946	101.9	3,411	1960	118.0	4,258
1947	113.3	3,817	1961	117.2	4,268
1948	107.3	3,637	1962	112.2	4,167
1949	107.1	3,649	1963	108.5	4,098
1950	106.2	3,632	1964	105.0	4,027
1951	111.5	3,823	1965	96.6	3,760
1952	113.9	3,913	1966	91.3	3,606
1953	115.2	3,965	1967	87.6	3,521
			1968	84.8	3,470

Source: U.S. Bureau of the Census.

Relative salaries will probably not rise as fast, and junior colleges and high schools will be able to attract more highly trained faculty, but the mere fact that they are more highly educated does not necessarily mean that they will be better for the job. In any case, as we move toward the eighties, the pressures for expansion of higher education will diminish, and then may be a time to catch our breath, to bring our facilities up to date, and to improve the quality of our education. This opportunity is, however, by no means a foregone conclusion.

The Economics of Higher Education

In this sector of the American society loom some things that look more like a crisis. Education has been rising sharply as a proportion of the gross national product, from 1.8 percent in 1944 to 6.6 percent in 1968. Higher education has risen even faster. The reasons are not too difficult to fathom. We should expect a long rise in the proportion of the economy devoted to education simply because of the growth of human knowledge. The more knowledge there is in the absence of fairly radical technical improvements in the cost of transmitting it, the more resources have to be devoted to transmitting it. A great part of this increase in knowledge, furthermore, is not what might be called "consumption" knowledge, knowledge for pleasure or for its own sake, but knowledge that is intimately bound up with the functioning of the whole society. In a quite literal sense, for instance, if the present corpus of mathematical knowledge were not transmitted from one generation to the next, our whole society would grind to a stop and we would be forced to retreat to much lower levels of living.

There has been no marked change in the productivity of education, that is, knowledge gained per unit of real resources spent. The increase in the expectation of life cuts down a little on the amount of knowledge that has to be transmitted, assuming that knowledge is not lost much before the age of seventy, though not many gains can be expected from this source in the future short of quite unforeseen breakthroughs in the biological sciences. The fact that education is a technologically unprogressive industry—indeed, one might almost describe it as a craft— means that technical progress in other parts of the economy will raise the relative price of education, for educators can expect to share the gains in overall productivity. In terms of current dollars, therefore, we may expect the total amount of the GNP devoted to education to increase continually, both because of the increase in knowledge and because of the rise in the relative price of education.

A system of finance of education, however, which is workable when education, say, is 5 percent of the GNP, runs into severe strains when it is 7 percent, as it is now, and may break down altogether when it becomes 10 percent, as it may be in another generation or less. Education is still financed to a very large extent by what I call the "grants economy," that is, by one-way transfers of "exchangeables." Furthermore, the grants are usually given to institutions rather than to students, although there is a notable exception to this rule in the GI Bill of Rights. The grants economy, however, is an economy in the sense that the total of grants is limited. The willingness of people to make grants or to pay taxes is not indefinite, even though it is somewhat flexible. There has been a remarkable tendency over the last twenty years or so for the total government sector of the economy, which is largely in the grants economy, to run at about 20–22 percent of the total. This may reflect something rather fundamental in the psychology of the American people, and while there is certainly no absolute rule that government cannot go to, say, 25–30 percent, there seem to be strong psychological and political obstacles to increasing the proportion.

Under these circumstances, as education rises as a proportion of the economy, and especially as a proportion of the grants economy, it runs into increasing competition with other claimants, particularly national defense. It is possible to interpret many activities of the past year or so, such as the Proxmire subcommittee of the Joint Economic Committee, the Committee on New Priorities, and even the Vietnam War Moratorium, as in part an expression of crossing a very fundamental watershed in current history which represents the psychological end to the Great Depression. The Great Depression was an enormous and traumatic experience for American society, much more traumatic than any of the twentieth-century wars. The people who were traumatized by it are now mostly fifty and over and are a rapidly declining proportion of the population. A generation has arisen indeed which knew not Joseph, or at least knew not Franklin.

We have had approximately full employment now for over twenty years, and one of the paradoxes of the full-employment economy is that it reintroduces scarcity. As long as we have unemployment, we can expand, let us say, national defense without contracting anything else. Under full employment, a dollar on one thing is a dollar off another, and the sense of competition and conflict among different segments of the economy becomes much more acute.

We have, furthermore, reached another watershed in American history with the virtual disappearance of any reserve of labor in agriculture. Agriculture now contributes less than 5 percent to the gross national product and employs 6–7 percent of the labor force. Not even massive technological improvements in agriculture over the next thirty years, as we have had in the last thirty years, will release many people. The doubling of agricultural productivity would release only 3 percent of the labor force.

When we have a segment of the economy, like education, then, that seems due for almost continuous expansion, the question of where the expansion is to come from in real terms becomes increasingly pressing. Manufacturing is not showing any spectacular increase in productivity, and, in any case, its products seem to have such a high elasticity of demand that increased productivity in manufacturing increases output rather than diminishes labor force. The service trades are notoriously unprogressive technologically—with one or two exceptions—so that the only labor force reserve left in the economy is in national defense. It is not surprising, therefore, that an acute conflict is developing between education and defense, both ideologically and economically, and there seems little doubt that any major expansion of national defense would have a crippling effect on the growth of education. Almost the only other place where substantial expansion in education could come from is household consumption, in the private sector, which has already been sharply reduced as a proportion of the economy over the last forty years, and I suspect we would run into sharp resistances to further reduction.

These considerations raise the question whether some radical changes in the finance of education, and especially of higher education, are in order if the crisis is not to be continually deepened. The general case, first, for subsidizing education, and, in the second place, for making it a public good, is quite strong. If we suppose that education were left entirely to the market, there is good reason to suppose that there would not be enough of it, simply because it would have to be financed by parents, whereas the benefits would be received by the children. Parents have a good deal of altruism for their children, and where a society is without social security and other provisions for old age, the support of children is an important investment for parents. In our society, however, children are expected less and less to support their parents in old age; education then becomes less an investment for the parents, and the children, of course, do not have the resources to invest. Furthermore, if education were turned over entirely to the market, this would tend to perpetuate the existing class structure and stratification of society, for the rich would be able to afford to give their children education, and hence the children of the rich would be rich and the children of the poor would be poor. There is, furthermore, a community function of education in the sense that community is created by people having similar experiences. Thus the great case for public education is precisely that it gives virtually everybody in the society a rather similar experience in the formative years and hence creates that sense of community which is necessary if society is to hold together.

These are weighty considerations, and I am certainly not advocating either the abolition of public education or the abandonment of the subsidization of education. Nevertheless, we do need to take a hard look at how education is being financed and whether it might not be done better. If education is a financial investment for the student, as in a very large number of cases it is, with a fairly high rate of return, there seems no reason why we cannot create financial institutions and financial markets of a kind that would take care of the problem. Something like the so-called Killingsworth plan,[1] for instance, has a great deal to recommend it. According to this scheme, for higher education at any rate, the colleges and universities should charge the full cost of their education, so that essentially they are financed by market sales. Then, we should set up an educational banking system under government sponsorship which would be prepared to lend the student the full cost of his education, if necessary, as a loan to be repaid over the course of his life by a certain proportion or surcharge on his income tax. It is estimated that this surcharge could be as little as 1–2 percent and would be quite bearable. A plan of this sort would mean that those who benefited most financially from

---

[1] Charles C. Killingsworth, testimony to the United States Senate on Employment of Manpower, Sept. 20, 1963. Also, "How to Pay for Higher Education," presidential address to the Economic Society of Michigan, 1967, mimeographed.

their education would contribute the most, which in a sense they do now under progressive taxation. Those who did not benefit financially from their education would not be under any burden about it, for they would not pay so much income tax. The surcharge could easily take the form of a proportion of the total tax, and the surcharge itself could also be progressive.

Educational banks might make little change in the real incidence of the subsidies to education, but they would take education out of the grants economy, which is exhibiting marked inelasticities, would remove it from the implication of being "charity," would recognize it for the real investment it is, and would also permit better accounting and decision making in the education industry itself. Hidden subsidies are a real obstacle to rational decision, and education is full of them. If we were to charge for education at least more in proportion to its costs than we now do, we would see more clearly what the real costs, for instance, of making doctors are, compared with making teachers. Cost analyses might well lead to more rational decision making in these areas.

Furthermore, a system of educational banks would permit the poor to participate fully in the benefits of education. At the moment a great deal of our education subsidy goes to the rich, as we see especially in state universities, which are really scandalous subsidies to the rich. The families of the students who tend to go to the better state universities, for instance, are often in the top 10 percent, certainly in the top 20 percent, of the income distribution; yet they are heavily subsidized.

An educational banking system would put everybody on a more nearly equal footing. It would not preclude, of course, additional subsidies for the children of the poor, and perhaps to the parents of the children of the poor, where the alternative costs of education may easily be greater in terms of the utility of immediate income forgone and in terms also of psychological alienation from a family culture. Subsidies of this kind, however, are easily within the range of the grants economy and would be much more honest and productive than the kind of subsidies we have now.

Some economists, especially in England, have argued for a scheme of this sort for financing students' education should be applied at the high school level, or even lower. What is called the "voucher plan" proposes to give every child a voucher to cover the cost of his education which could be exchanged for the fees of any recognized school.[2] The case against this proposal is that it might introduce too much diversity into education. Nevertheless, the idea of introducing a little competition, especially with the public schools, is quite attractive. The educational banking system for higher education would, of course, act much like the

[2] See E. G. West, *Education and the State: A Study in Political Economy* (New York: Transatlantic Arts, 1965), pp. 206–8.

voucher plan and would put public and private institutions on equal terms. In fact, it could easily eliminate the difference between public and private institutions, except perhaps in the methods of appointing trustees or regents. There is still something to be said for the state university as a symbol of the community of the state. Under an educational banking system, however, state subsidies could be used more for symbolic purposes, such as creating a beautiful campus of which the state might be proud, rather than for the nuts and bolts of education, which states seem increasingly unwilling to provide.

Institutional Governance and Quality

Even if we solve the problem of educational finance, a great many problems remain which revolve around the governance and quality of the educational enterprise. Just as the shoemaker's children are traditionally supposed to have the worst shoes and physicians have been known not to be able to heal themselves, so universities which are research institutions, among other things, do surprisingly little research into the university as an organization. One problem here is the paucity of adequate theory about the university, though there is beginning to be an interest in the subject. Certainly within the last generation economists have spent much more time on the economics of trade unions and corporations than they did on the university; sociologists spent more time on the sociology of the family or of the law than they did on the sociology of the university; political scientists have spent much more time on the politics of governmental bodies than they have on the politics of the university, and so on.

ADMINISTRATION

The governance and organization of universities is an accretion from the past, deriving partly from medieval patterns and partly from the corporate model. The governing principle of the American university indeed has been defined as that of a corporate oligarchy tempered by an active labor market, by contrast, shall we say, with the producers' cooperatives of the Oxford and Cambridge colleges.

The governing bodies have been either self-perpetuating boards; boards appointed by outside agencies, such as the state governor or a church; in some states, boards of regents elected by the people of the state; and in rarer cases, boards that have alumni members or even student members. The governing boards appoint the president and usually have some sort of veto power—rarely exercised—on other appointments.

The faculty has a curious quasi-independent status with a great deal of departmental autonomy. Appointments, promotions, and firings are generally initiated by departments. Tenure and the watchful eye of the

American Association of University Professors increase this faculty independence. The main power of the administration is exercised through control over all budgets and veto over novelties. The administration, however, has very little power over the actual conduct of the faculty or the promotion of novelties. In this respect, universities are, of course, not unique; almost all large organizations tend to develop a structure in which novelties originate somewhere below the middle of the administrative hierarchy, and the further up the hierarchy one goes, the more the role becomes that of adjudication and veto rather than that of initiation. I cannot refrain from quoting a little poem I once wrote:

> In every giant corporation
> Are channels of communication,
> Along which lines, from foot to crown,
> Ideas flow up, and vetoes down.[3]

The university corporation is no exception to this rule.

STUDENTS

The most ambiguous role is that of the student, and it is at this point that most of the uproar has been generated in the last few years. The problem here is whether the student is a customer or whether he is a member of the community. The difficulty is that he has characteristics of both roles. He does help to pay the bills and consume the product, although insofar as he is subsidized and especially insofar as the institution as such is subsidized, the role of the student as customer is thereby diminished. Yet the relation of the student to the university is much more intimate than that of a customer to a department store. He lives on the premises, the university involves him in a major portion of his life: it is his employer, his country club, his landlord, his restaurant, his church, his judge, and even his enemy in guerilla warfare.

In regard to the relation of the student to the university, we find movements in divergent directions. In loco parentis has become extremely unpopular and seems to be in process of being abandoned. We no longer pretend that the university is one big happy family and that the students are children. Students have increasingly insisted on the right to their private lives, as witnessed by the growing unpopularity of dormitories, the tendency for students to move into apartments where they are not subject to regulation, and the general assumption that by the time a student comes to the university he is an adult and no longer needs parental supervision is increasing in popularity. The abandonment of in loco parentis indeed seems to be satisfactory to everybody: the university gets out from under a troublesome and disagreeable responsibility,

---

[3] K. E. Boulding, "The Brandywine River Anthology," *Michigan Business Review*, March 1958, p. 7.

and the student achieves an adult freedom. There is not much evidence that he abuses freedom more than older adults. In loco parentis in a sense assumes that there is a great moral improvement with age, an assumption for which the evidence is at least skimpy.

The university may be abandoning the notion that it is a family, but it cannot quite escape the fact that it is a community and that students are in some sense part of it. Except during vacations the students are around much more than customers are around in department stores. The contrast, indeed, between the beautiful churchyard peace which settles on a campus during a vacation and the sweaty turbulence of terms suggests that students by their very overwhelming physical presence involve the university in problems of community in which the students themselves are involved. Community, however, means polity, and a good many of the upheavals which we have had in the last few years are a reflection that students have been part of the community but not part of the polity of the university. Student government has been a puppet state, with all the frustrations that involves, and students have quite rightly felt that they were in some sense disfranchised members of the community. If they are customers, of course, they do not have to be enfranchised; if they don't like it at one place, they can simply go to another one, and competition will modify the rigors of authoritarian rule, as it does indeed in the case of the faculty labor market. A nice letter from another dean is more politically effective than any amount of constitutional power. There is, of course, something like a market in students, and students do shop around. Universities, however, tend to penalize this practice and there are quite strong pressures on students to stay with one institution.

Student unrest at their powerlessness within university polity has been compounded, of course, by the fact that students are young people, and in general, young people in society are disfranchised and pushed around. The draft is a particularly notorious example of the powerlessness of youth in the society, which is largely run by people over fifty. The draft is a system of taxation in kind, grossly regressive, and disobeys virtually all of Adam Smith's canons of taxation, and bears particularly heavily on the young. The draft has certainly increased the student sense of disfranchisement, even though the student has been largely exempt from it. It has made him feel, however, that he is forced to go to college and to stay in college for fear of being drafted, and this creates a prisonlike community of the coerced.

The educational banks system would make the student much more a customer and hence would relieve some of the pressure that he now feels to become a citizen of the university community. It would not and should not relieve all this pressure, for in some sense the student is a citizen of the university community and should be recognized as such.

Nevertheless, he is a citizen with an ambiguous status. The history of consumer cooperation suggests that customers may be citizens of an organization, but that the relationship is not easy. Even in the case of consumer cooperation, the customers tend to remain customers and exercise a rather nominal governance over the organization.

Similarly, with students, their most effective governance is probably through their effect on the reputation of the institution and their capacity to quit and go somewhere else—invisible governance, but governance nonetheless. The usual case made against organizing a university polity in which students become active citizens and exercise real power is that students are not around long enough and hence they cannot take real responsibility for the continuing welfare of an immortal institution. The way faculties gad about these days, it is not wholly clear that faculties are around very much more than students. Still a real problem remains: every institution tends to be governed by its core of committed personnel, that is, people whose whole life patterns are bound up with the success and continuance of the institution.

FACULTY

It may be that a major predicament of the university is that it doesn't have such a core. The faculty tend to be committed to their own professions, not surprisingly, because the life career of a faculty member depends much more on the judgment of his professional peers than it does on the judgment of his superiors in the university hierarchy. Naturally enough, then, departments tend to be largely autonomous, and universities consist really of federations of quasi-autonomous departments and research institutes. We rarely find, of course, a whole department quitting an institution to go to another one. Occasionally, however, a closely knit research group within a department or even within a research institute develops enough independence to go from one institution to another, or even from government to the universities.

The case for faculty and departmental independence is, of course, that the only judges of professional quality are people in the same profession. There is enough truth here to make the status of the faculty member as an employee almost as ambiguous as that of the student as a customer. An employee is hired to do something. In a very real sense, a faculty member is hired to *be* something and to "do his thing," this is, to do whatever is consistent with the role as it is visualized by himself, usually with some sort of approval of his colleagues and professional equals. This does mean, however, that the university cannot be organized like a firm as a productive organization of employees. The wise administrator is usually resigned to this distressing fact and does not attempt any startling educational innovations. Innovating administrators indeed, like Robert Maynard Hutchins at Chicago, usually come to grief on the rocks of faculty independence and professionalism and trustee and alumni suspicions of anything that looks much out of the ordinary.

This profound contrast between the firm and the university—the firm is an organization for producing something; the university is an organization for being something—is also exhibited in the longstanding problem of the relation of teaching to research. Everybody recognizes and laments that research and publication are much better rewarded than good teaching, despite recognition that teaching is the prime function of the faculty of the institution. The reasons lie partly in visibility. When a man comes up for promotion with a very impressive list of publications, and another man comes up with no publications but a letter from his department chairman saying that he is a wonderful teacher, the sheer problem of information becomes acute. Teaching is regarded partly as a craft and partly not even a craft, but an art—a skill almost inborn—and is hard to reward partly because its effectiveness is hard to measure.

I have sometimes thought, but I confess not very seriously, that we might solve the problem of reward for good teachers by reorganizing the pay system for faculty members. They might be hired on a modest retainer basis for committee work and general overhead. Then if a man wants to teach, he should apply for a "teaching grant," these grants, of course, being given to the individual from the general teaching fund. Even if this system were not used generally, it might be used for special teaching experiments.

The fundamental handicap here in undertaking to revise the rewards for teaching is the absence of any clear theoretical model of the nature of human learning. We know little about its physiology and we know still less about the essential variables of the process. The results of most educational experimentation are disappointing and suggest that the "Hawthorne effect" is common: that is, the student is stimulated by the mere knowledge that he is being experimented on, and none of the variables currently being looked at makes much difference. Programed instruction has made some gains, but is most suitable for material that is fairly close to rote learning. The crucial problem of what determines the motivation of the student is still quite unsolved.

Legitimacy and Power

There may be considerable disagreement on the depth of the crisis of universities. Clearly, however, it is part of the general malaise of our total society. The sense of malaise is widespread and it is in some ways paradoxical. We have had two decades of almost unprecedented prosperity and continued economic growth; poverty is diminishing rapidly simply by the sheer growth of the economy, for we have not changed the distribution of income very much. Yet there is a real crisis of legitimacy, especially among the young, and a loss of faith in many of the traditional institutions. Part of the blame can be placed on the foreign policy of the last generation with its, what I have called elsewhere, "mantle of Elijah complex"—the belief that we inherited the mantle of the British Empire and we have made a Pax Americana. This conception, combined with our uneasiness about communism and about the Soviet Union as a potentially expansive force, has pushed the defense budget up to 9 percent of the total economy and has perpetuated the draft. And the latter institution has probably done more to undermine the legitimacy of the nation state than anything anybody's enemies could think up.

Our governing elite, and especially our governing intellectuals, have failed to understand the fundamental principle that legitimacy is more important than power. And the pursuit of power by means which many people regard as essentially immoral has undermined the legitimacy of the users of the power. Part of the student revolt is a revolt not so much against the university as against the whole Establishment. If some of this revolt exhibits a lack of understanding and immaturity, we should hardly be surprised at that. Actually it is more the serious-mindedness of this generation of young people which has frightened the adults. Panty raids and football riots are all right; they do not threaten any legitimacies and they can be encapsulated under the caption "Boys will be boys." Student activism, which has some of the qualities of a panty raid, also has this profound overtone of seriousness. This is frightening, for there is no greater threat to any establishment than a challenge to its legitimacy.

Part of our difficulty, both in universities and in the larger society, is a failure to recognize and distinguish between two very different types of patterns of social dynamics. A certain amount of protest and challenge is directed toward what I have been calling the "integrative system." The protesters are saying, in effect, "This is the way we see it; don't you agree?" The appeal is to persuasion, to the sense of community, to the need of the powerful to feel that they themselves are legitimate and are doing a good job. A certain amount of activism, however, is couched as threat: "If you do not do something that we like, we will do something that you won't like." Internally, we may now be reaping the returns of having emphasized the threat system in our international relationships almost to the exclusion of any other. The sheer principle of cognitive dissonance comes into play, and what is sauce for the foreign goose also becomes sauce for the domestic gander. We may be paying a very high price for the unrealistic realism of those who framed our foreign policy.

The universities are particularly ill-equipped to deal with situations where the threat system has been suddenly invoked. On the whole, in universities it has been muted though, of course, it always exists. The escalation of threats on the part of any party may result in initial victories for it and confusion on the part of the unprepared threatened parties, such as university administrations.

Threat, however, always produces counterthreat, as universities are beginning to learn fairly rapidly. One of the problems of the university is that it has very little in the way of "graduated deterrence." Where the essential realities of the social system are misunderstood, a rise in deterrence could be as disastrous in universities as it has been in Vietnam. A real problem may be created, however, when, in the disciplining of students, there is really no intermediate sanction between the rap-on-the-knuckles reprimand and the blockbuster of suspension or expulsion. I recall an institution at Oxford, called "caution money," which the student had to pay at the beginning of his residence and which was returned to him at the end if he had done no damage to property, but which was used by the college to pay the cost of any such damages. I am not suggesting such a solution for American universities, inasmuch as monetary penalties inevitably bear unjustly upon the poor, who are least able to pay them. As an alternative, I have sometimes thought the university might set up a meditation chamber for unruly and disruptive students where they could continue their studies for a period of uninterrupted, though not too uncomfortable, quiet. The Japanese experience suggests that the traditional university is almost defenseless against the onslaughts of genuinely disruptive minorities. I confess that recent disturbances have made me look on Gothic architecture in a somewhat new light. I was at Union Theological Seminary giving some lectures at the time of the first Columbia disturbances and the fortresslike quality of that architecture suddenly took on rather a new meaning.

The highest cost of disturbances, however, is the destruction of trust. If the university becomes a fortress, something very precious has been lost. Disturbances are a profound challenge to the Establishment because they demand an awareness of, and a degree of discrimination among, different types of social phenomena, phenomena to which university administrators and faculty may come ill-prepared by experience and training. To be sensitive to real grievances and to integrative protest, and at the same time to be prepared, in case of threats, to take countermeasures that will not destroy more than would the original threat—all this requires wisdom and perception perhaps beyond what it is reasonable to expect. Nevertheless, if administrators can hold firmly in mind that the outcome of the threat depends more on the cool of the threatened party than on the passions of the threatener, and if they keep in mind also that the dynamics of legitimacy is the key to all these problems, then at least we can get a sense that we are not at the end of our problem-solving resources.

Proposal for a New Function

Perhaps the most important practical suggestion is that we give serious study to the university as an object of research into social systems. If schools of education had had the prestige and support attained by schools of agriculture, medicine, law, and engineering, such study would have been initiated long ago. We need an interdisciplinary profession of studies of higher education. Small efforts have been made in three or four universities, but we need a major effort during the next generation toward developing both an adequate theory of human learning and of the university as a social system and toward developing a much better system of data collection than we now have. There are few intellectual operations to which I would give a higher priority.

We might then be able to vizualize teaching as consisting in part of a research program in student learning. We might be able to integrate the testing and teaching operations and see testing as an integral part of the learning process. We might set up an organization apparatus through which faculty members would continually improve themselves, more effective than the haphazard or routine granting of sabbaticals. We might integrate community service with teaching and make the university a center for a large social and political learning process to supplement the political system and make it more effective as a problem-solver. Or we might decide that all or some of these things would not work, and that what we are doing now is just fine.

What is certain is that the university as an institution has unused potential, and that it should itself be a major instrument in realizing that potential. The only real source of rational optimism in this world is the reflection that the capacity of the human nervous system is very far from exhausted. The progressive realization of that capacity is the greatest task of the university.

WILLIAM M. BIRENBAUM

Planning
Qualitative Disruption

UNREST AMONG OUR YOUTH and especially on our campuses is a direct function of two unusual sources of the tension that has developed in American society and in its universities.

In the management and direction of American life, in all of its main parts—in industry, government, religion, the local community, education—the distance has grown between what we say and what we do. The quality of conduct is the issue here. And inasmuch as conduct presumes, first, the possession and, then, the exercise of power, the quality of political life is the ultimate issue.

The university is meant to be a community based on a relationship between people and knowledge. But because of the ways universities are organized and directed, many of them have deteriorated as working or workable communities. Vietnam, as a principal source of one of the deepest tensions in the larger society, permeates everything. But Vietnam, as either an abstraction or a symbol, is quickly translated on the campus into a large number of daily, operational human relationships illustrative of the critical gap between American preachments and practices.

Campus life, therefore, becomes a living critical commentary on the

» » « «

William M. Birenbaum is President, Staten Island Community College, and former Vice-President and Provost of the Brooklyn Center of Long Island University. He is author of Overlive: Power, Poverty and the University.

quality of national life, especially on the quality of national political life. Unless the unrest is understood this way, prescriptions for coming to grips with it may, in fact, aggravate the problem rather than contribute to its solution.

Thinking and Acting

The university's special claim for a growing portion of the nation's treasure and in behalf of a unique kind of autonomy (freedom) is based upon its assertion that it, and it primarily, is specially organized to convey the knowledge of our civilization and to create new knowledge in behalf of the progress of our society.

Our nation is the most mature in its dependence upon the use of knowledge in sustaining industry, the military, the conduct of government, and almost everything else. Access to and possession of varying kinds of knowledge are central to economic survival in the United States. Our nation is also among the most mature in the development of its aspirations for equality and freedom among its people. This fact links access to, and the possession of, knowledge to effective political participation in American life. Successful conduct in almost every aspect of American life especially depends upon the citizen's access to and possession of varying kinds of knowledge. Knowledge is tied in an imperative new way to conduct. Thus, when one now says that Knowledge is Power, he is saying something which has a unique operational significance.

Given the university's traditional claims and pretensions, the significance of knowledge casts academic operations in a different perspective. Academic operations will especially be looked at in a different light by those for whom this society has traditionally planned a nonparticipatory role—by middle-class white youth who arrive at young adulthood having never been empowered to make important decisions and thus having virtually no understanding of what it means to be responsible for conduct pursuant to making decisions; by black youth who have been raised to young adulthood in homes, on streets, in neighborhoods and communities which are and have been, in American terms, powerless environments.

Recognized are the present state of our knowledge in key fields, what must be done to acquire and master that knowledge, and the conditions required for mastery of the successful use of that knowledge. But dangerous gaps have opened between these elements and the medieval and archaic ways most of our academic institutions are structured and operate with regard to getting access to the knowledge, mastering it, and applying it. Most of our academic institutions continue to maintain walls between themselves and the environments upon which their existence depends, between systems for the mastery of thought processes and arenas for the expression of thought pursuant to the processes. Most continue to deny the relationship educationally between thinking and conduct pursuant to thought.

The persistence of these academic attitudes results inevitably in an escalation of the causes of campus unrest.

These attitudes lead us directly into volatile, new hypocritical situations. For example, on some of the most prestigious campuses which have been disrupted, where the quality of the faculties and the programs offered in political science are the most distinguished nationally and even internationally, the most inept and even corrupt self-government among the students and the faculties has been exposed. While the students on such campuses have earned their As in the superior curricula devoted to the art of government, they have demonstrated an F ability for governing themselves on their campuses. And although their faculty members travel to Washington to give advice, they turn out to be ineffective as advice-givers or as participants in their own campus communities at the moments of governmental crisis there.

Again, for example, I believe that the majority of those teaching in the field of sociology, and especially urban sociology, in the metropolitan New York City region, have had only the most casual and mediocre experience with regard to the life dynamics of Harlem and Bedford-Stuyvesant. Most of them, by the nature of the system which produced them as professionals, are white and detached from the realities they purport to teach. I find a surprising number of them who do not even have a visual impression of these communities: they've never been there. Yet, it is these teacher-authority figures who stand in front of the increasing number of black and Puerto Rican students entering their classrooms—students who travel every day from Harlem and Bedford-Stuyvesant—to tell them how, academically, it is. One of my students, a graduate of the Harlem Prep Academy, told me after his first eight weeks on my campus that he had been taught at the academy that college success would depend most upon learning how to listen. "I have been on your campus eight weeks," he said, "and above all else, I have listened. I have learned something you ought to know. Your faculty around here has never learned to listen."

Who are the teachers and who are the taught? The clear answers we have brought to this question are no longer clear. Will the real campus please stand up? What stands up now is often shockingly surprising to those in charge. At Berkeley and Columbia, at City College and Harvard, the most disturbing initial action was at the gates in the walls. Naturally.

Once the action shifts, if it ever meaningfully does, to the campus legislative and conference rooms, where the redistribution of decision-making power is negotiated, where the new content of the curricula is decided, where a somewhat different view of the humans involved is defined, where the meaning of *campus* is reconsidered, the main issue will be: Who shall possess the key to the gate, and on what terms; and what shall be the future of the walls, of the architecture and the plan of the future learning community?

Law and Order; Due Process

Law embodies a practical version of what the community to which it pertains accepts as being just. Due process refers to the ways that the community's version of justice may be administered. A community's "order" at any particular time will reflect the popular understanding of what is just—a popular sense of jurisprudence. An orderly community is one in which either the people think their laws are just, or the people are kept powerless through successful tyranny. A disorderly community is one in which there is a breakdown between the meaning of the law and the popular understanding or acceptance of it.

Education, in essence, if it succeeds, is a disruptive process. It is not simply a case of training people to play basketball well according to the NCAA rules as administered by NCAA approved referees. Education, when it succeeds, raises fundamental questions about the validity of the NCAA conception of the game, about how referees are authorized, and about how they should perform. By its nature, education raises these questions even while the game is being played. Education may even raise the question of whether the coaches, who have a vested interest in the way the game is played, should dominate the NCAA legislative processes.

On the campuses the trouble with the academic law has been two-part: (*a*) its obsession with the projection and defense of ancient elitist versions of academic justice, and (*b*) its failure to delineate and embody processes, now overdue, for change.

Academic law has gotten terribly out-of-tune with popular notions of what is just. These notions are being reshaped in the larger society mainly as a result of the powerful new connections between economic survival and political participation, on the one hand, and fair access to, and effective possession of, knowledge. Academic freedom—a concept which traditionally assumed that freedom conditions in the larger society were qualitatively inferior to those required inside the academic walls—must be reexamined now under conditions where the freedom enjoyed in significant areas of American life is qualitatively superior to that prevailing inside the campus walls. This situation can lead to serious misunderstandings on the part of lay, political authorities when they think about law, order, and due process with regard to the academic scene. The layman may be thinking—as he legislates, makes political speeches, or administers the laws of the land—of the traditional American notions of law and order and due process; but on the campuses law, order, and due process often follow lines sharply departing from the American traditions.

Faculty democracy is usually described as the keystone for the administration of academic freedom on the campus. But faculty democracy, where it exists at all on our campuses, involves something less than a third of those who teach our students on a full-time basis. The right to vote on the salient curricular, personnel, and budgetary matters is usually reserved for those who possess tenure. This means that the residency requirement for the franchise in our faculty "democracies" is anywhere from five to ten times longer than we require for those who may vote for the President of the nation. The young faculty are generally precluded from the most important processes for programmatic or personnel change on the campus. And by the time they qualify within the present terms, they have often become vassals of departmental disciplinary systems for promotion, either incapable or fearful of performing the important acts for revision or reform. Those members of our faculties closest in age and in temperament and understanding to those to be taught are most effectively cut off from decision-making power within the academic community.

Further, the breakdown of the processes for curricular change and revision in the university can be understood only in terms of what must be decided and who has the power to decide. What must be decided is dominated by a version of education which assumes, in a way designed to create despair, a surplus of knowledge and a shortage of time. Six thousand years of recorded human history must somehow be packaged within the boxes of the prevailing credit hour system, the present nine- or ten-month conception of the academic year, the existing notions of appropriate teaching loads, and the current conception of the right balance between teaching and research.

Curriculum development has always been and always will be a sophisticated art of selection. But under the existing circumstances—given prevailing academic prejudices about the people who want to learn, how people learn, about what should be excluded, and how decisions should be made in academe—the art is almost impossible to practice. The key issues now are: Within what frameworks of value should the selections be made; and who should participate in the power to interpret and select? These issues are put in perfect focus by the current efforts of essentially senior, white faculties, operating through conventional academic channels, to devise black study programs, while maintaining that the distortions in existing curricula are not the result of their own scholarly abuses of academic freedom.

Of course professional qualification and experience are critical in the practice of the art. But unfortunately, professional self-interest—the maintenance of professional status and power—is involved; and the interests of the consumers, who often represent uniquely different fields of experience and qualification, are excluded. The younger adults (faculty and students), who are the main sources of the unrest, are excluded. The exclusion of those who are the most potential generators of unrest is a powerful and sure way to insure the intensification of the causes of unrest. The failure to provide for the effective expression of their views will naturally lead them to challenge more intensely the expression of self-interest by those now empowered to decide.

The maturation of professional self-interest in American higher education, and the pursuit of it by those in charge, leads to serious distortions of reason and justice in academic law and order, and of the capacity of academic managers to reach wise and just decisions. Indeed, the academic managers, almost willingly, have become a part of the process of distortion. They are the monopolists of the vital data upon which so much of the administration of campus justice depends and are the partners of the governing boards of the academic corporations—who, because of ignorance, remoteness, or intention, sustain and promote the distortion.

Nothing illustrates the distortion more incisively than the national tendencies in higher education regarding the relationships among faculty salaries, teaching loads, class sizes, who teaches what, and the deployment of the physical resources throughout our colleges and universities. Generally, what has happened and continues to happen is: faculty salaries are going up, and teaching loads are going down, at rates faster than the expansion of overall institutional budgets (or, on a national scale, than the rate of increase of the proportion of the national treasure devoted to higher education).

This imbalance in growth rates means that as salaries increase, and contact teaching hours decrease (from fifteen per week to twelve and nine in the two-year colleges and to nine and six or less in the senior colleges and graduate and professional schools), class sizes have necessarily increased. As junior faculty are usually assigned the least desirable teaching loads, and as the lower years of both undergraduate and graduate teaching are considered, according to prevailing prejudices, the least desirable, the largest class sizes are usually scheduled for those levels and are assigned to the least experienced teachers. These are, of course, the critical ports-of-entry for the new student clientele—for the large number of minority group youth and others getting into the system for the first time, most from faltering secondary systems which ill-prepare them for the initial collegiate academic discipline. Those getting in at a point when their needs are the greatest receive, in many ways, the least from the institutions admitting them.

The reduced teaching loads are developing into a national pattern of three- or even two-day work weeks on the campus. And in the urban areas beset by major transportation problems, the three-day weeks are increasingly scheduled, especially for senior faculty, between the hours of ten in the morning and three or four in the afternoon.

Of course, this pattern seriously distorts the use occupancy of physical facilities, creating peak periods of congestion in the assignment of classroom and laboratory facilities, and other periods of underutilization. If this situation were corrected, and if evening hours, Saturdays, and summer periods were brought into full utilization, our nation would probably confront an immediate oversupply of higher educational physical facilities, notwithstanding the horrendous and expensive waste built into much of the present academic plant.

An even more serious consequence of this situation is its subversion of remaining opportunities to develop a sense of community among those who teach and those who are taught. The system puts all personnel in fast motion and at greater and greater distances from each other. Within the framework of complex and harried schedules and larger and larger classes, the people on the campus pass each other like ships on a foggy day—tentatively, remotely, suspiciously, and with horns blowing louder and louder. The credit-course system for packaging the knowledge emerges as the one sure, computerized beacon breaking through the fog. It tells everyone exactly where to go *unless* the destinations sought are the ones that bear most on the popular sense of justice— the desire for self-government, self-control, and self-identity or common political causes.

This pattern of pursuing self-interest finds a part of its justification in the performance of the other functions of the mature academic professional. But there is evidence that less than 15 percent of the full-time faculty ever publishes anything, good or bad; and there is virtually no evidence bearing on the quality of most of the academic research produced, whether it is qualitatively better or worse than most of the so-called research produced through the Ph.D. thesis machinery.

To these aspects of campus order, academic law, and due process, must be added the more conventional complaints about the conditions that govern student life: the invasion of, and disrespect for, their private affairs; and the artificial rigging of their campus civitas. Finally, the disconnections between the entirety of the campus and the corporate and legal fictions ultimately responsible for it in the eyes of the state complete the picture. It is a picture that encourages some students to occupy buildings as a base of power for a do-business conversation with presidents, deans, and trustees they have never met. It is a picture that encourages the majority either to drop out of school in fact or to drop out of everything going on there except the credit-course game.

It is a picture that leads the young to misunderstand what the older mean when they lecture about law and order and due process. It is a picture that casts a hypnotic and paralyzing spell upon all who look at it at a moment of truth, great pressure, crisis. At such moments, faculties, student bodies, and administrators are either appalled, disarmed, and incompetent, *or* they are stampeded into an admission of the breakdown of their own laws, their own processes, the order for which they have stood. Unhappily, when the injunctions are sought and ordered or when the police are called and arrive, the public power is applied to enforce what appears to many young Americans to be unjust law, tyrannical order, and processes that no American could honestly defend or accept as due.

Cities and Segregations

At this stage of our history more and more young Americans are growing up in cities and suburbs and are going to urban colleges. The majority will choose to work and live in great metropolitan centers. The majority aspire to life styles these centers can best accommodate, life styles which require an urban mentality to implement.

American youth, white and black, now know more by the age of eighteen as a result of life experience in the technological environment than most of our schools give them credit for. Most schools, designed in the image of the monastic enclave, champion a stereotype of middle-class American culture and morality inside their walls. But most middle-class white youth have penetrated the realities of the practice of this culture and morality where they come from—at home. And for most black and Spanish-speaking youth, what is championed is either utterly alien or, for many reasons, unacceptable or irrelevant. (For most blacks, the college campus is their first sustained community exposure to white society. Consequently, in their eyes the distance between preachments and practices appears in bold and exaggerated relief.)

Seventeen or eighteen is the demarcation line (drawn long ago in a different era) between the lower and the higher educational monopolies. The line is meant to separate the boys from the almost-men (who can be drafted at nineteen). This line no longer corresponds to experience quotients of the urban-oriented clientele.

The senior year of our high schools is a wasteland dominated, for the college-bound, by the importance of preparing for the final College Entrance Board Examinations. The first semester is filled with the anxieties of applying for college and taking the final tests; the second semester literally counts for nothing—given a system that encourages counting things. The freshman college year is devastated by compromises resulting from the senior system's view of prestige and status and by the increasingly remedial content of what is offered. What we have here is a debilitated two-year span arching over a contrived and unrealistic threshold. We have done almost everything we can to ensure the upset of those involved.

The traditional wall separating the campus from the community is inevitably a barricade in the modern urban setting. Most urban students commute from the realities of where they live to the other "community" where they are supposed to learn. The meaning of the ghetto, the war, the urban economic turmoil, and all the rest cannot automatically be turned off and on twice a day when the line between the campus and the world is crossed. The continued attempt to compel students to turn off reality this way succeeds only in turning the students off.

The university in the city cannot possibly sustain its pretensions as a monopolist of the best teaching and learning talents and resources. In the arts, in industry, in government, and in a variety of technical institutions are configurations of talent and resource superior to what any urban university can mobilize on a full-time basis—by the ranks, with tenure. The university's insistence upon tradition and its deep prejudice against the learning arenas where powerful people in our society actually make decisions are dangerous barriers to the provision of the best learning opportunities our urban society can now provide. Insofar as the young and the lay public increasingly understand this, present academic prejudice and practice will magnify discontent and resistance.

Our campuses have been planned to segregate the younger from the older adults, the technologies from the liberal arts, the academic from the other relevant learning talents and resources, the black from the white, and the learning community itself from the city environment upon which it depends.

Planned Unequal Opportunities

The criteria used to keep some people out of higher education (the so-called admissions standards) have had the cumulative effect of projecting class (and thus race) differences into higher education.

In order to accommodate the new classes forcing their way in, institutions and campuses have been differentiated according to stereotypes of who can be taught what, when, and how. An elitist view of class and race has been built into quality distinctions between two- and four-year campuses and also through the physical-geographic segregation of students within single campuses.

In the defense of prevailing notions of quality, different curricula have been advanced to project academic stereotypes of the learning capacities of different classes and races. Consequently, the technologies are increasingly segregated from the traditional liberal arts, the sciences from the rest, the two-year degree clientele from the four, the aspirants for professional accreditation from those tracked in so-called parapro-fessional pursuits, the research-oriented from the teaching experts, the experts in the remediation field from the mainstream, and so on. Hetero-geneity is honored less and less in higher education, notwithstanding the clear warnings advanced in such studies as Coleman's about the anti-educational impact of social, cultural, and intellectual homogeneity in the learning community.

These developments reflect a serious confusion about what *equality* of higher educational opportunity means. A growing equalization of the opportunity to get into higher education is confused with the more or less static and tracked range of options open to people once they get in and the quality of the options available, especially to the new classes getting in. This tracking (academic segregation) is the seedbed of future unrest not only on the campuses, but also in the nation.

Everywhere in our great cities minority group youth is recoiling from the less-than-bachelor's degree, from technology-oriented, dead-end degree programs planned for them in the junior colleges. When Secre-tary Finch or Commissioner Allen spoke of the two-year college as the great equalization opportunity for black and Spanish-speaking youth, they misread the minds of that youth and estimated incorrectly the po-tential of the two-year colleges *in the cities*. They made some conven-tional assumptions that are now false.

It is false to assume that poverty is exclusively an economic concept. It is false to assume that the new clientele, whose ancestors manned the lower rungs of the American agricultural or industrial economy, will now settle for access only to the lower rungs of the technology economy. It is false to assume that the two-year colleges are preparing people for jobs that will exist ten years from now, or that the trade unions are sufficiently cooperative regarding access to some jobs for which these colleges effect an immediate preparation. It is false to assume that two years is enough, given the character of most urban secondary school systems. And finally, it is false to assume—faced by a clientele deeply disturbed about self-identity, the meaning of being American, and, necessarily, the mastery of American decision-making processes—that preparation for jobs is tantamount to education. Liberal education, assumed to be a necessity for middle-class youth, is an imperative sur-vival requirement (updated and modernized) for minority group youth. On my own campus there is growing evidence that the newly admitted black and Puerto Rican youth are performing from low *C* through *F* in the introductory math, science, and grammar courses, and from middle *C* through high *B* in significant parts of the social science and humanities curricula. The pattern says something important about the previous education to which they have been exposed and about their sophistication regarding actual life experience and current concern.

A recent study of the American Association for the Advancement of Science shows that in the typical technology-oriented junior college degree program—encompassing sixty to seventy credit hours over two years—the liberal arts component is between nine and twelve hours, barely enough for rudiments of American history, American literature, and the A, B, Cs of economics, psychology, or political science. Sociology and philosophy are almost lost. In any event, such curricula are hardly the staging grounds for future Americans willing, ready, and able to play the American game the way the majority wants it played. And the so-called liberal arts input is now dominated by remedial English, math, and science subject matter.

A clear distinction must be made between the two-year college located in the agricultural or small-town American setting, and the provision of higher educational opportunity for our young people in the great cities. Something new must be invented to meet the challenge of the urban situation.

Reconstructions

Planning for qualitative disruption—the essence of higher education —requires major policy shifts on the part of government and the academic community.

Grants and loans to students for advanced education should be made directly to individuals in a manner which ensures their independence from both family and institution and encourages competitive selection of institution.

Federal legislation for the assistance of the public lower schools and colleges and universities should in significant part be framed to compel a new collaboration between the two in the development of programs and the construction of campuses, especially involving the secondary and collegiate systems in urban centers.

A much more direct tie should be made legislatively between funds for Model Cities programs and funds for urban higher education.

Most academic residential construction, especially for students, persists in honoring discredited life styles and ends up resembling the worst of low-income project housing. Governmental loan and grant programs in support of such construction should begin to assert humane living standards involving the input of national panels of our best architects, urban planners, sociologists, and others.

Federal legislation for the expansion of the two-year college movement should carefully allow for experimental and innovative new collegiate starts in the cities, distinguishing the viability of the two-year college in the nonurban setting from its obvious limitations in the urban situation.

Programs that allow for the input of top talent into industry, government, and technical and artistic institutions should be developed and encouraged to further the intern and apprentice educational concepts throughout the urban environment.

Federal legislation should be encouraged in anticipation of the growing unionization of professional groups serving higher education—especially of those who teach—to require the representation of consumer classes in all negotiations between employees and management. In higher education, the consumer classes to be represented are students, alumni, and elements of the lay public beyond governing board representatives who are cast in these situations (by law) in the role of management.

National educational organizations should aggressively promote nationwide conversation in the profession aimed at the reconsideration of the relationships between salary trends and workloads, and the content and staging of educational programs, especially at undergraduate levels.

Beyond these items are other subjects that should enjoy priority treatment in a national dialogue about the future of our colleges and universities in an age of universal higher education. These include: the role of students in the government of their own learning communities; the use of student talent in tutorial education; the opening up of city-wide curricula for students based on the collaborative offerings of several educational institutions in the city; the intensive consideration of programs, both architectural and educational, for the intelligent and systematic demolition of the deteriorating academic walls between thought and action, the academic place and the city itself as a campus.

MARCUS G. RASKIN

What Is the New University?

THERE ARE two major and basic crises in the university. The first is a reflection of a political crisis that now manifests itself across the entire American society, the crisis in political authority. To put it another way: By what authority does A tell B what is right and wrong? By what authority does A tell B what to do? By what authority does A get to control his lifetime and B cannot? In the university this crisis manifests itself in efforts by groups hitherto unconscious of themselves to ask what authority others have over them, where their legitimacy comes from, and who granted it to them. Such questions—and they are ones endemic to the next generation—will force a redrafting of the social contract before 2000 in our major institutions, including the body politic itself. The problem of redrafting the social contract is especially acute in the university since its ideology and rhetoric (but not the reality) assure us that authority, legitimacy, and truth derive from verification and persuasion, not magic, threat, force, who rules, or delayed payoff.

The second crisis of the university, and just as important, involves the university's relationship to knowledge. This question is neither an ab-

》 》 《 《

Marcus G. Raskin is Co-Director, Institute for Policy Studies, in Washington, D.C. He writes frequently on foreign policy, political philosophy, and education.

stract nor a rarified one. Rather, it deals with what individuals and groups study, want to know about, and value. In other words, the present crisis in the university is also one of value and epistemology. Should knowledge reflect and cause problems, or is there another way that knowledge increases and leads to wisdom and new values?

Who Are the Customers?

Jencks and Riesman have suggested that a primary question to ask about the university is: Who are the customers? It is obvious that all universities and other institutions of higher education in America, whether they are junior colleges or the elite five, are influenced in their thinking by their audience and customers. Consideration was easier when there was no turbulence in the body politic itself, when the university protected itself from turbulence, or when it knew clearly that it served Authority. Once such turbulence occurred, the universities that had found themselves catering to a particular interest have also found their purposes questioned by other groups.

Historically, our liberal ideology has taught us that America is an upwardly mobile society. Consequently, the ultimate customer in an abstract sense was opportunity/opportunism. "In the land of opportunity we are all opportunists." Students tied themselves to the prospect of upward mobility. In the last generation, students who might not otherwise have gone to college were admitted and channeled into particular fields in order to run the complex corporate hierarchy, that is, the corporate or civil bureaucracies, the production line, and national security industries.

The customers of the university became those particular institutions with which students would find themselves finally connected. The goals of the students were Achievement and Opportunity. The customer was less the student or the parents who paid the bill for the student, and more the institutions that hid behind the skirts of the university or the government which now paid for the students. And most of the "visiting committees" and boards of trustees of universities tell us who the customers were. For practical purposes the universities viewed the students as goods which they certified to the corporate institutions. The students themselves—to continue the market analogy—had little choice as buyers once they accepted the values and the traditions of the university. They saw themselves as merchandise. Only recently have we come to see that the customers may be the next generation, who themselves have a different view of what they are buying.

What Is the University Tradition?

What tradition are we trying to protect for universities, for which groups in the university, or for which users of the university? Is it the process of freedom of inquiry wherein the scholar or student may study those questions and develop methodology that will produce new knowledge and wisdom? Or is it instead a place for channeling the ideology of opportunism and hustling? What does a student learn in class? Perhaps bad habits. Usually he learns that he needs "that" course in order to move higher in the credit scale. The tradition passed on is not, therefore, the tradition of scholarship or learning. Rather, it is a tradition that says if you want to go high in the organization, you must attach yourself to this particular course or series of courses because the values of the corporate organization or academic guild demand that such courses be taken. The individual, at best, masters mechanical requirements.

If we were to look more deeply into the problem, we would find even greater difficulty with the values of the humanities and social sciences. In Western thought and action it has usually been the martial values of the society which have been sung or studied by historians and philosophers. It is the rare philosopher or social scientist indeed who has taken the other side of this question. In our own time we see this fact in a very stubborn way. It wasn't the Mississippi tenant farmer who ordered the troops to Vietnam. More likely, and more specifically, it was the former professors/Harvard Junior Fellows—those who had maximum chance to develop intellectually. In the leading journals of philosophy, the question of war and peace had never been dignified until 1967 and 1968, when the philosophers did condemn the Vietnam war at professional conferences *as philosophers*. And so, too, in political science, sociology, ethics, economics, where major structural and institutional questions were eschewed to protect privilege and class interest.

Over this last generation the university supplied people as consultants and operators to the CIA, the Defense Department, and other National Security State functions, as well as useless goods enterprises. Of course, certain prestige universities continue to reward these men with trusteeships and presidencies. Besides developing a manpower pool for these institutions and getting professors to recommend students to the operation of war-making institutions, universities also found themselves, for example, in the business of adding problems as a result of the knowledge which they explored. Therefore, the question remains about what traditions in the university we want to protect and reward. Insurgent groups openly question whether there are traditions in the university which are worthy of protection, if the institution is racist, sexist, or militarist-oriented.

In a period when the basic social contract of the society is going through profound change, new groups emerge which attempt to use the resources and institutions of the society for their purposes. Such groups want to see themselves not as objects of study or problems for the middle class to look at, but as active participants (and directors!) of universities. Obviously, Roxbury would like to have a situation in which Harvard will work for it in ways similar to those that the engineers and scientists and bright, upwardly mobile students of the lower class were coopted by the Establishment of universities to work for the corporate and national security system. They see no reason, and the radical young agree, why the university cannot reflect the needs and values of insurgent groups.

Yet from another vantage point some from the working class would argue that the university has a style of life which by its nature is threatening. They see the university as a privileged sanctuary where people talk about great issues, do very little real work, and have arrived at a state of parasitism and trouble-making. The university appears to be a palace court where the professors live the good life without fear of struggle or challenge. They see the universities as robbing them of their children, who learn to reject their parents and the dreams of opportunity and status which the university itself is a part of. The contradiction is that, although the professors may preach against privilege, the university appears to a large proportion of the society as the very essence of privilege.

The University as Body Politic?

In ideal terms the university is not only a place of inquiry which concerns itself with the great theoretical-practical questions and extends mythically through our minds and the spirit of the times as the Source of Reason; it is also a community of *place* with passions, interests, and functions to be performed much like other peopled places. The university is the modern body politic, which itself is an experiment. It has model and exemplary significance because there is enough time, slack, and reason to experiment with ways people could live together in a community.

As a body politic the university is not only an association of equals-toward—that is, a community of scholars in search of truth; it is also an association of equals-in. Operationally this means that functions are performed or are raised which touch all the people in their magnitude and consequence and should throw upon those touched the democratic rather than the hierarchic principle of authority. Thus, for example, the janitor, cook, professor, and student must participate in the decision process of the university regarding aspects of life which are clearly concerned with the economic, political, and social rights within the university community.

There is an irony to members of the Progressive Labor groups and the SDS on a university campus, usually children of the upper middle class, attempting to find the working class by leaving the campus. Instead they should see the working class in their own body politic: the janitors, laboratory assistants, and cafeteria workers who are in the same situation, the same body politic as the students. I have suggested elsewhere that the basis of political organizing between the students and the working class may vary from place to place. But experience in that direction and attempts at legitimating relationships within a body politic—especially one so basic in America—is that organizing must go on within the university. The needs are not hard to define, nor are the demands. Students in private universities could hold onto parts of their tuitions and pay the workers directly.

For a young person, the university rights of citizenship would relate to him as a full member of a political community in which he has rights to privacy, against self-incrimination, freedom of speech and action, as well as sexual freedom. The university community would give new meaning to the federal Bill of Rights, and undertake to set a community to fulfill those rights. The Bill of Rights would no longer be a merely formal political matter between the state and the individual. Cognizance would be taken of the fact that corporate power has abrogated political rights. To be sure, people may have the power of free speech, but not in the corporate unit in which they live their lives. Thus, students may have rights to privacy, but not against an oppressive dormitory system or dormitories planned by administrations. Obviously, formal rights are necessary for creating the spaces to obtain reconstruction.

The reconstructed intent of a charter from the state for a university is to free it from the external controls of the state. But such freedom can only be predicated on such institutions operating democratically. Thus, universities would undertake to operate according to rules of community which are written by all members who work and study within the community. University charters would be rewritten or reexamined to guarantee that there were democratic controls, a definition of rights within the community, and incorporation of rights generally recognized in law such as the Bill of Rights. Where groups within the university could not get on within the charter of the university, they would receive a new charter for themselves. The right of exodus—without penalty—would be protected or the right of organizing within the university as a group would also be encouraged (for example, a black studies program).

To reinforce excitement in learning and knowledge, and to act politically in order to maintain peace in the university body politic, the universities would legislate a system of hiring in which students would have the power to hire a number of faculty whom they want on campus without control from either the faculty or administration. Students would receive an amount from their tuitions to bring to the campus people whom they want to learn from and over whom they have the power of the purse. The types of knowledge to emerge from this group of teachers would be different from the kind that ordinarily comes from the academic profession. Faculties themselves would continue to hire people for their departments (from their specialization or guild) with the likelihood that those hired by them would be more tradition-minded and "knowledge-as-property-minded." In this uneasy compromise the university president—especially if he has the electoral sanction of the community, rather than that of the trustees—would also undertake to hire professors who he believes should be at the university. This political stand-off between the groups could also result in the saving of the university as a place of inquiry. However, without such a political change in hiring and firing by new groups within the university, it is open to question whether the university will be a place for serious inquiry. As Whitehead has pointed out, the university's role in inquiry switches from time to time so that the most serious work is performed outside the university in one historical period and inside it at other times. Whatever direction that the university takes internally, it is now struggling to become an action community governing itself. Consequently, it becomes the natural organizational structure to confront the state.

If, as I have suggested in *Being and Doing*,[1] the reason for the state no longer fastens upon us intellectually or emotionally, the practical effect is that authority must rest somewhere. We may assume that authority rests in the human association among people rather than in abstract conceptions of obedience. In the university, where there is a possibility of building a community through association and common purpose, we may begin to understand why it may become necessary to exercise historic relationships which exclude the power of the state, and thus cause the confrontation of the reconstructed university community with state power. It can accomplish this end if the university sees itself as a community which is chartered to act outside the needs of the state but act on the needs of the community. The university, by virtue of what is taught by its teachers, should find itself in conflict with state power. It is man's hope that the long-term values of the university are reason and passion. The values of the state are authoritarian control and destruction (war). While reason and passion can lead to control and destruction (war), it is more likely that there will be conflict between the purveyors of these different values if the university functions as a place of inquiry to hold back control and destruction.

[1] New York: Random House, forthcoming.

The power of the university community externally toward the rest of society relates to the question of allegiance within the university group to activities, functions, and associations that are not reflected in the way the national state now operates or in the way sovereignty is used by the economic or violence system. Consequently, the university that functions internally as a body politic is now able to ask for or take those actions and rights which protect members of its community.

For a body politic to be acceptable to those living within its domain, the authority must be shared in a way that is acceptable to its citizens. Take a symbolic example: Why should a president of a university be chosen by a board of trustees? The choice of the president of a university is something which involves the entire membership of the university community. Through a system of voting and participation, it would be possible for students, faculty, workers, researchers, and administrators to participate in choosing a president. This procedure would help in changing the perception of the student as having no part in the governing of the institution in which he will live.

The outlines of the past become our political instrument for reconstruction. It is likely that students, workers, and faculty will seek a more active role in choosing the university president. There then is no need for trustees who are an appendage of the state watching over the college. Whether there is trouble or no trouble, they become representatives of the college to the outside world. In any case, once the university is a body politic, only those within—or elected from the outside—have a voice. Imagine a university including the president in its membership for a term of years. His task as leader of a political community is to extend the authority of the university against the state. First, under newly drawn charters, he will undertake to protect the members of the university and extend their numbers. The protection of the members becomes a worthy thing because the president and his faculty know that they speak with the authority of the community, not alone for the trustees. They know that the activities of the people in the university involve the highest aspects of the inquiry of man. Because the members of the university community see humane purpose to what they do, they now are ready to stand against the state for those purposes because, in so doing, they are aware that they are speaking for the greater human community.

With this confidence, the university community would demand immunity for itself as a separate governing entity, removed from state incursions. The people within it and the alumni of the institution would see themselves joined in a relationship in which they would recognize that the university has its own rights and powers when it ceases to do the bidding of the state.

The university would then acquire its own political purpose, which would be tied to the purpose of human inquiry and the solution of human problems. The political purpose could include its own judicial system. For example, a court having to do with disturbances of the peace might be made up of people from the city and students, if for no other reason than that defendants should have the benefit of being tried before their peers. The university might undertake a specific taxing system—such as is done with special districts that receive taxing privileges from the state—which would help in the support of inquiry. The task of a national legislature would then be the granting of endowment amounts to universities with the requirement that they be invested in rebuilding cities and that the researches be given over to the science and politics of ecology.

New Ideas and New Knowledge

The most profound question facing the university is that of attempting to define what is to be known and what should be taught. The question whether knowledge is a thing to be passed on or a method and process of inquiry is open to differing viewpoints. However, we expect universities to concern themselves with fundamental issues. It is necessary to reject a possible situation in which the universities serve particular purposes and classes which themselves become everyone's problem.

Suppose we were scientists during the last generation. During this period we would have been put the question, "How do we stop or make an ICBM?" We are told to invent formulas and methods for this purpose and then to suggest a technology which would put these formulas and methods into practice. A whole series of facts and factors are developed which then create new technology courses in universities to answer the original problem of how to answer the ICBM. But, by undertaking that mode of analysis and creating such a technology in the university, we have developed the sorts of knowledge that create problems. We find then that we develop systems of knowledge and facts that get us no closer to the solution of basic problems.

For example, a whole system of international relations was initiated over the last thirty-five years on the description of violence and force and their use. (To believe that students would not see violence and force, taught in the classroom as a method of response, as the way to relate to other nations or Third World people is a naïveté.) While teaching about violence does not mean advocacy, virtually no university department of social science or government has developed a program on nonviolence or nonviolent methods of relationships, and there have been few attempts to build a new system of values which would show how groups and nations could relate to each other in associative, nonhierarchic, or nonviolent ways. Instead the leading theoreticians from the universities have invariably talked about the use of force as the arbiter of disputes. They and their students were prepared to play out their elegant techniques of description and organization in the use of force with the *will* to use such force. As Michael Maccoby has said,

> The work in psychology in the United States beginning with Yerkes and Dodson at the turn of the century and continuing through Thorndike, Watson, Hull, Miller, and Skinner all have to do with controlling behavior by controlling the rewards and punishments. That of Hovland, Festinger and others represent a more recent emphasis on persuasion by controlling the message.[2]

The important epistemological point is that the new facts and values we need to develop at the universities are found in places and groups that until now have been excluded from the university.

Surely universities could begin to find lost traditions where they once existed. Such traditions may not be immediately apparent but they are there. Here I have in mind research into how different communities resolved their problems in the past, how we can begin communes on a national scale, how we transform the corporate system into a worker-community control system. (The whole system of industrial relations departments at universities is predicated on the corporate-union system maintaining itself in the present form. I would hope that in the near future students in industrial relations would demand that the professors learn something about worker-community control of corporations so that a participatory function for workers will be developed. Such researches will change the subject matter taught in the university as well as the values and facts developed. For example, the development of non-hierarchic antiauthoritarian relationships, grounded on man's potentiality as well as his nature, will need exploration.)

The development of new knowledge and methods of inquiry includes acceptance of a point of view upon which the university would stand. We might term this as the development of a new humanist tradition which one hopes would pervade higher education. For example, *empirical research becomes the attempt to find answers to those questions which celebrate humanist values.* Some will wonder just what "humanist values" are. And perhaps they are hard to know. But we are beginning to know what they are *not.* Dachau or Nagasaki did not reflect such values. Nor did the Vietnam venture.

And while our most clever academicians talked about preparing for war in order to make peace, the dialectics have turned out to be wrong and disastrous. More and more, people understand the need to reject the facts and values developed from such assumptions. Many young people continue—haltingly—to reach for such values (Peoples Park) and want

---

[2] "Erich Fromm's Radical Revision of Psychoanalysis," unpublished.

their universities to reflect them in what is researched and thought about. In this they are carrying forward the pragmatist idea that science and knowledge were meant not to enslave man further, but to liberate him. Students understand such principles when they occupy a radiation laboratory at Stanford University. They are attempting to say something about the subject matter taught in a university and what is a proper activity for the university. In other words, they are concerned with the basic question of the ethical value to knowledge. The question can no longer be avoided by the university, and the people within it can no longer hide behind the notion that it supports value-free research. Faculties and students will now have to think beyond specialized terms to ascertain the ethical value of the particular researches done.

A profound ideology surrounds the modern university—the ideology that the university is able to deal with the basic problems that confront man. The rule of relevance is then not that the universities have been irrelevant to the problems of man; indeed, the knowledge and technologies developed at such universities have *caused* many of them. But the reverse is the case. Is the university now able to find the researches and experiments necessary to end the war system or develop the knowledge necessary to protect the ecology and the environment and to develop the universal principles of man so that the status of some over others will be removed? In my view, to do this work it will be necessary to be highly theoretical and highly experimentally practical. The middle levels of problem reflection and expediential, momentary resolutions, which much university research now reflects, no longer have a significant place except perhaps as museum pieces. It is not without cause that young people reject science and reach toward astrology or reject the functional rationality which leads to organizational criminality in favor of feeling. It is because the university grafted unto itself the values of the state (whether those values were for personal opportunity or for national manipulation for conquest by a particular class or nation over others in which knowledge was the manipulative power tool) that the young have come to realize that such values and knowledge are destructive to man and nature. There is a life instinct, and as more formerly subjugated groups enter the university, the old system of privilege, opportunity, and knowledge causing problems might have to give way.

My own view is that the university may not have it within itself at this time to bring forward radical creative ideas to lead to such a new system of facts, values, and knowledge. The university would be required to challenge the corporate structure or the state. While some might have believed that the university by its nature must challenge the state, the political likelihood is that it would rather purchase its own internal and external peace in a "partnership" with the state. Because of the enormous amount of funds given to the university by the state, whether federal or state government, the likelihood of challenge by the university is small, and consequently the likelihood of the development of new knowledge which brings forward a new system of values with the university as the source is not very great.

New educational forms are required which then help in the transformation of the university.

PETER SCHRAG

"Provide, Provide . . ."

THE CRISIS in higher education bears comparison with conditions preceding the Reformation: a once relatively monastic institution grown rich and powerful, selling indulgences (degrees, credits, prestige); maintaining a hierarchy whose inherent commitment to, and competence for, the original purposes diminishes as the institution grows in size and temporal influence; and whose mystique is being punctured by the criticism of a growing number of sophisticated members.

As long as the university was small and catered to elites, as long as other media of information and learning were limited, the mystery was maintained. The university, it was believed, was a special place with certain unique attributes. But the mystery has been shattered. We (or our students) have discovered that the campus is a worldly place, not a place apart, that its inhabitants are fallible creatures, and that those who most resist these discoveries are often academic sentimentalists lamenting the passing of the old days on The Hill.

The crisis is related to events taking place everywhere else and especially related to fundamental changes in cultural style which are outrunning the university's capability and willingness to adjust. One can talk about a good many things happening Out There: the growing sus-

» » « «

Peter Schrag is an Editor-at-Large of Saturday Review *and was, until recently,* Editor *of* Change *magazine.*

41

picion among many young men and women about all cognitive operations (the distrust of history, and the like); the shift to intuitive patterns of communication and learning; the changing styles in dress, drugs, and music; the disenchantment with all institutions, and so on.

But there is also a shift within the academy: namely, the academy's own uncertainty about its function, its meaning, and its integrity. Put another way: as little as twenty years ago we all knew what culture was, and how we should discuss, divide, and analyze it. Phenomena like the explosion of knowledge were regarded as serious problems, but only technical ones. What has happened in the meantime is that we now find that it was not merely knowledge that was fractured: our culture was. Who can still say that a Ph.D. in linguistics is culturally more important, for example, than a few years' listening to the Beatles and the Rolling Stones? Who is the man and where is the institution that can safely and accurately prescribe curricula? What is the meaning of the title "doctor"? (I am not talking about the speciousness of Ph.D. requirements, but of their strengths—scholarly competence in a narrow field.) How can a doctor prescribe what is to be learned in anything other than his own field? The holder of the Ph.D. is a journeyman, capable of directing apprenticeships in his specialty, but has he any more claim on the direction of a general curriculum than the student? The academic crisis is not rooted in the problems of university governance, or in student protest, but in the university's failure to deal with those things it has always considered uniquely its own province: the organization, analysis, and discipline of knowledge. "Relevance" is only a minor part of the problems. There are other significant ones: To what extent are the traditional academic disciplines anything but vestigial interest groups within the university? And to what extent are the existing modes of inquiry self-protective devices invented by contemporary scholastics to preserve the mystique and emoluments of their own "learnedness"? The academy offers tremendous amounts of technical expertise, but what does it offer in the way of learning?

Certainly there have been attempts at reform: urban studies, interdisciplinary courses, internships, work-study projects, and so on. Most are tokenism, and in many cases those who direct the attempts are the least prestigious members of the institution (often for good reason), people who have not made it in the conventional hierarchy. The essential task of reorganizing approaches to learning, the design or invention of new disciplines, the willingness to risk honest, visible error—these things have generally been ignored. How many faculty members are prepared to be vulnerable, personally and intellectually, in the process of learning? How many administrators regard themselves—in any way —as the representatives, not of institutions, but of the students they are supposed to serve?

All of this is oversimplified. By now every college administrator must have a sense that his "crisis" is different from the next man's. Nonetheless, there are pressing items for all of us.

1. For the academy generally, there is an urgent and continuing need for a radical reexamination of the existing disciplines, and for the allocation of resources for the design of modern, relevant forms of intellectual inquiry. Not more curriculum committees, but an ongoing discourse —involving students—which brings to bear the expertise of journeymen (when applicable) on the mastery and organization of real experience. The task involves dealing with things that are not rationally manageable (as well as those that are), and hence involves all sorts of risk, among them the risk of exposing oneself.

2. For the individual practitioner, there is a requirement to separate what is valid and alive in the discipline from the encrusted accumulation of things learned *sui generis* and in isolation. How much of what is culture (in the form of history or literature, for example) is worth retaining, and how much is a dead exercise practiced for the sole reason that the practitioner doesn't know how to do anything else?

3. For the institution, there is, obviously, the need to encourage and reward the first two sorts of activity. But there is also the need for administrators to represent students against the demands of "society" which, almost inevitably, mean the demands of government, corporations, and other powerful interests.

4. For the nation, the most pressing requirement is to develop, as rapidly as possible, resources and facilities which offer alternatives to formal higher education, and to break down the artificial barriers between levels of education—elementary, secondary, higher—and between the hierarchies within them. Specifically, funds for educational opportunity (trade schools, universities, travel, etc.) should be made available directly to the clients—primarily *all* young men and women— rather than being channeled almost exclusively to institutions. They can use their money to "shop around."

5. The power to confer credentials (credits, degrees) should be separated from the institutions offering the instruction on which those credentials are supposedly based. Grades should be made optional for the student everywhere, at once.

All this adds up to dis-Establishment. And as Robert Frost used to say: "Provide, provide. If you don't provide, somebody else will for you."

PART TWO

Where the Students Are

KENNETH KENISTON

What's Bugging the Students?

ANYONE WHO AGREES, in any brief span, to analyze "what's bugging the students" and to provide "recommendations for resolving conflict" should be suspect. Suspicion should heighten if the charge to the writer suggests that recommendations are needed for "preventing or resolving conflicts among members of the campus constituencies or between them and the members of other constituencies (students, faculty, administrators and presidents, trustees)." For the charge takes for granted some of the assumptions that are today most questioned by dissenting students: for example, that conflict on campus should necessarily be prevented or resolved, that some inclusive or definitive statement can be made about the students, that it is appropriate for someone who is not a student to attempt to summarize the complaints of students.

By way of disclaimer, let me first note that I am not convinced all campus conflicts should be prevented or resolved. On the contrary, I believe conflict is an inevitable precursor, concomitant, and consequence of change—whether constructive or destructive. Under many circumstances, I believe one should deliberately create conflict: for example, psychological conflict within those whose behavior belies their professed values, social conflict between those who condone or ignore injustice and

» » « «

Kenneth Keniston, Professor of Psychology in Yale University's School of Medicine, is author of Young Radicals: Notes on Committed Youth.

those who wish to correct it. Furthermore, the most expedient way to prevent or resolve conflict is to eliminate or silence those who create it. None of this is to say that conflict, whether psychological or social, is inevitably desirable; it simply notes that the value of conflict cannot be judged apart from its contexts, objects, and results.

Second, the question "What's bugging the students?" suggests, at the very least, that psychological factors may be central in understanding the discontents of today's students. We more characteristically speak of being bugged by personal hang-ups than by social injustice, warfare, racism, or hypocrisy. Yet I must conclude that what bugs student activists are not only their intrapsychic problems, but even more the nature of American society, the world, and their colleges. Psychological factors play a major role in sensitizing some students to issues that do not concern others, but intrapsychic factors alone are not *causes* of student tension.

Finally, the concept of "the students" bears close examination. We have rightly learned not to speak loosely about "the Negroes," "women," or "the Russians," recognizing that the generic label obscures the great variety within such groups. But, for some reason, we have not yet extended this same caution to the students. I will argue that different things bug different students.

Although almost every conceivable cause of conflict has already been discussed and documented, often at great length, it is impossible to make recommendations for resolving conflict without identifying its causes, albeit in a sketchy and telegraphic way.

Youth in Two Social Revolutions

First, I believe that what are euphemistically called "campus tensions" result in considerable part from social and historical changes and political and administrative policies that do not originate primarily in colleges and universities. Much of the turbulence in highly industrialized societies stems from the two highly explosive social revolutions that are simultaneously under way. The first is the ancient process of "inclusion" in the industrial society—what Ralf Dahrendorf has termed "the extension of citizenship." [1] The first revolution involves the demand that American society include as full citizens many persons who have traditionally been excluded from the mainstreams of social, economic, and political life: those who are not white, adult, middle class, Protestant, Anglo-Saxon, and male. Thus, from blacks, young people, women, Jews and Catholics, a variety of ethnic groups, and working- and lower-class individuals we hear ever more strident demands to be counted in as full

[1] Remarks made at a conference on "The University in Crisis," at Bellagio, Italy, November 1968.

members of society, granted full legal rights and equal psychocultural esteem. Because the rhetoric of American society is a rhetoric of democracy and full citizenship, and because of the high levels of material abundance, social security, and formal political freedom in our society, the demand for inclusion is today becoming more clamorous and insistent.

But overlapping, and to some extent opposing, this first trend are the less articulate but strongly felt demands of those who form part of a second revolution. This revolution, less sociopolitical than psychocultural, occurs in the children of those who have made it in the existing system: children of intellectuals, professionals, high-level government administrators, market researchers, and the cosmopolitan upper middle class of America, France, West Germany, Japan, and so on. For such men and women—most of them young—the promises of the first revolution seem already fulfilled; citizenship is attained; inclusion is assured. The new questions that arise for such young men and women concern the meaning and quality of life in a postindustrial setting. Their first provisional answers emphasize qualitative transformation; a rejection of the human, bureaucratic, and ecological price paid to attain high levels of industrialization; a search for fulfillment and more intense experience; and an effort to achieve new forms of intimacy, awareness, and community.

This contrast between the two revolutions provides the framework for much of my analysis of current tensions on the campus. It requires distinguishing the psychohistorical position of those who are so solidly *in* the existing society that they take its accomplishments for granted, the position of those who are still effectively excluded from society, and the position of those whose place in society is still so precarious that their major efforts go to secure stronger footholds. It requires a contrast between those who are "solidly in" the System on one hand and those who are "tenuously in" or "excluded" on the other.

I do not assume, however, a community of interest between all who share the same or contiguous sociohistorical positions. There are enormous differences between those who are tenuously in and those who are excluded. The tenuously in (the great majority of the "silent Americans") feel threatened from two directions: by those who are solidly in (the "experts" who allegedly control everything) and by the excluded (who appear to threaten the status and values of those who are tenuously in). But no matter how explosive socially may be the demands of those who are still effectively excluded from the rewards and esteem of full citizenship in society, these demands are essentially traditional and pose no revolutionary threat to the prevailing social and value system (although, indeed, they challenge existing political alignments). In contrast, the inarticulate aspirations of those who are solidly in the society but have begun to question its values and worth seem ultimately more revolutionary, though less politically explosive.

A second factor behind today's student unrest is the prolongation of psychological development—specifically, of adolescence. Its extent is apparent in the crudest social indicators. Since the turn of the century, the average amount of education received by each student group has increased by approximately one year per decade. Also, the average age for the onset of puberty has decreased by approximately one-fifth of a year per decade. Finally, the average student of any given age today appears to score approximately one standard deviation above the average student of the same age a generation ago on most standardized measures of intellectual performance. A student in the middle of his class today would probably have stood in approximately the top 15 percent a generation ago; put differently, he is approximately one grade ahead, at any given age, of his parents when they were that age.

Translated into individual terms, this means that the average sixteen-year-old of today, compared with the sixteen-year-old of 1920, would probably have reached puberty one year earlier, have received approximately five years more education, and be performing intellectually at the same level as a seventeen- or eighteen-year-old in 1920. Today's high school and college students are about a year more mature physiologically and a year more developed intellectually than their parents were at the same age, but on the other hand, they must defer adult responsibilities, rights, and prerogatives five years longer.

These changes have revolutionary implications for higher education. There are more than 7 million full- and part-time students involved, an increase of well over 100 percent in the last fifteen years. The better students are even better prepared than they were a generation ago, and upgraded secondary education (at least in white, suburban, middle-class areas) has meant an increase not only in achievement levels, but also in levels of sophistication, cosmopolitanism, moral reasoning, and intellectual comprehension; these advances are especially marked among the most privileged white young Americans.

There is incomplete but growing evidence that these changes have resulted not only in a quantitative increase in the knowledge of the average student, but also in qualitative changes in the reasoning capacity and moral development of many young men and women. The qualitative psychological changes entail greater autonomy, individuation, and interpersonal maturity; they frequently involve a relativistic or postrelativistic outlook on knowledge and a highly principled style of moral reasoning. To oversimplify, today's students are more likely to challenge, to question, and to think for themselves than were students of earlier generations.

A third factor in student discontent is what Kingman Brewster, Jr., calls the "involuntary" nature of university attendance for many students.[2] The present Selective Service System makes college education virtually a sure-fire way to avoid the draft, whereas dropping out of college is an excellent way to assure induction. Furthermore, this same system imposes upon morally sensitive students the guilt of being spared military service, at least for a time, solely by virtue of family background, previous education, or intellectual endowment—factors for which the individual himself has little or no responsibility.

But, as Brewster has noted, the draft merely aggravates pressures that existed and will continue to exist, even were it to be abolished or become more equitable. The indiscriminate use of college degrees as passports for occupational entry, the strong social pressure upon middle-class children to attend and complete college and often graduate or professional school as well, and the opprobrium heaped upon students who discontinue or interrupt advanced education, all mean that colleges abound with students who have no particular reason to be there and who would quite consciously prefer to do something else somewhere else.

As one consequence, these involuntary students put pressures on their colleges to serve a variety of needs that colleges are not well equipped to meet. A student who is pressured to attend and fearful of leaving college, but who would rather be involved in a worthy program of social reform or political action, inevitably presses the university to allow him to undertake this program for academic credit. The student who finds academic learning irrelevant is likely to demand relevance, even though it may involve kinds of experience which college cannot well offer. In brief, colleges are essentially rather limited institutions, and their captive audiences today create unbearable pressures upon them to be all things to all men, including a variety of men (and women) who would much prefer to be elsewhere.

A final factor—perhaps the most important—that profoundly affects the campuses today and provides the immediate target of much activist protest is the emergence of major contradictions in American society. Some of these contradictions, like racism, have long existed but have only recently been fully exposed; others are the product of changes in American society, economy, and international position. It has become clear, for example, that industrialization was achieved at no small price in terms of human regimentation and ecological despoliation. It has become more obvious to white Americans that the legacy of slavery has never fully been overcome, but is still translated into psychological and structural forms of racism which effectively exclude blacks from full citizenship. It has become more patent that there is a contradiction between

[2] "The Involuntary Campus and the Manipulated Society," *Educational Record,* Spring 1970, pp. 101–5.

America's traditionally democratic and peaceful view of herself internationally and her increasingly imperial role in the modern world. Some may argue that the extent of repression, hypocrisy, injustice, or cruelty within society has increased; in my view, it has in general decreased. Yet the level of *awareness* of injustice has clearly increased, and the sense of living in an unjust, irrational, hypocritical, and cruel world is undoubtedly growing, especially among the thoughtful young.

These factors affect students unevenly and, in many cases, do not consciously affect them at all. In particular, the emerging contradictions of society are noted and deplored by only a minority of today's more than 7 million college students. With the vast influx into community colleges, two-year colleges, upgraded state teachers colleges, and a variety of other public and private institutions, millions of students today are attending college who would not have done so a generation ago. As new kinds of students enter higher education, the level of those who attend the most selective colleges rises steadily. An educational system that once was explicitly elite has now become increasingly democratic, enrolling almost half the secondary school graduates. One consequence, inevitably, is that as the social composition of higher education becomes more diversified, any generalization about the students becomes increasingly impossible.

Some Types of Students

There are many useful ways of classifying students, but I will discuss three broad groups, classified largely according to social background and position vis-à-vis the existing society.

THE PUBLIC IMAGE OF DISSENT

The popular imagination, fed by the mass media, is attracted by oversimplified images of the students. A decade ago, it was still the tail end of the "silent generation"; today it is the "now generation," the "angry generation," and so on. These images often reflect real trends and are socially important in themselves, since it is the image of students, not the facts about students, that tends to determine public and legislative action. Yet any discussion of students must begin by noting that in the academic year 1968–69, *most* of this country's 2,400 colleges did not have a group of Students for a Democratic Society, *most* colleges experienced no protest over anything more serious than dining hall regulations or parietal hours, and *most* students, as of December 18, 1969, believed that Richard M. Nixon was doing a good job as President. Indeed, data from the American Council on Education's Office of Research suggest that during the present academic year, *most* freshmen arrive even less sympathetic to student radicalism than in the past.[3] Seymour Martin Lipset has, in several articles, pointed out that, until the last year or so, students appeared to be fully as hawkish as the general public on the war in Vietnam. At most colleges, student activists and radicals spend much time deploring the apathy of the majority of their classmates, who persist in being interested in dates, football, and getting ahead in the world. Similarly, despite much discussion and some reality behind talk of the generation gap, recent studies suggest that this gap is nowhere nearly as wide as it is made to appear, that most students say they admire their parents, get along well with them, and agree with a great many of their basic values. This is as true of student radicals, most of whom come from left-wing families, as it is of student conservatives, most of whom come from conservative families.

The media, of course, have a vested interest in dramatic and sensational "news": thus, pot parties are staged at Northwestern, motorcyclists are induced by television cameramen to roar across the campus at UC-Berkeley, while a focus upon the most volatile campuses gives an impression of constant student uproar, dissent, violence, and disruption. Selective editing invariably exaggerates the extent of violence, and selective aiming of the camera in the first place confirms the popular stereotype of the bearded, nihilistic, anarchistic, acid-head revolutionary.

Such images are important in themselves as well as for what they tell us about American society. Their prevalence determines public reaction to students; many policies are guided by such stereotypes, even when the author consciously knows better. The widespread mood of public indignation against students, long-hairs, intellectuals, and other "subversives" cannot be understood without appreciating the power of the stereotype of students. And the widespread currency of this stereotype points to fear of the young, to the extent that activists and hippie youth constitute a psychological challenge to the existing System, and the degree to which the students are joining and, perhaps, even replacing blacks as the objects upon whom adults project their own fears and repressed desires. Students, too, are affected by the stereotype, accepting its basic correctness and often feeling out of it because they are neither militant nor angry nor present-oriented.

Although the prevailing stereotype of the students is inaccurate, it is important to note its kernel of truth and to account for its prevalence. For one, the stereotype is far more accurate when applied to the most selective, liberal, and "progressive" institutions of higher education than

[3] J. A. Creager et al., *National Norms for Entering College Freshmen—Fall 1969* (Washington: Office of Research, American Council on Education, 1969). In fall 1969, 60.3 percent of all entering freshmen in all institutions agreed with the statement, "Most college officials have been too lax in dealing with student protests on campus." The percentage had increased over the fall of 1968.

when applied to the vast majority. A recent ACE study shows that the second best way to predict whether or not a campus will have protests over United States policy in Vietnam is to calculate the proportion of National Merit Award winners in the freshman class.[4] (The best way is to calculate the percentage who mark "none" for religion.) A casual survey of the institutions that have had the most publicized confrontations during the past two years demonstrates that the list is a roster of the most distinguished colleges and universities. If we were to eliminate the Ivy League, Berkeley, Madison and Ann Arbor, Cal Tech and MIT, and a dozen or so private, "high-quality," and "progressive" liberal arts colleges from the current portrait of student dissent, that portrait would virtually dissolve. Yet these colleges together enroll well under 5 percent of the college students in the United States.

The widespread impression of revolution on campus springs partly from the fact that the most visible, selective, and prestigious institutions, which by and large recruit students of the highest intelligence and the greatest independence, are the same colleges where student protest is growing. These institutions have traditionally trained a disproportionate number of the leaders of business, government, and university life. They are the pacesetters of higher education, the colleges that other colleges emulate in their struggle for status and visibility. Students at these colleges, furthermore, often constitute models for students at institutions of lesser status, who emulate the dress, slang, and political outlooks of those at the pacesetters. Trends begin in institutions like Berkeley, Antioch, or Harvard, spread throughout other institutions, and simultaneously into the secondary schools that send students to the elite colleges. In some cases—for example, white bucks and pink shirts in the fifties—by the time the chain of dispersion has been completed at the lowest level, those in the pacesetting institutions have abandoned the fashions they began.

We may now consider the dissatisfaction of three rather different groups, noted earlier. The discussion here deals with types, not individuals, and, therefore, it applies exactly to no one person.

THE EXCLUDED

The first thing to be noted about the excluded is that they are, by and large, excluded from colleges as well as the existing society, and until recently were especially excluded from colleges of the highest visibility, prestige, and selectivity. In 1968, only 6 percent of all American college students were black, while 3 percent were members of other nonwhite minorities. In 1969, the percentage remained the same, although there

---

[4] Alexander W. Astin, "Personal and Environmental Determinants of Student Activism," *Measurement and Evaluation in Guidance,* Fall 1968, Table 6 (p. 159).

was some shift toward the high-status colleges. The proportion of blacks that completes graduate and professional schools is even smaller. Furthermore, many blacks in college attend all-Negro institutions whose academic offerings and institutional climate have been pungently described by Jencks and Riesman.[5] Even the massive efforts to recruit black students into the high-prestige institutions have had extremely uneven effects today; at very few elite institutions are blacks represented in numbers proportionate to their percentage of the national population. The same is largely true of Chicanos, American Indians, and members of other excluded minority groups. Underrepresented in the university population as a whole, they still attend the colleges of the lowest institutional quality. Although race and color enormously aggravate the educational problems of black, Indian, and Mexican-American students, low social class and poverty in general, even in the absence of color, have a similar effect not only upon structural exclusion from the mainstreams of society, but also upon university or college attendance.

If any one theme runs through the demands of the excluded, particularly black students, it is for an end to exclusion and for full citizenship, with respect and esteem, in the university and society. Despite the angry and at times revolutionary rhetoric of many black students, and despite the adoption by a few small groups like the Black Panthers of a quasi-Marxist analysis, the position of black students is essentially that of the individual outside the System who demands immediate and full admission.

The vehemence and form of black students' demands spring partly from the fact that oppression and exclusion have taken not only political, economic, and institutional forms, but psychological and cultural forms as well. Perhaps the most degrading consequence of racism is that its victims come to believe in their own inferiority. One of the most bitter consequences of American history as generally taught has been to deprive blacks of any sense of an honorable past. And one result of many well-intentioned and, at times, insightful analyses of "Negro personality" and "Negro culture" has been to confirm blacks in their fear that their psyches were inadequate, while their "culture of poverty" was really, in Oscar Lewis' words, a "poverty of culture."[6]

Inclusion, for black and other so-called Third World students, comes to be defined not only in terms of admissions policies, scholarships, and so on, but also in social-psychological terms. Demands for special programs, control over black studies appointments, separate residential facilities, and the like are centrally impelled by the desire to right the

---

[5] Christopher Jencks and David Riesman, *The Academic Revolution* (New York: Doubleday & Co., 1968), chap. 10.

[6] Lewis, *La Vida* (New York: Random House, 1966), Introduction.

balance of self-esteem and respect. Nevertheless, black students as a group, especially those from working- and lower-class backgrounds, remain highly motivated by a desire to enter the System and to share in its benefits. As compared to white students at the same colleges, they tend to be more vocational in their educational goals, more skill-oriented in their definition of curriculum, less experiential in their educational and curricular demands. At colleges that recruit large numbers of relatively alienated, cosmopolitan middle-class white students (for example, the State University of New York at Old Westbury), black students object strongly to the experiential outlook of white students, which they contemptuously describe as "grooving on the grass."

Black students, indeed, present a major short-run challenge to the structure of higher education. The ACE's Office of Research has shown that demonstrations by black students become likely once a "critical mass" of about thirty black students have congregated on a campus.[7] When this happens, one can almost routinely expect demands for increased black admissions, special black studies programs, special and sometimes separate residential facilities, and so on. These demands are rarely impossible to meet, but doing so, especially in public institutions, may have severe political consequences both in faculty backlash and legislative reactions. Yet in a more fundamental sense, black students do not, in my opinion, constitute a revolutionary threat to American society or colleges and their prevailing values. The attack on careerism and materialism found among affluent white students is rarely as intense among blacks. To oversimplify: black students today reject the university and the college only because it deprives them of esteem, dignity, and a sense of their own value, even as it may exclude their brothers from admission. But they less often challenge the fundamental assumptions of higher education, the mode of teaching and learning prevalent at universities, or the traditional work-oriented values of American society.

THE TENUOUSLY IN

Higher education has always been an avenue of upward mobility in American society, and has become increasingly so since the passage of the Morrill Act establishing land-grant colleges. More than half the country's students define their college education primarily as a means of acquiring the skills and credentials essential for success *in* the existing society. Their approach to higher education is thus vocational, in contrast to the liberal arts emphasis on understanding the world, gaining insight into oneself, and finding one's identity. If there is a "silent majority" in higher education, it is in the vocational group.

[7] Alexander W. Astin, "Campus Disruption, 1968–1969: An Analysis of Causal Factors" (Paper presented at the American Psychological Association meeting, September 1969), Table 10.

A vocational approach to higher education is not, of course, perfectly correlated with any one socioeconomic background or psychohistorical position. Excluded blacks, for example, tend to be highly vocational in their view of higher education. Yet as a group, the white "vocationalists" in colleges and universities tend to have a number of common characteristics. They are, by and large, the first in their families to attend college, and they generally come from lower middle-class and, increasingly, working-class families. They attend community colleges, junior colleges, and those upgraded teachers colleges that Alden Dunham aptly calls "colleges of the forgotten Americans." [8] Often, the women in this group are preparing to be teachers, and the men may be interested in teaching (especially at the secondary school level), engineering, business administration, agronomy, and related fields.

Within this group, there is, of course, enormous variation. Politically, the vocational group includes most students who believe ardently in law and order, believe in the wisdom and morality of American policies in Southeast Asia, and regard the speed of racial integration as excessive. But most often, students in this category exhibit that political apathy so frustrating to the minorities of activists and hippies who attend the same colleges. Relatively uninformed about the world, conservative (usually without being reactionary) but essentially nonpolitical in outlook, these students constitute a more or less unpoliticized mass upon which the stability (or inertia) of most college student bodies rests.

The life styles of vocational students also vary extensively. Many attend commuter colleges, and their life style is still primarily determined by their parents and high school friends. Others in residential colleges accept older collegiate patterns focusing upon fraternity life, dating, and the fun-and-football syndrome. Still others view college in primarily social terms, defining social skill and "contacts" as the prerequisite for occupational advancement in modern society.

Although few of these students are politicized, it is from this group that the greatest danger of a student counterreaction against left-wing student activism exists. As the research of Brewster Smith and his colleagues at the University of California and San Francisco State suggests, politically conservative and inactive students tend to be at a different level of moral development than political activists: inactives define right and wrong largely according to conventional community standards and the requirements of law and order.[9] Student activists, who tend to be

[8] E. Alden Dunham, *Colleges of the Forgotten Americans* (New York: McGraw-Hill, 1969).

[9] N. Haan, M. Brewster Smith, and J. Block, "Moral Reasoning of Young Adults: Political-Social Behavior, Family Background, and Personality Correlates," *Journal of Personality and Social Psychology*, 10 (1968): 183–201. For a more speculative interpretation of these findings, see Keniston, "Student Activism, Moral Development and Morality," *American Journal of Orthopsychiatry* (1970), in press.

more "advanced" in moral reasoning, evoke a mystified response from most of their apolitical classmates who, like the general public, confuse the principled reasoning of the activist with hedonism and egocentricity. Thus, the apolitical vocationalist is likely to perceive the activist as an opportunist and, in times of crisis, to focus upon him the full force of moral indignation. Furthermore, campus conflicts, disruptions, building occupations, and protest marches are seen by the vocationalist as willful distractions from the main business of college, which is acquiring vocational skills and getting a good education. Thus, the demands of activists and radical or hippie students for more experiential education, for greater student participation, for student voice in curricular planning and even faculty appointments are interpreted as subversions of the primary purpose of education and, in addition, as disrespectful violations of the authority of the faculty "who really know."

The dominant motivation of most vocational students, then, is not to challenge the System, but to enter it without much questioning the price of admission. The discontents of such students are largely focused on immediate and personal issues. Often this focus is realistic, for their family backgrounds deprive them of the unquestioned affluence upon which upper middle-class, second-generation students can fall back, while their lower social status and less adequate secondary school educations mean that a college degree, indeed, may be for them prerequisite to a good job and upward social mobility. In current campus conflicts, the tenuously in students have remained largely invisible. They rarely join with activists in attacking the war in Vietnam, allegedly racist policies, militarism, or even the hegemony of the faculty and administration. In fact, they rarely even attend the colleges and universities where activists are found in large proportions.

If the recent spate of campus disruptions continues, however, the resentment of vocational students will probably grow apace, just as the resentment of their lower middle-class and working-class parents is growing. The universities and colleges they attend are competing—generally unsuccessfully—with the elite institutions; the resulting institutional inferiority complexes extend to many vocational students, convincing them that their degrees are really not as "valuable" as those from the prestige institutions. Thus, a variant of the traditional American resentment against experts, intellectuals, and East Coast snobs is often found among such students and could be readily mobilized, at least for brief periods. Already, the conservative coalitions that spring up to oppose radical students—even on many elite campuses—at times of campus crisis contain a disproportionate number of vocationalists.

Interstudent conflict is, of course, unlikely at colleges that draw very few vocationalists or nonvocationalists; it is likely only at colleges where they are interested in exploring the world, bringing critical judgment to arts colleges there are so few vocationalists that they are virtually silenced, and their resentment expresses itself indirectly, for example, through transferring or dropping out. And at most upgraded state teachers colleges, there are so few nonvocationalists (and, specifically, so few radicals or hippies among them) that they must usually resign themselves to chronic complaining about the apathy of their fellows. But at large, usually public institutions that draw big groups of *both* vocationalists and nonvocationalists, possibilities for interstudent conflict will be great in the years to come.

Just as intellectuals in the elite colleges and universities have generally lavished sympathy upon the excluded but withheld it from the tenuously in, a too-common failing of intellectual students and their intellectual professors and administrators is simply to condemn out of hand the apathetic or careerist students. Yet these students also have real and legitimate discontents. They see their values eroded, undermined, and mocked by more intellectual students; they must absorb the undeserved anger that many adults direct toward *all* students; and—most important—they often find their goal of learning technical skills and instrumental abilities blocked by activist-inspired experiential courses that not only fail to turn them on, but also leave them with little knowledge they consider substantial or useful.

In the future, then, we may witness a growing polarization within the student group as a whole, with the lines between vocationalists more sharply drawn. The student silent majority may find at least an intermittent voice, with the result that the existing polarization between hawks and doves among the general public, administrators, and faculty may find a counterpart among students themselves. Put differently, the divisions and angers growing throughout society will be felt increasingly within the student population; and there may arise a more vocal student constituency that believes—with considerable justification—that its interests are neglected because of a too-exclusive preoccupation with the clamorous demands of minority groups on the one hand and the insistent pressures of intellectuals and activists on the other. As those who attend college approach a majority, the traditional resentment of the less educated for the college educated may be increasingly transformed into a new resentment by the vocationalists against the intellectuals *among* college students.

THE SOLIDLY IN

The solidly in receive the overwhelming bulk of attention, approbation, and censure in any discussion of American higher education. These are students who define their educational goals in nonvocational terms: they are interested in exploring the world, bringing critical judgment to bear upon its problems, finding their identities, or defining new life styles.

Socially and economically, such students (called "forerunners" by *Fortune* [10]) are drawn from the children of college graduates who are now professionals, executives, teachers, social workers, lawyers, and the like—that is, from families where economic affluence and social status were virtually guaranteed facts of life from birth onward. Such students are more often graduates of the academically high-powered secondary schools, have a more intellectual orientation to college, get better grades, and attend the prestige colleges. Remunerative, secure, and even politically powerful positions in society are open to them. What is in question is whether they *want* such positions.

A liberal arts, nonvocational, intellectual, or identity-seeking outlook is, of course, not identical with dissent. On the contrary, most nonvocational students, whatever their criticisms of the existing society, hope that somehow it will prove capable of reform, and that they will be able to enter it as active participants. Such students, however, usually maintain a critical, skeptical distance from the System and see their educations not as a form of socialization or skill training, but as a chance to explore both themselves and the world around them. Most do not finally reject the System, but neither do they embrace it. They have not made up their minds yet.

But it is from *among* students in this category that most active dissenters are recruited, and also from among this group that "sympathizers," willing to join with activists around specific issues or experiment with hippie life styles, are largely drawn. The *Fortune* poll (Table 1) estimates that approximately 20 percent of the forerunners (about 700,000 students) are potential supporters of the New Left, when "support" is construed as disenchantment with American society. This group of 700,000 overlaps another group of about the same size which identifies with the less political counterculture that the hippies have come to symbolize. From the nonvocational group, then, are drawn not only most political activists, but also most drug experimenters and advocates of encounter groups, meditation, astrology, I Ching, communes, and the plethora of styles, values, fads, and fashions that together define dissenting college students.

The two groups within the solidly in category that most concern the general public are those I shall call *activists* and *hippies*—recognizing the inadequacy of the labels and the overlap of the groups. Several dozen research studies have yielded strikingly consistent results about the

---

[10] "What They Believe: A Fortune Survey," *Fortune*, January 1969, pp. 70–71, 171 ff.

TABLE 1: *Selected Differences between "Practical-Minded" (Vocational) and "Forerunner" Students* [a]

(N = 334)

Beliefs	Percentages	
	Vocationals (58 percent)	Forerunners (42 percent)
No favored presidential candidate in 1968	25	50
United States is a "sick" society	32	50
"Dove" on war in Vietnam	45	69
Draft resistance is justified under some circumstances	36	67
Civil disobedience is justified under some circumstances	32	66
The police were not justified at Chicago in 1968	40	60
Too little is being done for black people	38	71
Would not enjoy being in business	26	46
Containing the Communists is worth fighting for	59	28
There should be more emphasis on law and order	78	39
There should be more respect for authority	73	41
Accept the prohibition on marijuana	69	37
Desire more emphasis on technological improvement	75	56
Factors influencing career choice:		
Family	48	25
Money	58	21
Job prestige	33	13

Source: "What They Believe: A Fortune Survey," *Fortune,* January 1969, p. 70.

[a] Groups identified by self-defined "purpose of college education."

student activist.[11] Compared to his classmates in the same college, the activist is characterized by his intellectual viewpoint; his high socio-economic status; the likelihood that his parents will be politically active and left-of-center professionals, intellectuals, teachers, artists, or ministers; and his nonreligious outlook. Similarly, the likelihood of protests themselves can be relatively well predicted simply on the basis of the characteristics of the student body as a whole. The more students who fit this description, the more probable are protests over Vietnam, racism,[12] and student power. Research studies of political activists also emphasize the relative solidarity between them and their families, and fail to support the popular view that student political activism in general is a form of rebellion against parental values.

With regard to the hippie, however, the evidence is different. Like the activist, he comes from a family with relatively high socioeconomic

[11] For summaries of recent American research on the psychology of activism, see Seymour M. Lipset, "The Activists: A Profile," *Public Interest,* Fall 1968, pp. 39–61; Richard E. Peterson, "The Student Left in American Higher Education," *Daedalus,* Winter 1968, 293–317; Kenneth Keniston, "Notes on Young Radicals," *Change,* November-December 1969, pp. 25–33; and Jeanne Block, Norma Haan, and M. Brewster Smith, "Activism and Apathy in Contemporary Adolescents," in *Contributions to the Understanding of Adolescence,* ed. J. F. Adams (New York: Allyn & Bacon, 1969).

[12] See Astin, "Campus Disruption," and Astin, "Personal and Environmental Determinants of Student Activism."

status and is likely to be the son of college-educated parents. But his parents are less often politically active, less often in the helping professions, and more often in marketing, public relations, advertising, or entertainment. He is more likely to define himself as a critic not only of society's practices, but also of his parents' values and life style. In such students, the element of rebellion or rejection of parental values is indeed strong.

The discontents of the nonvocational group are more sharply articulated and more often expressed in social and political terms. Three issues above all have concerned these students and have constituted the direct focus of virtually every campus protest, confrontation, or disruption. The two primary issues are the war in Vietnam and racism in America, especially as the college or university itself seems implicated. One study of 71 campus protests that occurred between October 1966 and April 1968 found that 69 of them involved one or both of these issues.[13] But increasingly in the last year, the issue of student participation in decisions about college life has begun to appear as the third major focus of student discontent.

This is not the place for a discussion of the war in Vietnam, of psychological and structural racism, or of student involvement in college decision making. The point is that for dissenting students, each of these issues involves a sincerely held moral conviction, from which dissent grows. For example, the fear of being drafted and killed in Vietnam, however real, is rarely the basic cause for student objection to the war. The objection is primarily a moral one; for many students, this includes objection to a Selective Service System that allows most students *not* to be drafted. Similarly, opposition by white students to racism is less often based on direct experience with blacks than upon moral considerations (one of many factors that anger black students in dealing with whites). Finally, the advocacy of student power reflects the moral indignation of the student who feels himself to be a *part* of a university community in whose governance he has no voice.

Many observers have argued that the underlying causes of campus tensions lie outside the campus and that, consequently, little can be done on campus to alleviate these tensions. This view is, in my opinion, partly correct, but it should not be taken to mean that student protests are merely a "displacement" of concerns that might better be directed elsewhere. For most student protests are directed against college policies that appear to involve collusion with immoral forces in the society at large. To call these protests merely symptomatic is to ignore the fact that colleges and universities have, indeed, been highly involved in the

---

[13] E. J. Shoben, "Demonstrations, Confrontations, and Academic Business as Usual," *Western Humanities Review*, Winter 1969, pp. 63–72.

war in Vietnam, and that many or most have, to greater or lesser degree, acquiesced in the prevalent structural racism of American society. It is not accurate, then, to dismiss the student tension as nothing but a reflection of war and racism *outside* the campus, when what many protesting students explicitly object to is the influence of war and racism on the campus. The prevailing thrust of protest has been in the direction of the disengagement of colleges and universities from the "immoral" policies and practices to which activists object.

But there is another sense in which the dissent of the nonvocational college student indeed reflects a major crisis in American (and Western) culture. The old motivations that still sustain the vocationalist are no longer adequate for the forerunner. Upward mobility, career success, prestige, money, family togetherness—these goals no longer serve to animate a growing minority of students. When this happens, two routes are open. The first is to extend to others the rights and opportunities taken for granted by the affluent, secure, and politically free white student; this leads to sociopolitical activism, to a concern with the deprived at home and abroad. The second route is the cultural revolution of the experiential counterculture, with its search for significance and transcendence in the here-and-now. This route leads to the commune, to drugs, to meditation, and the antiscientific outlook of some students. As more and more students enter college from families that are solidly in the System, we can expect increasing experimentation with both these routes, each influenced by the changing social and political scene.

One factor that will influence the choice of routes is the organization and strength of the student political movement. As of January 1970, it seems fair to say that the New Left, as it was constituted between 1962 and 1969, has ceased to exist. SDS has become a set of explicitly Leninist-Maoist factions, divided over tactics and details of analysis, but sharing a dogmatically revolutionary position. The splitting and "ideologization" of SDS means that most students attracted to the older style of the New Left now have no organization. Many are repelled by the schisms, doctrines, or tactics of SDS factions, but they are equally skeptical about the coalition politics of liberal left groups.

Furthermore, the public backlash against student activism; the ascendancy of political figures like Ronald Reagan, John Mitchell, and Spiro Agnew; the trial of the Chicago Seven; the widespread fear and, to some extent, fact of repression of political dissent served, as of January 1970, to turn an increasing number of students away from political action and toward more private forms of dissent. The first half of the academic year 1969–70 has seen an extraordinary proliferation of the nonpolitical counterculture among dissenting students and the rise of many groups, communes, cults, and sects dedicated to the transformation of consciousness, new modes of experiencing, and unalienated relationships. This could presage a wider trend: a tendency to deal with the contradictions of American society not by active social and political involvement, but rather by withdrawal and "internal emigration." [14]

A second factor relevant to the future of student dissent is the administrative response to student protests and—even more important—the general mood, climate, and policies of colleges and universities. The small body of research on institutional characteristics and student unrest reaches the apparently paradoxical conclusion that unrest is greatest at those institutions that are the most liberal, permissive, and flexible. This finding, of course, results from the fact that the most protest-prone students attend the most liberal institutions. More detailed studies of the relationship between protests and specific institutional policies vis-à-vis student participation, the surrounding community, recruitment of minority students, university-military contracts, and so on are urgently needed. So, too, are comparative studies of the effects of institutional response to student protest and disruption.

Recommendations for Change

My own experience suggests, first, that responsive administrators and faculty members can often prevent destructive conflicts by prompt and reasonable responses to student complaints, grievances, requests, and demands—or, even better, by anticipating these grievances before they become focused into demands; second, that slow and nonpunitive response to actual confrontations and disruptions, including efforts to respond to student grievances and to avoid police intervention, often serves to deescalate student protest and at the same time to facilitate needed institutional change; and third, that external control or limitations on the capacity of a college to define its own solutions to its own internal tensions almost always aggravates these tensions.

But whatever happens to the student movement, or on the campuses, I doubt that it will basically lessen the level of discontent. To some ex-

[14] The rapid turnabout toward political activities following the invasion of Cambodia, the Kent State deaths, and the Jackson State deaths after these lines were written may reflect a reversal of this trend. What in effect happened in May 1970 was the politization of large numbers of "sympathizers" not previously involved in protests and activism. On many campuses, the sympathizers were so numerous that they overwhelmed the more dedicated radicals, producing a larger, more politicized group with less radical and more narrowly "political" objectives. But the absence of any national organization to coordinate student political activities, coupled with the extreme factionalization of the New Left, suggests that many of these students, however politicized during the spring of 1970, will become rapidly depoliticized, especially if peace candidates are not elected in large numbers in the congressional elections of November 1970. If this happens, a number of students have already announced their intention to "drop out" into the apolitical counterculture.

tent, student tensions can be channeled into more or less productive routes, but even channeling is likely to backfire. What is happening on American campuses is also happening in the universities of most economically advanced nations, and it will continue in one form or another.

In general, I believe that the grievances which students have brought to our attention are real and in urgent need of correction. But I also believe that American colleges and universities have been (and, I hope, will continue to be) among the most vulnerable and least oppressive institutions in society. Their principal contribution has been to provide sanctuary (and even stipend) for a great variety of deviants, creators, misfits, innovators, crackpots, and geniuses who have found their way into the student bodies, faculties, and presidencies. I see the greatest danger to higher education today not as arising directly from students, but rather indirectly from the backlash of a public increasingly disenchanted with the "products" of higher education. Colleges and universities are highly vulnerable in the long run because they cannot be self-sustaining: they depend on outside funding that can easily be cut off. And I view the greatest danger to this country, within the universities and outside, as the increasing polarization of the tenuously in and the unstable alliance of the solidly in and the excluded. If this polarization grows, I fear that the tenuously in will triumph. It therefore seems to me critical, not only ethically but also politically, to attempt to understand and to respond to the grievances of those who believe their interests have been neglected.

I make the following recommendations:

1. The rage of the excluded, like the disaffection of a portion of the solidly in, can be changed only by major changes in national policies. These should include (1) an end to the war in Vietnam and a change in foreign policy so that any other such war becomes impossible, (2) a reallocation of national resources to end structural racism and to begin to eliminate poverty, (3) a commitment to provide assistance to the impoverished nations of the world, (4) a sustained national effort to preserve a livable environment, and (5) an intensive examination of the adequacy of the existing political, social, and economic institutions of American society in light of the needs of the last third of the twentieth century. Were this country to move toward these objectives, campus tension would still persist, but it would be less enraged, less disaffected, more constructive.

2. American higher education must learn to tolerate and, at times, encourage conflict, rather than avoid it. Tolerating conflict may require developing new institutional mechanisms for its on-campus expression; it will certainly require from faculty members, administrators, and the public a more relaxed and less panicked attitude toward confrontations, demands, and even disruptions. Contrary to some opinions, neither

Western civilization nor American higher education will crumble because a college yields to student demands or fails to call the police. Contrary to other opinions, students are often wrong or inadequately informed; at times they violate the rules of the college so basically that they must be separated from it. Campus conflicts at present generate more agitation than they deserve; we must grow used to them.

3. American colleges must become more voluntary and open to "traffic" in and out. At present, only a third of those who enter four-year colleges graduate from the same colleges four years later; the uninterrupted undergraduate career is a myth. Socially approved channels for interrupting, discontinuing, and resuming higher education must now be created. A more equitable Selective Service System, embodying early service and abolishing student deferments, must be developed. Students who do not want what college offers should be encouraged to leave and seek valuable and relevant experience elsewhere.

4. Colleges and universities should not attempt to provide all things for all men. There are many experiences, desires, goals, and achievements that are humanly and socially worthy and important, but have no place in a college or university. Specifically, preparation for military service, psychotherapy, active involvement in social change, and so on may all be worthy objectives, but they should be implemented outside the college and not within its formal structure. The pressure for "relevance" and "experience" from students should be acquiesced to only when consistent with the institutions' educational goals and resources.

5. Colleges and universities should maintain and increase their autonomy and independence. Specifically, this means that institutions of higher education must retain the capacity to respond in their own manner to their own tensions, free from outside interference or pressure. Direct or indirect pressures from externally appointed or elected boards of governance, state legislatures, and so on must be minimized. To merit this autonomy, colleges and universities must resist the pressure from students and faculty to become political agencies for social change through community action programs. At the same time, they must refuse to become agents or executors of government or military policies, should not undertake secret defense contracts, and should not be involved in teaching or research whose primary purpose (or most likely intended consequence) is the destruction of human life or the impairment of human development.

6. Students should be maximally involved in the governance of each college and university. The precise meaning of "maximal involvement" must vary from institution to institution, depending on its traditions and the nature of its faculty and student body. Both minimally, participation should involve student representation on major faculty committees and policy-making bodies, student representation on boards of trustees, and

the systematic gathering of student opinion concerning faculty teaching ability. Actual student participation in decisions concerning faculty appointments, promotion, and tenure, while presenting many problems, deserves to be tried in some colleges on an experimental basis.

7. American colleges must deliberately seek a "mix" of student types. Present enlistment, recruitment, and selection processes tend to make student bodies at each college homogeneous. In the long run, this promises to create an educationally reinforced characterological split in the American public. An atmosphere of diversity, openness, and respect must be fostered within each college, whereby the rights and outlooks of students with distinct orientations to higher education are preserved.

8. The needs, grievances, and tensions of that majority of college students which views education in vocational terms should be heeded. Programs of genuine worth, use, and relevance to such students should be continued and strengthened. In the rush to respond to the urgent demands of the excluded and the activists, the educational needs of less vocal, more respectful, and less militant students must not be slighted. Indeed, there are many nonvocational students who would prosper more in college were they to work elsewhere until they can return with a more instrumental definition of educational goals.

9. Student political involvement should be supported. If presently unconvinced students are to be shown that American institutions can create meaningful social change, it must be because students can share in producing such change. To make this possible, the voting age should be lowered to 18 and residence requirements should be altered to ensure college students and others of their age group the vote. Students should be encouraged in the expression of opinions and in mounting actions directed at off-campus issues. At the same time, a mood that makes political involvement mandatory should be avoided, and the right of students to be "apathetic" should be respected.

GWENDOLYN PATTON WOODS

The Black Student Movement

FOR THE LAST FOUR YEARS, black students have been engaged in a vigorous program for educational reform. They have challenged the black university to create an educational experience that is more relevant to them and to the people they wish to serve. In many instances, students at neighboring colleges have been unaware of their protests. Since such struggles generally take place in isolation, black students have felt compelled to make their struggle dramatic; and since the university is, in many cases, reluctant to respond to proposals for change from the students, the struggles have tended to be disruptive and violent. There is a real need to develop a national forum for black students so their efforts can become more unified and so that, as a national body representing a cross section of the black university community, they may examine viable alternatives to their present struggle. The extreme lack of communication among black students must come to an end. We must create real alternatives for students, or we must risk increasing social disorder on the black college campuses. The same holds for black students within the large multiversity.

》　》　《　《

Gwendolyn Patton Woods, National Coordinator, National Association of Black Students, is a graduate of Tuskegee Institute, where she was student body president.

We need to study seriously the means and methodology that black students have used in fighting for educational reforms. We need to systematize these data and, from this information, develop concrete programs that students can employ to accomplish their goals. We need to examine ways of preventing educational and administrative problems from requiring militant action. This needs to be done from the students' point of view and with their direction. This kind of research would require a large facility, such as the National Association of Black Students, which could maintain contact with the activist groups erupting increasingly within the black university.

We also need to collect and examine the large body of information which is now in existence on the black university, to correlate and systematize it, and then create a research arm to study the problems of the black university from the students' point of view. We need to look into the cases of violent student rebellion to discover the legitimate ills which lead to these rebellions.

The university administrations recognize that their schools face extinction, either through the lack of operative funds or through the integration of the Negro. Yet the black institutions offer almost the only means of education to black students, especially in the Southeast, where most of them are located. These schools must be preserved, and at the same time they must rise to the challenge of the educational needs of the black community. Black students, who are becoming increasingly aware of the inadequacy of these schools, must have some organized method to articulate their concerns; they must develop means of transforming the schools into institutions which are more relevant to their needs.

Problems Facing Black Students

All of us know that educational institutions in this country were originally developed for the white middle and upper classes. In the past, Negro students did their best to ape their white counterparts. With the awakening of black pride and black dignity, students no longer feel that this ritual is necessary, and they are, in fact, questioning middle-class notions, ideas, and way of life.

The black students in the black university find themselves in a very complex situation. Motivated to get an education because there is no other means of survival in an increasingly technical society, the black student is appalled to discover that often he does not acquire the skills he came to college to learn. He also discovers that the black university makes no attempt to relate to the problems of the community from which he comes. Today many students go to college with a view to returning to their own community to help lay the foundation for a stable black community. The black university has made no positive response to this new feeling of the black student: it is much easier to convince the administration of New York University to develop a black studies program than it is to convince the administration of Tuskegee Institute. The irony of this does not escape the black students who begin to feel that their educational experience becomes less and less related to their goals. They discover that the student publications and the student government apparatus are held in firm control by the university administration so that there is no longer a legitimate forum through which to articulate growing apprehension. Given no positive means of reacting to what is rapidly becoming an unreal and intolerable educational situation, students are led to form secret insurgent groups which emerge only when they are ready to confront the college administration in a deadly and implacable situation. The university, when confronted by these groups, usually attempts to destroy them by dividing the students or by calling in local police, who are already convinced that the students want to destroy the university. The groups usually are looked upon by local officials as armed guerrillas and are treated as such by the police organization. These attitudes and actions convince the young blacks that nothing can be done; they tend then either to become discouraged or more creative in their approaches. The ultimate result is identical to the violent disruptions which take place in the urban centers during the summers. If this trend continues, we can expect the black university to become the real center of revolutionary action for Black America.

The black student in the multiversity finds himself in an odd situation indeed. He goes to the best schools in America and discovers that, as part of a small subgroup within a large university, he has no voice. He finds that he can acquire the skills he needs, but that the values of the institution are at odds with the development of a meaningful relationship to the black community. He has difficulty in maintaining a clear perspective of his role in the struggle of black people. Further he feels that the university exploits him to demonstrate its own progressive and liberal nature. He is forced to protest his cultural and social values by joining forces with his black brothers and sisters. He forms organizational structures to grapple with the situation—Afro-American societies, black student unions, and the like—however, he is still isolated within a large university. He has absolutely no understanding of the broader problems of his counterpart in the black university and of his ability to aid and to help reinforce the efforts of those within the black university. The National Association of Black Students hopes to bring these two groups together to work on their mutual problems.

Recommendations

Black students must be given decision-making positions commensurate with the ideas they are putting across. The students, like the black community, have grown increasingly knowledgeable, sophisticated, and creative. Further, black people occupy the focal point of all the great unresolved questions of American society. Because of the pressure and presence of black people, the country is moving toward the kind of social self-care that is characteristic of every industrialized society other than the United States. Even West European countries, for example, have family allowances.

Black people are responsible for the creation of a whole new language of politics and economics as well as art, medicine, architecture, and so on. American politics is forced now to deal with the necessity for participatory democracy at a time when governments all over the world are becoming more remote and impersonal. An index is the fiasco of the Democratic Convention. This event is traceable to the initial pressure put on the Southern Democratic hierarchy by the Mississippi Freedom Democratic Party. New ideas and tactics, the result of the pressure and presence of black people, were transmitted through idealistic young people, once involved in civil rights work, to the very core of this country's political process and system.

Any policy formulated with respect to black students should take the above items into account. Administrators, of course, may do a disservice to black students and to the black community by failing to require students to communicate their demands in an articulate and meaningful fashion. A sit-in or other demonstration provides a good indication of how accessible the faculty and the administration are to the student body.

This is not to say, for example, that the deviousness of Ivy League administrations is to be applauded, though it results in fewer demonstrations. In these institutions, demands have been granted and then lost in committees as soon as the heat was off. The problem here is that the frustration and energy generating the original demands are never siphoned off.

A realistic approach would be for the administration to help black students create their own Black Student Association, which would concern itself with the unique problems of black students. The National Association of Black Students proposes to help black students move in this direction. The intent is not that we will have no relationship with white organizations. On the contrary, the possibility would be opened for black and white students to work together in areas of mutual concern while being free to work in other areas unique to each group.

The development could ultimately lead to the formation of a truly National Student Association of equals, not a secondary group within a large organization that does not have the capability of dealing with the problems of the secondary group.

Specifically, and in the context of what has gone before, the following are recommended:

1. Direct grants to black student organizations for programs upon their making the same kind of presentation as is required for funding any other operation.

2. The creation of a pool of black speakers, talent, and materials to facilitate the study of blackness, such as black studies. The program should include movies, repertoire groups, nationally known black persons, film making, and music and art.

3. A black student newspaper. This medium is the easiest way for black student thinking—seemingly enigmatic to many people—to become clear. Articles on black people selected to appear in national magazines of editorial opinion are chosen, quite naturally, to conform with the spectrum of opinion with which editors feel comfortable. That is certainly their privilege, but it is not a meaningful source of insights into the affairs of black people.

4. Seed money for students instead of administrations. The effort needs to be made to move recalcitrant, conservative, and generally ossified administrations and faculty in these colleges and universities out of their ivory towers to deal with real issues.

EDWARD SCHWARTZ

Less Radical Programs, More Militant Tactics

THE STRATEGY of the protest movement has changed substantially since my term as president of the U.S. National Student Association in 1967–68; and the shift has altered the politics of the university as well. Students today, in a sense, are less radical yet more militant than they were two years ago. In order to set a context for my suggestions, then, I must delineate my impression of what is happening, then outline the ways in which educational leadership should respond to the changing conditions.

In 1967–68, a large number of campus activists viewed the university as a place to organize students not simply around specific issues of American political life—the war, the cities—but around fundamental questions of America's cultural and social future. We talked about Vietnam, about racism and poverty, of course. Yet, as often, we talked about the country itself—its values, its drives, its predominant institutions. We asked not merely, "How did the Vietnam problem, the race problem, the poverty problem develop?" but, "What is the nature of a society which enables Vietnams, racism, and poverty to develop?" Why was it, we asked, that most of our classmates were unresponsive to the needs of the poor, indifferent to the demands of black people, and unconcerned about the suppression of revolutionary movements elsewhere in the world? The

» » « «

Edward Schwartz is a graduate of Oberlin College and a former President of the United States National Student Association.

73

indifference struck us as being as serious a problem as the so-called problems themselves.

In exploring the roots of this indifference, we began to ask questions about the nature of the culture itself, particularly as it applied to the universities with which we were familiar. We began to see that higher education was wedded to the process of production, explicitly through its reliance on research grants for funding, implicitly through the structure of curriculum and courses. Universities trained students in styles of thought, behavior, and ideology appropriate to problem solving—to Ellul's notion of "technique": "the translation into action of man's concern to master things by means of reason, to account for what is subconscious, make quantitative what is qualitative, make clear and precise the outlines of nature. . . ." [1] That the product of that system was geared to meeting middle- and upper-class needs for private consumption, that its ethic sustained a competitive spirit which alienated men from one another, that the blind worship of production was itself becoming a serious crisis in the growth of man—these were unimportant issues to most people in these universities, as they became, in Hubert Humphrey's words, the handmaidens of society.

The movement for university transformation, as we tried to build it, addressed itself to these cultural-social issues. Our strategy derived from the belief that if we could alter the patterns of central educational institutions of the society, we could create new kinds of people who would rebel against other institutions as well. Consequently, we encouraged students to challenge the social relations, the power relations, between the various factions of campus governance—faculty, administration, trustees. We challenged grades, tests, credits, courses—all those arrangements which duplicate the competitive process of the corporation. We attacked the process, or lack of it, by which students determine their course of study as well as the curricula offered to students in making that determination. We attempted, in general, to open students to the notion that learning is self-development in interaction with other people, that communities can be created to sustain and enhance personal growth, that the university itself can be a resource to this process, rather than a competitor with it, or, at worst, a stifler of it. We envisaged not simply a free university in a free society, but a new, communal university, in a new kind of society, with a drastically altered balance between private and public, competitive and cooperative, rational and affective values.

[1] Jacques Ellul, *The Technological Society* (New York: Random House, Vintage Books, 1964), p. 43.

The Grievances Remain

Today, little of this thinking animates the university struggles—not consciously, at least. The urgency of fighting against the war in Vietnam and the precise demands imposed upon the university by black students, among other issues, have simultaneously directed students away from universities to the political process, while restricting the undergraduates' attack against universities themselves to demands which relate directly to the immediate political issue. Thus a McCarthy liberal is satisfied if the general faculty votes support of a moratorium; a black student group settles for the admission of new black students, larger scholarship funds, the creation of a new department or a new dormitory; the Boston student radical community goes after the Massachusetts Institute of Technology, not because it is a leading national center of the national technical complex, but because it takes its funds from the government.

It is wrong to assume, however, that the channeling of even radical students into demand organizing will enable easy resolution of the precise issues between the young and the universities. The basic grievances, which in earlier periods encouraged programs for fundamental restructuring, remain even if students have become less able to articulate them clearly. In the absence of broad strategy for the transformation of the university, the newer activist will fix upon one demand as being "revolutionary" (even if it is not) and pursue it with tactics equal to the revolutionary spirit. Liberals, who see the demand as being offered as a proposal for reform, grow confounded that the revolutionary radicals fight for it with such violence. The liberals refuse to see the *symbolic* nature of certain left demands, such as the elimination of defense research. They do not understand that wrapped up in a few demands are the frustrations over the war in Vietnam, the bitterness over the collapse of the movement to build a decent society at home, as well as the anger that universities themselves have done only what they have had to do to "readjust" to student initiatives. This is why the movement has become less radical in program, but decidedly more militant in tactics.

Ground Rules and Premises

What, then, can universities do in response to this shift in strategy? My basic suggestion is to forget that it has happened—and to realize that the precise demands are symbols of the broader crisis that has existed, and to treat the problems of universities as being greater than the sum total of the immediate conflicts. What those who pleaded for institutional transformation said a few years ago still applies—the power structure, the curriculum, the program of the university must be transformed if the institution is to survive its period of revolution and revolutionaries.

The sort of transformation we seek was outlined in brief by Wolin and Schaar:

> The great intellectual task of the present is the task of rethinking every aspect of technological civilization. That this civilization inherently moves toward self-destruction is now clear, and any radical rethinking must start from the premise that its manifest destructiveness will not be stopped by a broader distribution of the values or a more intensive application of the methods and processes which constitute and sustain the evil itself. If the universities were to dedicate themselves to this rethinking, they would not only serve society in the most valuable way possible, but they might even save themselves. . . .
>
> What it will require is a new focus, and the courage to withdraw human and material resources from the subjects which have high value on the current market, re-allocating them to the task of rediscovering and redefining the humanity and sociability which have become twisted and frustrated by the "single vision" of contemporary modes of organization and public purpose.[2]

Wolin and Schaar do not outline the ways in which this rethinking process might be effected except to say that it should be a focus more than a specific curriculum. I will suggest, therefore, a few possible ground rules and premises:

The route to the restoration of the *authority* of the universities lies in the ability of its leadership—administrative and professorial—to demonstrate competence in handling the questions which matter to students. At present, university professors can demonstrate competence in handling questions which do not matter to students (such as meaning of various words in Shakespeare's sonnets), without dealing intelligently with questions that do matter (such as the issues of love, death, and time explored in those sonnets). A university president interested in building his "authority" would be speaking out on the problems of creating community, of transforming bureaucracy, of building equality, of redirecting international priorities of the United States, rather than lecturing students on the need for one generation to "communicate" with another, or on the necessity for "restraint" and "reason." Such a redirection, in fact, is the only sort which will convey authority, as opposed to power, which is all that university presidents display when they flaunt the police.

College presidents should see themselves as gadflies—as activist mayors of the campus community. They are the ones who should be challenging the faculty into rethinking their approaches; focusing the community's attention on new needs, new demands; exhorting legislatures, alumni, and trustees to see what kinds of changes are occurring which demand a new kind of educational system. Clark Kerr's mediator-presi-

---

[2] Sheldon Wolin and John Schaar, "Education and the Technological Society," *New York Review of Books*, Oct. 9, 1969.

dent may have been a passable administrative model in 1963, but now, after a decade of moral crisis, the flabby bureaucrat, the vacillating Uncle Tom, it will gain the respect of no one.

Nor will the university president who argues that political decisions of the university are *not,* in fact, political be believed any longer. The structure of investments, support, curriculum, research grants—the whole enterprise by which a university relates to its surrounding society—must be dealt with as a complex of *political* decisions, and considered, at least in part, in political terms. To be sure, there are many cases in which the political and educational arguments for a change intertwine. One can contend, as many do, that heavy research grants from the Defense Department skew the ability of the faculty to examine critically the ways in which defense policy functions. Yet even when these educational arguments cannot be brought to bear on a situation, the political ramifications of university-society relations must be faced squarely.

In short, educational leadership concerned about the way in which this society is moving would be fighting to turn their institutions upside down. At this point, the models are all there—from learning teams, to independent study programs, to the elimination of grades, to the creation of living-learning dormitory complexes, to the admission of a high percentage of Third World students, to the accordance of academic credit for action undertaken in the community, to the development of new decision-making structures in every area of university life, to university-wide councils to handle issues raised by the war in Vietnam, to the use of film and new media in instruction, to tutorials. The list of proposals and real programs is endless. The problem now is political: finding the willingness on the part of educational leadership to move toward this new kind of university capable of providing assistance to students in coping with the changes of a new kind of world.

The student movement, it is true, has shifted in strategy and focus. It is more militant, if less radical, than it was two years ago. Yet the issues which divide the generations are the same. They involve the public crisis of domestic and foreign priorities, juxtaposed over the broader social crisis of a society in which masses of men and whole complexes of institutions have lost the capacity to respond morally to human beings in desperation and to a natural environment being ravaged around us. The response which educational leadership must make now is, as it always should have been, to keep its eyes on the prize, and hold on.

DAVID A. KEENE

Dissent
versus Disruption

THE DISRUPTIONS that have plagued many of our colleges and universities in recent years have forced many people to reexamine American higher education. This reexamination has been good in many ways. Structural problems have been highlighted and, in some cases, dealt with. Outdated and unrealistic rules and procedures have been eliminated or revised, and in some ways the educational experience has been made more relevant.

I have maintained and continue to believe that students should be treated as individuals. They should receive no special privileges by virtue of their status nor should they be subject to extraordinary penalties. Like other citizens, they should be expected to observe the laws of the larger society and the reasonable rules of the institution they attend.

This view has made some headway in recent years. Few administrators now see themselves in loco parentis and fewer still are likely to involve themselves in the individual student's personal affairs. Still, many do see themselves as protectors of a special and privileged class. They are too willing to dismiss their students' crimes and to intervene to protect unruly students from the consequences of their own volitional action. Some

>> » « «

David A. Keene, law student at the University of Wisconsin, is National Chairman, Young Americans for Freedom.

administrators tend to blame themselves, the larger society, or unnamed culprits for disturbances caused by young people acting on their own choice. They strive to "improve" our schools so that they will conform with the wishes of the disrupters in the naïve belief that this will lead to campus peace.

Although educators must continually work to improve the quality of education and the value of the educational experience, they should not assume that their efforts in this direction will stop the radical assault on our colleges and universities. Unfortunately, there are educators who make the serious mistake of assuming that the attack is directed against the imperfect nature of the university rather than against the university as an institution and as a symbol of the larger society.

Disruption and Institutional Response

Radical leadership has, of course, been willing to exploit institutional imperfections to attract moderate, nonradical support in specific situations. But when administrators assume that the leadership is primarily interested in dealing with these imperfections, they make it virtually impossible for themselves to understand or cope with the problems facing their campuses. Many radical leaders see these imperfections merely as issues to be exploited rather than as problems to be solved. The demands they make on the institution are often irrelevant to their real purpose. Thus, Mark Rudd's answer to the reporter who asked him what SDS would have done if the Columbia administration had granted all six of its demands during the disturbances there is illuminating. He replied that SDS would simply return with "six more."

Two years ago the Center for the Study of Democratic Institutions published an "Occasional Paper" devoted to student unrest. The paper consisted of the transcript of a dialogue among a number of New Left types who gathered at the Center for the occasion. Every college administrator should read it and think about it, because the assembled students do an excellent job of communicating their view of the world, of the revolution, and of their roles in both.

Most of those present saw themselves as revolutionaries dedicated to the destruction of an evil society. Since they were also students, part of the discussion was devoted to rationalizing the importance of the student in the coming "revolution." In their view, the student is important because he has the potential power to close down the university and thereby stop a society so complicated and interrelated that an attack on its universities is an attack capable of bringing it to its knees.

The absurdity of this analysis isn't really important. What is important is that a large number of young people believe it to be valid and are acting on that belief. These people—hard-core radicals—cannot be dealt with by improving the quality of education. They see the university as a battle-ground and as a revolutionary staging area or a sanctuary. Their gripe is not that the university is involved in politics, but that its politics are wrong. They cannot be satisfied, but they must be thwarted.

To deal with these kinds of people, college administrators must know what they are up against and have some idea of what a university should be. I fear that many administrators fail on both scores. They certainly don't understand the threat, though they are beginning to as time goes on, and I doubt that many of them really have any idea of what a "good" or "perfect" college or university would look like.

A university is, of course, many things. It is a place where people are trained, but it is also a place where they can educate themselves. It is at once the most conservative and the most radical institution in our society. Thus, while most universities are dominated by establishmentarians, they are also sanctuaries for men like Herbert Marcuse and Milton Friedman. In this way the institutions both train the people who maintain the status quo and shelter those whose ideas might alter it. To do these things a university must be both free and civilized. Those who attend or teach its classes may be ideologues and partisans, but the institution must main-tain its neutrality. It must be a place where all ideas can be discussed and where people can pursue their own lines of inquiry in any way they desire.

Those who would "purify" the university by driving out those with whom they disagree would eventually destroy it. To fire a man because he was associated with the Institute for Defense Analyses in 1969 is no less reprehensible than it would have been to fire him for being tied up with the Institute of Pacific Relations in 1949. McCarthyism of the left, like McCarthyism of the right, is not really consistent with free inquiry and discussion.

Those people responsible for running our colleges and universities must draw the line by saying that disruption of the educational experi-ence cannot be tolerated. They must learn the difference between dissent and disruption and between debate and street fighting. When they draw that line and see those distinctions, they will be in a better position to preserve and improve the institutions they administer.

Lewis Feuer has observed that the real crisis comes, not when the university as an institution is attacked, but when it fails to react. It's at this point, he observes, that the institution becomes "deauthorized" in the eyes of the attacker, who from that point on is more than likely to escalate his attack.[1] I think that Mr. Feuer's point is a good one and may describe what does in fact happen. To illustrate this point one need look only to the different ways in which two universities have dealt with

---

[1] Lewis S. Feuer, *Conflict of Generations* (New York: Basic Books, 1968).

disruptions. The institutions are the Universities of Wisconsin and Chicago. The different results achieved at these institutions are significant. Wisconsin officials tolerated leftist disruptions over a number of years until they were forced to deal with a situation so serious that force had to be used. Chicago officials, on the other hand, moved deliberately and authoritatively to handle a similar crisis at an earlier stage. The success of the Chicago experience contrasts sharply with the continual crisis atmosphere at Wisconsin.

It should be noted also that Chicago officials were not forced to rely on the police. The police are sometimes necessary, and college officials should not hesitate to call them when they have to, but they should recognize that they become necessary only when administrative policies have failed to deal effectively with the problem. Officials who have drawn the line before being forced to the wall have generally been able to preserve the integrity of the institution without calling the police. As a rule, only those who have negligently allowed the situation to deteriorate find themselves in a call-the-cops-or-capitulate position.

Administrators must be prepared to deal with situations as they develop and be ready to bring action against disruptive individuals before they become a threat to the existence of the school. To do this they must, in many instances, revise outdated disciplinary codes with often archaic goals and unconstitutional procedures.

Further, administrators must work toward a situation in which the hard-core radical will be hard put to recruit much of a following. Few college administrators are in contact with their students and many find it difficult to communicate with them at all. A few have been forced to bypass campus newspapers in order to communicate directly with their students. More of this may be necessary. Radicals are able to recruit as well as they do because they have the student's ear. Their side of the story is often, if not always, the only side given a real hearing. As a consequence, they inevitably recruit some—and often many—followers.

Institutional Purpose

The situation can be improved. Perhaps college officials should adopt their own "Boulwarism"—their own nonnegotiable terms—in dealing with radicals and openly seek the sympathy of the masses of students. This requires more than PR; it also requires a dedication to improving the educational experience. This dedication should not be born of fear, however, but of concern.

Peter Drucker has suggested that there are thousands of faculty members around the country who "stopped working the day they got tenure" and that we might consider requiring all faculty members to tape-record and listen to some of their own lectures. He feels that the latter proposal would drive many out of teaching—and I suspect he is right. Something must be done to put competition into the educational system, to provide incentives for good teaching, and to eliminate some of the canned irrelevancies that characterize much of what passes for education.

Perhaps people are required to spend too much time in college. Mr. Drucker has observed that college degrees in many fields are merely keys to job opportunities and really have little to do with how a person performs once he gets the job. In fact, he has compared similar positions in America and West Germany and found that in Germany people with the equivalent of an American junior high school education fill positions that in our country require college degrees. Further, there seems to be no difference in performance. This discrepancy should be looked into for it certainly reflects on the value of educational experience as it relates to job performance.

Drucker's observations might apply to something more important. Perhaps our colleges are attracting people merely looking for degrees as licenses to work rather than people interested in learning because the learning itself is needed in later life. If this is the case and if our colleges are becoming licensing agencies in this sense, then it would seem that some review of our purposes and goals is in order.

I make these points to highlight a few areas in which colleges and universities seem to me to be failing. They relate to the institutions' role and functions and must be viewed in that light. Perhaps a step preliminary to any real reform would see administrators, faculty members, and students sitting down to discuss the purposes of the institution.

PART THREE

What about Faculty?

SEYMOUR MARTIN LIPSET

The Politics of Academia

THE NUMEROUS ATTEMPTS to understand the growth in politization in the university have largely focused on student unrest. Clearly, student activism has been the most dramatic, the most visible form that politization has taken. But it should also be evident that increased concern with politics has also involved the faculty, both as initiator and as reactor.

Various critics of American faculty behavior have written harshly, in moralistic terms, about the causal role faculty members have played in undermining the authority of the administration by approving of the "objectives if not the tactics" of the campus militants.

The claim that faculty have directly stimulated or supported campus unrest is documented in an American Council on Education survey of 281 institutions of events that occurred in 1967–68. Of the 181 schools in which there were demonstrations, faculty were involved in the planning

》　》　《　《

Seymour Martin Lipset is Professor of Government and Social Relations, Harvard University. He is coauthor of The Politics of Unreason: Right-Wing Extremism in America, 1790–1970. *This paper has been cut considerably; the original, longer version will be published in a volume of essays commemorating J. P. Nettl, ed. Tom J. Nossiter (London: Faber & Faber). The author expresses thanks to the Carnegie Commission on Higher Education for support of research on faculty politics, of which this paper is a product.*

85

of more than half of the protests, and in 11 percent they were among the leaders. In close to two-thirds of the demonstrations, the faculty passed resolutions approving of them. Conversely, however, deans report that faculty gave the administration prior information about the protest in about a quarter of the situations. Faculty were most frequently involved in actions defined as "physical, but nonobstructive" or "diplomatic," somewhat involved in "physically obstructive" demonstrations, and not involved in those in which the demonstrators used violence.[1]

Faculty members, of course, differ on issues stemming from student unrest. Probably no other matter has so divided the university, to cause the severing of social and intellectual relations, as the internal faculty controversy over student protest on a given campus. As yet, little research is available—in fact, even begun—to help us understand student protest. This paper will bring together what we do know about the sources of faculty political involvement in the current situation, and suggest various hypotheses, most of which require further elaboration and research.

The Culturing of Activism

In the most general sense, I would argue the case that the major contribution of the faculty to student unrest in the post-1964 period is not found in the various malefactions of which its critics accuse it, such as not teaching, ignoring students, spending time in extramural money-making or status-enhancing tasks, but rather that a significant section of the faculty in the institutions which have been the largest centers of student radicalism have encouraged the political values underlying such protest. In this, they closely resemble the parents of the student activists. The many surveys of the social characteristics of student activists agree on the whole that they tend to come from relatively privileged families who formed a liberal-to-left political commitment as a reaction to the depression of the 1930s, the anti-Fascist war, the (Joe) McCarthy period, or aspects of their own family cultural background. The children of this large minority of the middle class spent their formative years hearing about the reactionary, racist, undemocratic character of the United States. Beginning in the late 1950s, as they came of age, and in response to various historical events which encouraged moral protest, the scions of the liberal segment of the privileged class increasingly turned to protest politics. Studies of parental reactions indicate that such behavior won their approval, or at least their tacit acceptance; rarely did it result in familial opposition. The parents approved of the goals of their activist children; their primary concern was that they might get jailed or hurt in their activities.

[1] Robert F. Boruch, *The Faculty Role in Campus Unrest* (Washington: Office of Research, American Council on Education, 1969).

On the campuses to which they went, which were the better schools of America in terms of wealth, facilities, faculty scholarship, entrance requirements, and the like, these students found many professors who shared their parents' social and political values. The liberal-left students tended to take courses in the liberal arts, particularly and increasingly in the politically relevant social sciences where the assumptions of their professors again coincided with their own. But some of them found, to their increased dismay, that their teachers not only resembled their parents in social values, but also fostered a polite gradualist version of reform politics. That is, both their affluent parents and their prestigious liberal professors appeared to do little to change America, to get rid of the evils they talked about. Thus, the student activists hurled the charge of hypocrisy against both their parents and the university. The very charge testifies to an agreement in values. One does not attack as hypocrites those with whom one is in disagreement. The liberal students found kindred spirits among their fellows, and found encouragement for their moral concerns among the faculty. Ultimately, when they turned to the use of civil disobedience against the university, they discovered that the university—unlike the Southern states where the tactic emerged or the public authorities elsewhere—was unable to defend itself, that the faculty and even occasionally the administration acting in loco parentis could not endorse the use of force against their own students, acting for moral ends with which they agreed. Once the activist students made this discovery in Berkeley in the fall of 1964, the wave of comparable disturbances across the nation and even the world was inevitable.

It is true, of course, that in a number of cases university administrations or the public authorities have resorted to calling in the police against student protesters who have violated the law, particularly through sit-ins in university buildings. But at Berkeley in 1964, at Columbia in 1968, and at Harvard in 1969, the faculty as a body refused to support the action. In each case, they called on the university to request the public authorities to drop the charges against the arrested students. In each case also, large segments, perhaps the majority, of the faculty turned against the university administration, equating, in effect if not in form, as immoral the initial law violation by the student demonstrators and the sending-in of the police to remove the protestors. In other universities, faculty groups played a major role in pressing the administration not to call in the police.

To a considerable extent, a major reason students can be a potent anti-Establishment force is the existence of norms that insist on autonomy from outside police interference, and that restrict efforts to punish students for behavior which for nonstudents would frequently result in severe penalties. Daniel Cohn-Bendit, the leader of the 1968 French student upheaval, argued that students are obligated to be politically active precisely because they are protected against the much more severe sanctions which would be meted out to other groups for like actions.[2]

More important in general consequences for the politics of universities has been the predominant sympathy of intellectuals generally, and the academics among them in particular, for liberal-left political causes and ideologies. Such sympathies both stimulate their antagonism to sanctions against activist students and lead them to welcome actions ostensibly designed to implement comparable political sentiments by a section of the student body. The leftist students—a youthful group without the responsibilities inherent in career and family, uninured to the pressures for compromise, and without experience concerning the complexities and unanticipated consequences stemming from rapid and major change —press through the implications of the ideological positions they share with much of the faculty in a more absolute and total fashion. The adult faculty liberal-left will, on the whole, disown and oppose the drastic tactics and more extreme objectives of the student activists. Such opposition will, however, be voiced from an ideological stance generally sympathetic to these objectives.

The Anti-Establishment Role of Intellectuals

The commitment of academic intellectuals to an anti-Establishment position has been deduced by many writers from aspects inherent in the very definition of the concept of the intellectual and scholar. Intellectuals, as distinct from professionals, are concerned with the *creation* of knowledge, art, or literature. Many writers have pointed out that inherent in the obligation to create, to innovate, has been the tendency to reject the status quo, to oppose the existing or the old as philistine, to reward the avant garde. Intellectuals are also more likely than those in other occupations to be partisans of the ideal, of the theoretical, and thus to criticize reality from this standpoint. The pressure to reject the status quo is, of course, compatible with a conservative or right-wing position as well as with a liberal or left-wing one. In the nineteenth century, when one found in the United States the two often antagonistic emphases on populist egalitarianism and on business growth, observers at the time noted the conservative opposition of American students and intellectuals to both.

Although important segments of right-wing intellectual criticism remain, it is clear that since the 1920s, in the United States and increasingly in other Western countries as well, intellectual politics have become left-wing politics. The American value system, with its stress on egalitarian-

---

[2] Daniel and Gabriel Cohn-Bendit, *Obsolete Communism: The Left-Wing Alternative* (New York: McGraw-Hill Book Co., 1968), p. 47.

ism and populism, fosters criticism from the left which challenges the system for not fulfilling the ideals inherent in the American creed.

Most recently, many prominent academicians have publicly stressed the inherent innovative and critical role built into the university and intellectual role. Milton Friedman, the doyen of conservative economists, approvingly quoted an unpublished manuscript of his colleague, George Stigler, to this effect:

> The university is by design and effect the institution in society which creates discontent with existing moral, social and political institutions and proposes new institutions to replace them. The university is, from this viewpoint, a group of philosophically imaginative men freed of any pressures except to please their fellow faculty, and told to follow their inquiries wherever they might lead. Invited to be learned in the institutions of other times and places, incited to new understanding of the social and physical world, the university faculty is inherently a disruptive force.[3]

Similar comments and analyses have been suggested over the years by men as diverse as Joseph Schumpeter, Robert Michels, Reinhold Niebuhr, Crane Brinton, Carl Becker, Sidney Hook, Edward Shils, and Lewis Coser in their efforts to account for the "critical attitude" of intellectuals, both academic and nonacademic.

This stress on the critical anti-Establishment role of the intellectuals would seemingly imply much more support for student activism and protest among the faculty than in fact exists. Most descriptions of faculty reactions on specific campuses characterized by student activism have properly pointed to the tremendous divisions among the faculty, to the fact that only a part of the faculty appeared sympathetic to the student demands or sought to protect them from civil or university sanctions. During the first four years of turmoil at Berkeley (1964–68) the faculty was divided in its support, however qualified, for the student or administration demands and positions. The great majority, however, reluctantly intervened only at moments of great crisis, sought a reasonable compromise that would allow the campus to "return to normal" quickly (and allow the faculty to return to unfinished work). When faculty support to both the administration and activist students is qualified and erratic, it erodes the authority of the university without satisfying the activists.

On almost every campus faced with a major crisis, the faculty has split, sometimes formally, into two or three major factions or faculty political parties. At Berkeley, Columbia, Cornell, Harvard, and San Francisco State, to cite a few cases, these groups have usually operated with elected executive committees, have prepared strategies for dealing with faculty meetings, and the like. Three general faculty positions have been de-

[3] Stigler, unpublished memorandum, quoted in Friedman, "The Ivory Tower," *Newsweek*, Nov. 10, 1969, p. 92.

noted by Spiegel, of the Lemberg Center for the Study of Violence: (1) liberals support goals of the aggrieved students to the extent that the university does not lose face through surrender; (2) the conservatives or hawks want to defeat the activists while minimizing the university's loss of face for "overreacting"; (3) there exists as well a middle ground position which attempts to balance the demands of the faculty hawks and doves with those of the students, a feat of no mean skill.[4] In many schools, although these three basic positions may be perceived, a two-party system has emerged with the leadership of each party tending to be chosen from the more moderate members, thus facilitating compromise and cooperation. Although the groups have obviously differed sharply in their estimate of responsibility for the campus crisis, both groups as a whole seek a return to campus peace. Thus, the "hards" tend to become a vehicle of faculty communication and pressure on the administration and trustees, and the "softs" tend to act as an intermediary with the radical students. From time to time, therefore, these roles lead critics to see the other party as a tool or stimulator of radical student or administration policies.

These descriptions of division among the faculties clearly raise the question of why the supposedly critical, liberal, and anti-Establishment professoriate divides when faced by a challenge from the student left which seeks to use the university to implement liberal-left objectives. Part of the answer, of course, is that American academics vary considerably in their commitment to intellectual and hence "critical" functions. Most of them are, in fact, primarily teachers, not scholars, dedicated to passing on the existing tradition, not the enlargement or critical rejection of it. Many are involved in teaching or doing research in narrowly professional and vocational fields, not so absorbed with the basic core of ideas centered in the so-called liberal arts faculties. But beyond these variations linked to the dimension of intellectuality, professors, like others, vary considerably in social outlook, differences stemming from the host of experiences they have had from birth to the present moment. These other factors or experiences impel them in different political directions, so that, though predominantly liberal, they include almost every possible political position.

The Academic as Political Man

While a general analysis of the political outlook of American academe is relevant to any concern with student activism and political protest, there is clear evidence that the sources of variation in political orienta-

[4] John P. Spiegel, "The Group Psychology of Campus Disorders: A Transactional Approach," mimeographed (Waltham, Mass.: Lemberg Center for the Study of Violence, 1969), pp. 13, 17.

tions along liberal-conservative, radical left to reactionary right dimensions also go far to account for differences within the academic community on ways to treat the issues stemming from student protest. In one study of faculty opinion in six diverse colleges and universities, the respondents divided sharply whether students had the right to participate in decisions concerning social and academic matters and, if so, to what degree. Attitudes on these issues were strongly associated with general political orientation:

Those who supported an equal vote for students were overwhelmingly (78 percent) liberal or radical, while 78 percent of the *No voice* group described themselves as moderate or conservative. The *Equal vote* group was also more likely than the *No voice* group to have discussed campus issues with students. A similar study at Columbia University concerning the sit-in and student strike in spring 1968 found that "21 per cent of the [self-identified] conservatives, 49 per cent of the moderates, and 88 per cent of the [strongly liberal] and radicals were high [in their support of the activists]." Clearly, then, the political attitudes among faculty before a crisis are important in explaining subsequent campus-related divisions of opinions.[5]

The evidence that the dominant mood on the campus is liberal and hence predisposed to favor student politics dedicated to equalitarian social change is clear and decisive. The most recent and massive (N=61,000) evidence bearing on ideological identification of American professors is contained in the data collected in the spring of 1969 for the Carnegie Commission study. These findings, together with the results of similar studies of American students, the U.S. public, and British academics, are presented in Table 1. Both groups of faculty and American students seemingly gave comparable distributions of responses. They were each much more liberal-left than the U.S. public.

Studies of voting patterns in every presidential election since 1936 show a disproportionate number of professors expressing preference for the more liberal major party candidate. Academics have also been disproportionately high in backing for left-wing third parties.[6] The Car-

[5] Robert C. Wilson and Jerry G. Gaff, "Student Violence—Faculty Response," *Research Reporter* (Berkeley: Center for Research and Development in Higher Education, University of California), 4, No. 2 (1969): 3; and Stephen Cole and Hannelore Adamsons, "The Student Demonstrations at Columbia University: Determinants of Faculty Support," mimeographed (New York: Bureau of Applied Social Research, Columbia University, 1969), p. 3.

[6] Lawrence C. Howard, "The Academic and the Ballot," *School and Society*, Nov. 22, 1958, p. 416; for other years, see Paul F. Lazarsfeld and Wagner Thielens, Jr., *The Academic Mind* (Glencoe, Ill.: Free Press, 1958), p. 402; Robert Yee, "Faculty Participation in the 1960 Presidential Election," *Western Political Quarterly*, 16 (1961), Supplement: 43; Edward Noll and Peter H. Rossi, "General Social and Economic Attitudes of College and University Faculty Members," private report (Chicago: National Opinion Research Center, University of Chicago, November 1966), p. 20.

TABLE 1: *Political Ideology Responses of National Samples of U.S. Faculty, Undergraduates, and of British Faculty, 1966*

Faculty	Percent	Students	Percent	U.S. Public (a)	Percent	(b)	Percent	British Faculty	Percent
Left	6	Extremely liberal	12	Liberal	*17*	Liberal	15	Far left	5
Liberal	43	Fairly liberal	41			Moderately liberal	18	Moderate left	48
Checked both	.3	*Total liberal*	*53*	*Middle-of-road*	*32*	*Total liberal*	*33*	*Total left*	*53*
Total liberal	*49*								
Middle-of-road	*24*	*Middle-of-road*	*24*	*Conservative*	*38*	Moderately conservative	28	*Center*	*28*
Moderate conservative	22	Fairly conservative	19	No opinion	13	Conservative	23	Moderate right	18
Strong conservative	2	Extremely conservative	2			*Total conservative*	*51*	Far right	1
Total conservative	*25*	*Total conservative*	*21*			No opinion	16	*Total right*	*19*

Sources: United States: Faculty data from Carnegie Commission survey in spring 1969. Student data from a Gallup survey from April 23 to May 17, 1969, as reported in "Special Report on the Attitudes of College Students," *Gallup Opinion Index,* Report No. 48 (June 1969), p. 37. U.S. Public (*a*) Louis Harris poll taken Nov. 1–3, 1968, as reported in "Conservative Mood Discerned by Poll," *New York Times,* Dec. 4, 1968, p. 31; U.S. Public (*b*) Gallup survey taken in July 1969, as reported in *Gallup Opinion Index,* Report No. 50 (August 1969), p. 9. British faculty: A. H. Halsey and Martin Trow, "A Study of the British University Teachers," mimeographed (August 1967), chap. 7, p. 6.

negie Commission's national survey inquired about voting choices in 1964 and 1968, and found widespread support for Johnson and Humphrey, who received 80 percent and 60 percent of faculty votes, respectively.

RELATION OF DISCIPLINE TO POLITICAL POSITION

Almost all of these surveys dealt with the whole of academe: they include those in liberal arts departments as well as faculty in professional and vocational education. They covered institutions ranging from the major graduate training and research centers of America to small church-controlled colleges. In a real sense, as noted earlier, a very large proportion, if not the great majority on whom these studies report, have not been "intellectuals," "scientists," or "scholars," if these terms are arbitrarily limited to those involved in *creative* scholarly and artistic endeavors. The hypothesis that intellectual scholarly pursuits predispose their incumbents to a left or liberal critical position in America would imply that such an orientation should be found most heavily among those in the more "intellectual" disciplines—the liberal arts, as compared with the more "practical" professional fields. Within the liberal arts, it may be suggested that "innovative intellectual" orientations should have more bearing on political attitudes in the more politically relevant social sciences than in the natural sciences, with the humanities falling in between.

Differential voting preferences are discernible in various academic fields. Social scientists and humanists are preponderantly and increasingly Democratic, while the engineers, education, and business professors lean more toward the Republican party. A 1966 National Opinion Research Center (NORC) national survey, which differentiated by major groups of disciplines concerning the social worth of government control of business and labor, found that social scientists were most favorable to increased controls over business and least supportive of such policies with respect to labor. Respondents in the education, business, engineering, and natural science disciplines were more disposed to favor greater increase in control over labor than over business.[7] British faculty exhibited similar voting patterns, with a clear preference for the Labor party among social scientists, and with decreasing Labor support in the arts, natural science, technology, and among medical school faculty.

Special studies of sociologists, political scientists, psychologists, and social scientists as a group reinforce the conclusion that these fields tend to be the most liberal in the American university. Political scientists as a group are slightly though consistently less liberal Democratic than sociologists. Comparisons of party affiliations indicate that more sociolo-

[7] Noll and Rossi, "General Social and Economic Attitudes of . . . Faculty Members," p. 89.

gists identify with the Democratic party than do political scientists or psychologists. The reverse is true for identification with the Republican party. More psychologists than political scientists or sociologists are Republicans.

These studies also examined the differences among groups of disciplines to find if they are primarily inherent in characteristics of the fields, rather than background factors (for example, family, community, or party origins) or environmental conditions (quality of school, rank, income) as shown by disproportionate distribution among the subject areas. In fact, if differences were controlled for, the association between academic professional and political orientation was stronger.

Concern of academicians over the Vietnam war follows a similar pattern. As opposition to the war is related to liberal attitudes, the incidence of dissidence is highest among liberal arts, and particularly among humanist and social science faculties. In examining the content of antiwar feelings within various social science fields, Ladd found that politically identified anti-Vietnam war sociologists are more likely in 1968 to have supported McCarthy than Kennedy, who was supported more by political scientists. Further, in their opposition to the war, the sociologists are more likely to make a "moral" argument, while the political scientists are "realists." Sociologists more than any other social science field are likely to voice support for student activists. Psychologists appear to fall closer to the "moralist" approach, while economists produce more antiwar "realists." [8]

There have been various efforts to account for the greater emphasis in sociology on support of reformist tendencies in the body politic. The discipline in the United States was founded by reformers and continues to deal with topics which inherently remain a focus for discontent—race, urbanism, stratification, poverty, power, crime, delinquency, and so on. Political science lacks a comparable tradition. Studies of prospective sociology concentrators, both entering freshmen and beginning graduate students during the 1950s, found a high proportion of them oriented to social reform.

In addition to the manifest concerns with reform, these studies have noted strains inherent in the supposedly marginal position of the field— uneasily located on the border between humanism and science, between qualitative and normative concerns—and a desire to be perceived as a science that involves a high degree of quantitative rigor and formal theory. These two factors may make the sociologists feel more like outsiders, possessors of a low level of "legitimacy," of low prestige within academe generally.

[8] Everett C. Ladd, Jr., "Social Scientists and Opposition to the Vietnam War: The Petition Campaign Revisited," mimeographed.

Another interpretation has been offered by Cohn-Bendit and his fellow sociology students at the University of Nanterre. They argue that sociology's very claim to be a "leftist" field, that is, "its faculty like to pass for Leftists," while deprecating political action, fosters political protest, particularly since in their view sociology has adjusted its theory, concepts, methods, and problems of research to facilitate the growth of a stable capitalist system. Thus, Cohn-Bendit and his colleagues argue that the left-leaning sociology serves the needs of the system more directly than any other discipline, as it seeks to account for basic social problems such as racism, unemployment, delinquency, and slums as if they were isolated social phenomena, not inherent in the nature of capitalism. And by explicitly condemning various social evils while adapting to capitalism's needs, sociology has forced its students to oppose the university.[9]

Lazarsfeld and Thielens suggest that American professors are relatively left politically because they *believe* they are underprivileged, in part because they use the deference accorded to all holders of high status, including academicians, in Europe as a reference point from which to judge the status of American intellectuals. They also explain the special case of the liberalism of the social scientist as tied to his ability to visualize a radically different state of human affairs, which requires a critical anti-Establishment intellectual stance.[10]

SELECTION OF FIELD OF STUDY

Perhaps the major source of political differentiation may be selective recruitment. This factor plays a major role in determining the predominant political orientation of different disciplines. In a study of undergraduates' academic majors and political orientations, it was found that the strong relationship between these two variables was associated with changes in career plans or subject major. Thus, conservative students initially concentrating in liberal (in political terms) fields tended to change subjects where most student concentrators were more conservative. The same trend was found for liberal students as well. As yet, however, we know little concerning the images of different fields among students and the general public which produces such selectivity. In general, students from the lower socioeconomic backgrounds are disposed to see higher education as a means of securing the credentials and skills necessary for a "good job," whereas those from more affluent, well-educated, liberal, and intellectual environments see college as a way of gaining knowledge or finding ways to "do good" rather than as a means to economic success.

A study of Berkeley undergraduates in 1959–61 found that interest in

[9] D. and G. Cohn-Bendit, *Obsolete Communism,* pp. 35–36.
[10] Lazarsfeld and Thielens, *The Academic Mind,* pp. 150, 149.

college teaching, although related to socioeconomic status, was also associated with political identification. The more liberal-left college students were more inclined to become college professors than conservative ones.[11]

It is difficult to establish precise links between the political attitudes and behavior of professors and those of student roles which lead into different academic fields. Such relationships, even if sustained, do not demonstrate the causal effect of student political beliefs on the discipline variations among the professoriate, since much of this association appears to be a function of the recruitment process. We need to learn much more about the interplay between structural attributes and self-selection before we reach any definite conclusions about the politics of students or professors.

INTELLECTUALITY AND POLITICAL ORIENTATION

Presumably, although early social and political values may play a considerable role in dictating fields of study, they should not have a comparable effect in determining who among prospective scholars and intellectuals will be most successful in the role. Yet the thesis that a commitment to "intellectuality" predisposes men to a critical political stance should mean that those most involved in creative activities will be more liberal or left in the American political context. The data bearing on this proposition tend to sustain it. The more distinguished professors have been more liberal-left or irreligious (two closely interrelated attitudes) than those less involved in creative scholarly endeavors. Various studies have established a clear relationship between scholarly productivity and the propensity to vote Democratic within different age groupings or to take liberal-left political positions.

Another indicator of the relationship between creative intellectuality and political orientation is the predominant liberal-left political outlook at institutions which emphasize scholarship, as reflected in the prominence of their faculty, their devotion of a considerable proportion of resources to the support of scholarly endeavors in the form of good libraries, laboratories, and research budgets and which have high admission standards and are heavily involved in graduate education. The greater liberalism of the faculty at the high quality schools has been explained as congruent with the assumption that an emphasis on intellectuality or scholarly creativity is linked to such political values. The higher quality schools are more likely to attract and retain scholars and innovative intellectuals, while schools of lesser quality have a larger proportion of faculty composed of men who are primarily teachers.

Income, rank, and age are major determinants of variations in political

[11] Ian D. Currie et al., "Images of the Professor and Interest in the Academic Profession," in *Sociology of Education,* ed. Ronald M. Pavalko (Itasca, Ill.: Peacock, 1968), pp. 540–41, 549–50.

orientations in the community at large. Within academe, they are inter-correlated with each other and are also affected by type of institution in which faculty are located and by their relative scholarly productivity. The better institutions are centers of greater liberalism and pay much higher salaries on the average than the less prestigious, more conservative schools. Whether, however, income as such is a major source of ideology has not been studied. Although the data are somewhat inconsistent, there is indication that, in general, younger and lower status faculty are more liberal and Democratic and the older and higher status members are more conservative, regardless of school quality. Similar patterns have been found in Great Britain. In high quality schools, however, senior faculty are among the most liberal in academe as a whole, although somewhat less liberal than their younger colleagues. The relative liberalness of the more visible and distinguished senior men in the social sciences at top-ranked schools, who presumably constitute important reference individ-uals for younger scholars, is an important contributor to the image of the profession.

RELIGION AND BACKGROUND

Most of the studies of the opinions and behavior of academics agree that religious orientation and background make a considerable difference in political choice. The contribution of faculty of Jewish background to liberal political groupings has been stressed in a number of surveys. Al-though Jews are only 3 percent of the national population, they made up 10 percent of academe in 1969 according to the Carnegie Commission sample. Further, they constitute much larger proportions in various dis-ciplines and types of institutions, because they are concentrated in a few professional schools, the liberal arts faculties, and at the more prestigious universities. Jews are relatively strong in psychology, philosophy, sociol-ogy, and political science and are weaker in fields such as geology and en-gineering. Jews are strongly represented in the most liberal fields and are weakly represented in academic disciplines that have the most conserva-tive attitudes. Close to 90 percent of the Jewish academics are Democrats, and they have contributed highly to the backing of leftist third parties and to the early opposition to the Vietnam war. It is hoped that the size of the Carnegie Commission sample will permit some specification of the interrelationship (hitherto ignored) among academic occupations, the sociopolitical orientations associated with them, and the cultural-ethnic-religious backgrounds of professors.

It should be made clear that the issue of causal weight of intellectual orientations on other aspects of belief systems is not eliminated by the finding that those who hold the hypothesized set of values come from specific, highly delimited backgrounds. We should expect a high degree of congruence between the personal values present disproportionately in various social milieus (class, religious, regional, ethnic, etc.) and the over- or under-representation of persons from such backgrounds in given types of jobs. The research on occupational choice or job placement indicates logical relationships between the values and special abilities of individuals and the jobs they prepare for and take. Those subgroups in American life which value intellectuality more highly than others should, all other things being equal, contribute in heavily disproportionate numbers to the intellectual occupations. Conversely, lesser contributions will come from those milieus which are anti-intellectual or where other forms of human activity are held to be of greater worth. Further, it should follow that those individuals socialized in a highly intellectualized family and cultural environment should do better in intellectual jobs than those who enter such pursuits without the advantage of strong family and cultural encouragement and early experience. The children of intellectuals, for example, regardless of religious background, should do better in intellectual pursuits and should possess more of the core values of intellectualdom than those of other backgrounds.

There is a general assumption among those who write about Jews that they are especially attracted to intellectual values and pursuits. This assumption is based largely on the considerable Jewish presence in intellectual activities, as well as on the relatively greater success of Jewish students in educational activities at all levels. A comparison of the values and behavior of Jews and Protestants lends credence to the hypothesis that Jewish liberal-left political orientations may form a part of a complex of attitudes with intellectualism. In one study, Jewish academics were more likely than a comparable group of Protestants to define themselves as intellectuals. Reading habits suggest that self-defined intellectual Jews read more serious nonprofessional magazines than do intellectual Protestants.[12]

The evidence clearly suggests the existence of a self-sustaining or even self-escalating cycle. Intellectualdom recruits from groups who value intellectuality and who, as we saw, are likely to come from relatively privileged, well-educated, and politically liberal backgrounds. Those from more lowly origins see education as a means of getting ahead vocationally, and are unlikely to enter academe. Those of this group who do decide on academic careers presumably would do so more for vocational and status reasons than because of a commitment to intellectuality. One would expect them to be both more conservative politically and less successful occupationally than those who came to academe or other intellectual pursuits with a desire to be creative.

These assumptions are congruent with the findings of several studies that creativity is linked with high self-esteem as an intellectual, and that,

---

[12] Charles H. Anderson, "Kitsch and the Academic," *Sociology and Social Research*, 51 (1967): 452, 447–49.

controlling for age, professors from high socioeconomic backgrounds are more likely to be highly productive and liberal. This suggests anew that a higher status background, presumably from more intellectually oriented families, is more conducive to such liberal views within academe than a deprived, typically less intellectual one.

The more successful persons within academe, also the most liberal, are more likely to see academe as a place in which intellectual and nonconformist styles of life may be best fulfilled. When an NORC survey asked for a comparison of academic and nonacademic jobs with respect to which they thought was better on a number of job characteristics, a consistent set of differences emerged between the answers by faculty at low quality and at high quality schools. Those at low quality schools were more likely to say that academic jobs were superior to nonacademic ones in opportunity "to work with people," "to be helpful to others," "to be helpful to society," and "to exercise leadership." Those at high quality schools were more prone to stress the desirability of academic jobs for the opportunity "to be creative and original," "to achieve recognition in own field," and to have the "freedom not to conform in personal life." These findings reinforce the thesis that there are two distinct groups of faculty, one concerned with the world of ideas, the other with the vocational and pragmatic uses of academe. Liberal teachers seem to be more "cosmopolitan," in Merton's terms, oriented toward their profession at large, while the more conservative social scientists are "local," that is, oriented toward the particular college situation, and thus less committed to the broader view of intellectualism.[13] Undisclosed, of course, is the extent to which faculty at different types of schools developed the varying orientations as a reaction to their experiences in differing academic worlds or perhaps brought so much of these values with them that their personal orientations helped determine what part of academe they would inhabit.

The values of the cosmopolitan liberal scholars continue to dominate academe because new recruits to the profession are socialized in the graduate schools. Those who most resemble their professors are most likely to be recommended for the best jobs, to be defined as the most promising. Graduate students clearly see their professors as valuing creative scholarship above all other things. Being original and creative is also seen as being highly valued. And relatively few graduate students believe that teaching ability gives them any prestige with their graduate professors. These values, of course, are in conflict with those now espoused by the activist students and their younger faculty sympathizers. How much, if any, change in faculty practice will result is an open question.

[13] Robert K. Merton, "Patterns of Influence," in *Communications Research 1948–49*, ed. P. F. Lazarsfeld and F. Stanton (New York: Harper & Bros., 1949).

STUDENT ORIENTATIONS

Perhaps the most impressive conclusion to be drawn from the studies of faculty opinion is the high congruence between the correlates of liberal-left points of view among faculty and among students. The studies indicate that liberal-left faculty come from social backgrounds conducive to intellectualism and liberalism, and are concentrated among the more highly intellectually committed disciplines and institutions. Similarly, Flacks has pointed out that student activists are characteristically from well-educated, professional, affluent, and Jewish or irreligious homes, whose parents stress intellectual involvement, humanitarian interests, and creativity.[14]

The congruence in values between liberal-left faculty and students, the strong relationship between a critical anti-Establishment ideology and a commitment to intellectual values has obvious implications for the political future of academe. It is quite likely that the activist students of today will be the faculty of tomorrow. Clearly, many of the younger academics today are alumni of the student "movement." Radical faculty and organizations, such as the New University Conference or radical splinter groups within the professional organizations in sociology, history, political science, economics, and many other fields, have attracted many of the younger academics. Most of their membership comes from junior faculty and graduate students. Many of the more senior faculty on the left tend to abstain from membership and public support because of opposition to the confrontation tactics employed by some of these groups or because they object to explicit politization, to the insistence by many of these radical academics that the ideal of "objective scholarship" is reactionary, that all research and teaching should be openly partisan. With indications that academe is attracting a disproportionate share of the most militant students because they are the most oriented toward intellectual careers, it will be interesting to learn how this more politicized group of prospective faculty react to the teaching-research dilemma.

Political Ideology and Campus Response

The above discussion rests on the assumption that the ideological predispositions which faculty bring to campus political crises have been major determinants of the way they have responded to the campus issues. However, a single factor cannot explain such complex modes of behavior, and, in any case, it is clear to all participants in internecine campus conflicts that the division has not been that simple. In almost every well-known conflict, prominent faculty liberals and even radicals have

[14] Richard Flacks, "The Liberated Generation: An Explanation of the Roots of Social Protest," *Journal of Social Issues*, 23 (1967): 66, 68.

strongly opposed confrontationist tactics as being destructive of the basic conditions for scholarship or as politicizing, and hence reducing, the academic freedom present within the university. Conversely, some men of conservative values have sharply opposed the policies of the administration in using force against student demonstrators on the grounds, among others, that the administration and faculty, as the adult members of the university, have a greater moral obligation than students to restrain their use of sheer power; that in the given situation, they should have negotiated much longer than they did or been willing to change outmoded policies, even under duress.

Although the survey of British faculty opinion was conducted before the current wave of student unrest and hence did not inquire into it, it showed that British faculty who were left wing and cosmopolitan were much more likely to favor the "democratization" of university administration than were the more conservative locals. The substantial predictive power of political and "cosmopolitan-local" factors together show that views on the structure of power in universities are tied to attitudes on more general issues than university governance.

FACULTY AGE AND RANK

The nonpolitical factors which give the impression of having had the most impact in differentiating faculty groups are age and rank. At most schools, the more left caucus is invariably reported to be heavily composed of younger and nontenured faculty, the more conservative one of senior tenured professors. Although such differences may largely reflect variations in general political ideology linked to age, possibly they are also related to clear-cut interest differences, as well as to a variation in the degree of involvement in and commitment to the institution. To the junior faculty, the administration and the university are often a "they," an employer who will probably require them to move on. To senior faculty who have spent most of their lives at the university, the university is "home." Perhaps even more relevant, the administrators who are under fire are men they have known for many years, who, they feel, deserve the benefit of the doubt, and may even be excused for blunders.

Rank and age have also been found to be important sources of differences in attitudes of faculty toward university governance. One study found that the lower the status, the more left the faculty vote on the issue of allowing outside recruiters on campus. However, when rank was controlled, longevity at the institution emerged as the decisive factor: those with high rank who were new to the university were more liberal than assistant professors of longer experience at the school.[15]

---

[15] Rosalio Wences and Harold J. Abramson, "Faculty Opinions about University Functions and Autonomy," unpublished (Storrs: Dept. of Sociology, University of Connecticut, October 1969), p. 13.

It is, of course, difficult to tell what the source of the differences between the locals and the "newly arrived" is. It may be a reflection that the latter, being more mobile, are more oriented to the larger values associated with intellectualdom and scholarship in academe discussed earlier. It may also result from the lesser ties of the newly arrived to the university administration and existing faculty leadership. In any case, this study suggests that universities which emphasize turnover through stringent requirements for tenure, seeking to build a high caliber cosmopolitan and scholarly faculty, may by so doing increase the sources of opposition to the administration in intramural disputes, a conclusion implicit in many of the previously reported findings.

Possibly the most rigorous effort to factor out the causal significance of the variables involved in faculty reaction to campus protest was conducted by Cole and Adamsons shortly after the police drove student demonstrators from Columbia.[16] They asked questions about faculty attitudes on administration policy, the justifiability of the sit-in, the goals of the demonstration, the general strike called after the police action, as well as their general political attitude, and assorted background factors. On the variables which have already been discussed, the Columbia faculty who responded to the questionnaire fit the expected pattern. The authors, however, went further in their analysis of the data. Using the technique of test factor standardization, they sought to separate out the independent weight of the different interrelated variables. The analysis indicated that when political identification (conservative to radical) is standardized, the effect of the other independent variables is considerably reduced. They concluded, for example, that much of the effect of religion lies in an early political socialization that sets an initial frame of reference; religion is much less potent in distinguishing within established categories of liberals and conservatives. The effect of party affiliation also was reduced within the ideological categories.

Standardization, however, did not reduce the relationship between age and support for the demonstration. That is, older liberals or radicals were much more opposed to the demonstration than younger ones who identified with the same ideology. This finding is, perhaps, the most interesting yet located inasmuch as it suggests the basis for a genuine division within ideological groupings. Because the meaning of terms such as "liberal" and "conservative" change over time, older radical faculty members, who are less likely than young radicals to support civil disobedience as a tactic, impute different meaning to the terms "liberal" and "radical." Thus, the young are differentiated from the old not by differences over goals, but concerning tactics.

Looking at factors internal to the university, Cole and Adamsons con-

[16] Cole and Adamsons, "The Student Demonstrations at Columbia University."

cluded that differences linked to rank and academic tenure can largely be eliminated when the two important external factors—age and political identification—are controlled. Salary, however, continues to differentiate supporters from opponents even when the two external variables are standardized. Although high income may have produced more conservative and pro-administration faculty, it is possible that the higher paid are also those who have had greater academic recognition. Thus, number of articles published and office in a professional association also continue to differentiate after the two major external factors are controlled.

Curiously, discipline group had little independent effect after standardization, except that the engineers were less likely to support the demonstration. Orientation toward research or teaching had no effect on support for the demonstration. This result, which the authors correctly call "surprising," may, however, reflect the cross-pressures of the student protest ideology (which denigrates research as compared to teaching) on the more liberal, intellectually oriented faculty, who previously would have been wont to favor research. In effect, the students now press their faculty supporters to include a preference for teaching as part of a liberal-radical ideology, so that this attack on scholarship from the left may incline more conservative and less intellectual faculty to endorse it..

Although Cole and Adamsons point out how a variety of university-linked experiences, including friendship patterns and opinion in one's department or school, may deflect faculty members from acting on the political predispositions they brought to the conflict from their nonteaching statuses and experience, they conclude that nonteaching statuses provide a political orientation that influences behavior on intramural issues for which there is little precedence. They also found that those who had attained the greatest success in academic life are less dissatisfied and more committed to the university system which has been the source of their reward, and they are presumably, therefore, less supportive of student demonstrations. This latter conclusion, however, awaits further specification of the effect of intellectuality on success and campus attitudes.

More studies of specific campus reactions such as the Columbia study are needed if we are to understand the complexities and dynamics of faculty reactions to campus political crises. The depth analysis of the Carnegie Commission sample should contribute much to this effort, since, in addition to tapping opinions on campus politics, the sample is large enough to differentiate among types of schools which had different conflict experiences.

FACULTY BEHAVIOR IN CONFRONTATION SITUATIONS

Observers of major campus confrontations have noted two types of temporal changes among both faculty and students: initial radicalization, particularly after police were called in, and a subsequent, much slower process of growing disillusionment with the activists. This change involves increased support for effective administrative measures to restore a normal state of teaching and research to a campus bedeviled by recurrent radical demands, confrontations, heated controversies, and frequent faculty meetings.

In the beginning stage of campus protest, many nonpolitical and even conservative faculty may join in the various meetings of ad hoc groups called to mediate the situation and prevent the police from being called in. Many faculty and nonactivist students are initially inclined to consider the activists' demands—on campus political rules, outside recruiters, ROTC, community housing policy, and the like—at their face value. That is, many not involved in the protest assume, quite naturally, that the only matter at issue is the one raised by the demonstrators. And the liberals among the university population will more often than not conclude that the protesters have a good point, that the policy they are objecting to is wrong, or that the reform they demand would probably be a good thing. Consequently, they agree that the university ought to negotiate, compromise if possible, give in if necessary. Since their major objection is to the tactics, not seemingly to the demands, they find it difficult to uphold strong action against the demonstrators. Others object to repressive tactics, even against law violators, because they perceive the conflict as one between (weak and politically inexperienced) students and (powerful and politically sophisticated) administrators. They, too, see the situation as calling for compromise on the part of the university. Hence, when the university or public authority sends in the police, much of the community is morally outraged. Many are "radicalized" in the sense of now accepting the view held by the more radical students, that they are the victims of the university's collaboration with reactionary social forces.

In this first stage, the left faction among the faculty gains heavily. Many join it who might be expected to take a more conservative stance. Among them, those who feel that the protesters represent a dangerous, politically astute, radical grouping, who have been able to outmaneuver the politically unsophisticated administration which has had no experience in dealing with revolutionists, find it difficult to endorse the tactics of the administration. They include, too, faculty who feel that the administration by its mishandling of the situation has lost its legitimacy—that part of its claim to authority which rests on the prestige and personal reputation for competence of the particular president, chancellor, provost, or dean. (As should be obvious, administrators in schools with distinguished faculties have relatively little power deriving from their formal office. They are in the position of political leaders of unorganized collectives; their power is to a large extent personal rather than institutional.) As a result, even many who are sharply critical of the activists will not seek to defend the incumbents, or if they do so because of personal loyalty or a desire to uphold authority, they will not do so enthusiastically or effectively. The upshot of such a series of events has often been the overthrow of the administration through the "resignation" of its most prominent officers.

The next stage frequently witnesses a revival of conservative or moderate strength, including the involvement in the more conservative groupings of faculty, of older men who have been quite liberal or radical in their general societal politics. This change occurs, in part, as a reaction to a continued state of disorder on campus. The student radicals have been both greatly strengthened or exhilarated by a sense of power and influence as a result of the after-effects of the first major demonstrations. Many of them seek new issues around which they can organize new protest demands. And some of the more extreme elements occasionally have initiated what appear to be provocative and disruptive activities—filthy speech campaigns, disruption of classes, raids on the library or faculty club, and the like. As a result, many faculty who had thought the settlement of the initial major confrontation, often by agreeing almost totally to the demonstrators' demands, would end the period of disorder, now shift to support more conservative policies and turn against the student movement and the faculty left. Thus, at Berkeley, the more conservative faculty faction began to win faculty elections after a relatively short period. At Columbia, close to eight hundred faculty signed a public statement demanding that the administration bring more order to the campus during 1969–70, the year after the massive sit-ins. At San Francisco State, the moderate-conservative faction won the elections to the faculty executive committee after a year of police on campus and faculty and student strikes. The Harvard faculty behaved similarly in elections in February 1970.

Obviously, such dynamic processes cannot be explained by static, cross-sectional analyses of the sources of diversity in faculty opinion. The diverse tactics of demonstrators, administrators, and faculty leadership during and after campus crises produce sharply different results. The "Chicago plan"—not calling the police, waiting out the demonstrators, and then enforcing university sanctions after order is restored—has been effective on two separate occasions, in 1966 and again in 1969, in preventing the undermining of administrative authority and community radicalization. Most recently, however, radicalization appears to be occurring among segments of the Chicago faculty who object to the expulsion and suspension of many students as unduly harsh. At San Francisco State and Cornell, liberal presidents (Summerskill and Perkins) who sought to handle the crises by constantly negotiating, by repeatedly compromising with activist demands, found their campus support declining because these tactics did not prevent increased activist demands and recurrent crises, and they resigned under pressure. At Cornell, very liberal administrative policies eventually resulted in a more "conservative" faculty, who felt that academic freedom was being undermined by concessions to student agitators.

Clearly more studies in depth which combine sophisticated descriptions of the behavior of the different actors in the campus controversies with a dynamic procedural analysis are needed if we are to understand the complexities of faculty reactions to political crises. Yet we obviously know enough, both from the historical record and the large number of faculty and student surveys referred to here, to conclude that a major reason the university has been a center of unrest during this period in which the legitimacy of traditional authority has been undermined generally is the outcome of the incentives in intellectual values and occupational role requirements to take a critical and anti-Establishment stance. Ideally-typically, the university is inherently egalitarian and meritocratic in its self-conception. Discrimination against the talented because of background factors is destructive to its norms and values. It recruits, particularly in the liberal arts, from those who are critical of the Establishment. One may wonder that the university has so often been a center of conventional politics, not that it has supported unrest.

It remains, of course, that relatively few university faculty are political activists in "normal times." It is also true that most of the faculty, even when sympathetic to the goals of student protest, dislike seeing the campus used for political purposes. The majority of the social scientists who signed advertisements against the Vietnam war indicated their opposition to student demonstrations. Thus, the faculty seems to justify the charge levied by many activists that they are hypocrites, that they do not act in ways congruent to their beliefs.

The Issue of Value-Free Research

There are important reasons why many scholars have opposed politization, regardless of their political ideology. These reasons derive from the very nature of scholarship itself. Politics and scholarship are highly different types of activities even though they may overlap and complement each other.

The political activist, whether left or right, is expected to be an advocate of a particular point of view which excludes opposing ideas. Inherent in the effort of the activist to gain a following and win power is the need to convince potential converts of the essential correctness of his ideology. Political leadership calls for deliberate oversimplification and decisiveness. The political leader who is tentative and points out the complexities and uncertainties of knowledge will not last long in that role.

Scholarship emphasizes the opposite characteristics. A scholar should consider all existing points of view and all available evidence before reaching a conclusion. He is expected to take as long as necessary to come to a definitive conclusion. A scholar is required to present contradictory evidence and point to any methodological weaknesses in his material. In attacking a research problem, he is required to complicate the issue by introducing as many factors as appear at all relevant. Thus scholars writing on such applied politically relevant problems as poverty, inflation, foreign policy, and the like tend to emphasize that knowledge in these fields is complex and indeterminate in character and that the evidence rarely justifies any simple cause and effect relationships. Unlike the politician, the scholar's obligation is to present a broad range of knowledge with all its uncertainties and ambiguities.

It is in the social sciences that the clash between scholarship and politics has had the greatest impact. Because the social sciences touch so directly on politics, many students take social science courses in order to enhance their political objectives. Their interest, then, is not that of a scholar but that of the politician. In addition, the effort to engage in *objective* scholarship is much more difficult in the social sciences and humanities than it is in the natural sciences. The subjective nature of the social sciences does not lend itself to definitive conclusions about what kinds of courses should be taught, what the content of courses should include, and what issues should be studied. Hence the gap between the interests of the faculty and those of politically concerned students is much greater in the social sciences than in other fields.

Many social scientists argue that, precisely because their fields touch so directly on politics and are involved in subjects about which they, like all aware men, have strong feelings, it is important to separate their values from their research *as much as possible*. This stress on scholarship in the social sciences does not mean that objective or value-free scholarship occurs in any pure or absolute sense. Personal values and interests, variations in life experiences, differences in education and theoretical orientation, all will affect the scholar's choice of problems, the variables dealt with, the rigor with which he explores alternative explanations, and the like. However, a teacher, knowing something about his own political biases, must take great care to reduce the impact of personal preferences on research results. For a researcher to be committed to a political role in these fields increases the probability that he will judge scholarly work by its presumed political consequences. Of course, the ultimate test of scientific validity is the exposure of research results to the community at large. Conclusions that are held up as valid by all others who seek the truth must be the goal of the scholar. The possibility of reaching such scientific truth will be heightened by the commitment of social scientists to *objective* methods of inquiry.

The conflict between politics and scholarship also manifests itself in the issue of political involvement by the university or the faculty as a body.

In demanding and securing freedom from clerical and state control, the university argues that its members as individuals must be free to come to any conclusions about topics relevant to religion or politics. In turn, it implicitly commits itself to officially ignore religious or political commitments in its formal policies and in its appointments to the faculty. While the radical activists are the most vociferous in their demands that university bodies publicly endorse or condemn government policies, it is they who stand to lose the most from such politization of the universities. Under the umbrella of autonomy, the university serves to protect unpopular minorities, that is radicals, who would find it hard to earn a living elsewhere. Once a university loses its autonomy by lending its prestige to political advocacy, it will also lose its position as a sanctuary for these unpopular minorities.

Yet it is important to recognize that many of the faculty, administrators, and trustees who now would emphasize the inherent need for university autonomy against pressures from leftists manifestly to combine politics and scholarship have contributed to the current situation. Since the 1930s, the American university has increasingly become a major center of political involvement. Many faculty have engaged in applied, policy-oriented research, and have not taken care to separate their academic from their policy adviser role. Professors and institutions have lent their prestige to Establishment as well as other causes. Universities, through their choice of politically involved men to receive honorary degrees and other indicators of esteem, have implicitly endorsed the value of the work these men have done. And if the name of the university has been used in ways that have clear political consequences, it is difficult now to argue that leftist efforts to use the university should be ruled out, even though they may involve more overt forms of politization. The argument that the defenders of the status quo can be more subtle in their politically relevant endeavors clearly has merit. Now that the issue of politization and university autonomy has been joined again, there is a clear need to think through the rationale behind the involvement of academe as such in nonacademic concerns.

The Issue of Teaching

The issue of teaching versus research, although dating to the nineteenth century, did not take on a political character until recently. In fact, if any deduction concerning the ideological correlates of those on different sides of the question may be identified, it is that the conservatives have favored more teaching. The data presented earlier concerning the links between intellectuality and political liberalism clearly point in this direction. Conservatives have defended the teaching function of the university, seeking to preserve the classical ideal, to stress the need to absorb the wisdom of the past, the "great books," but not the creation of new knowledge. The pressure to make the university a center of research and innovation has more frequently come from those imbued with the idea of progress, of social change.

Student movements, however, insofar as they represent "class" sentiments of students have perceived professors primarily, if not solely, in their role as teachers. They want more time from them. And they have seen grades as mechanisms of social control, as means of getting them to conform to the authority or whims of the teacher. The leftist students have added to this criticism the idea that grades help maintain the "capitalist" emphasis on competition, on achieving ends and devaluing means, on the struggle for success, rather than on learning for its own sake.

STATUS OF TEACHING AMONG FACULTY

The faculty, of course, also divides on these issues. Many younger professors in recent years have accepted the view that research is often self-serving careerism. Some resolve to devote their careers to teaching, to working with students. Those who disagree with this position argue that an emphasis on teaching can be a way of escaping from being judged in the necessarily highly competitive intellectual world. It has also been suggested that stress on teaching as the primary function of the academic job makes the task of "succeeding" easier. There is less strain in devoting oneself to lectures and discussions with students than in seeking to produce research which is regarded as first-rate.

There would appear to be an "interest" factor in this discussion which is partially generational. The older more "successful" faculty, who have acquired academic distinction through their research, have an obvious reason for defending the existing system, including the ways in which support has been distributed. Those who have "failed" or are too young to have succeeded are more prone to stress the virtues of teaching. Yet the inherent requirements of an intellectual career will press many younger faculty to seek jobs which facilitate their concentrating on research and writing. Presumably, it will be precisely those who are high in intellectuality, in scholarly competence, and hence also in political liberalism or radicalism who will want this. As a group, at the moment, they are clearly in a cross-pressure situation. They, in effect, are the one group in academe who are pressed to resolve the dilemma between degree of emphasis on teaching or research in their own behavior.

Thus far, there is little evidence that the increased concern for undergraduate education which is manifest in the myriad of articles, books, national commissions, and local campus surveys has, in fact, changed the dominant practice of the American academy. Some years ago the Israeli sociologist Joseph Ben David suggested, as a general proposition concerning American academe, that any event which reduces the attractiveness of a given university to retain or attract faculty would necessarily result in an increase in the bargaining power of faculty vis-à-vis the administration. A major internal crisis or a change in the ecological environment of a campus meant that the university had to pay more to gain or maintain a high-level faculty. For example, at Berkeley after the loyalty oath crisis of 1949–50, the teaching load was cut. And after the Berkeley revolt of 1964–65, loads were further reduced, especially in the politically vulnerable, and therefore competitively less attractive, social science fields. A similar drop in teaching load and increased salaries occurred at the University of Chicago in the late fifties and early sixties, seemingly linked to the decline in the attractiveness of the neighborhood surrounding the school. And at Columbia, a reduction in teaching load from three courses to two per term followed the activities of spring 1969.

Crises, as Ben David suggested, mean greater bargaining power for faculty, and faculty use such power to reduce their teaching obligations. Thus, though many, probably most, of the faculty at these and other institutions honestly believe that they are more interested in and dedicated to teaching since the emergence of student protest in 1964–65, the evidence as reflected in time given to students at major American institutions does not bear them out. The reasons are obvious, and no amount of moral advocacy that is not accompanied by a change in the reward structure will affect practice. As long as faculty rely on research for status and income, spending time with students must be regarded as less attractive.

It is important to recognize that the teaching issue is one in which the student activists can expect more support from administrators, trustees, alumni representatives, and politicians than from the faculty of major universities. The former are much more disposed to view the university as a school, are more concerned with the way it treats the students than are the professors. The highly competitive, nationally oriented research faculty are seen by the administrative classes of the university in much the same way as the radical students see them, that is, as self-centered, self-serving individuals, who are using the university to benefit themselves, and who give as little as possible to the more campus-centered activities.

A similar political line-up on issues such as these occurs among the faculty. As has been noted, the less research-oriented faculty tend to be more politically conservative and locally oriented to campus affairs, and are more concerned with teaching as an institutional function. They, too, deprecate what they consider to be the exaggerated emphasis and rewards given for research. They are the people who staff the committee system, who assist the deans, who keep the place going in normal times. Hence, when student groups raise the teaching-research issue, they are likely to confound the basis for faculty political cleavage. The "conservatives" and the Establishment agree with them while the more research-oriented "liberals" will, if they honestly speak their minds, disagree.

POLITICAL PHILOSOPHY OF CONSULTANTS

The same apparent contradiction exists with respect to outside involvements as consultants for government agencies or business firms. The radical students assume that both sets of institutions are reactionary, and presumably those faculty who are involved with them have "sold out" and should be among the more conservative members of the faculty. But in fact the 1966 NORC national survey indicates that professors who had *never* worked for extramural organizations, whether business or government, were most disposed to *back* government policy on Vietnam. Those who had served government were most opposed to the policy. An even stronger relationship between having been called in as a consultant to business and political liberalism was indicated in the study of social scientists' reaction to (Joe) McCarthyism. Holding age constant, those who strongly favored academic and civil liberties for Communists and other unpopular minority dissidents were most likely to have been consultants for business. At every age level, the "clearly conservative" had the lowest level of involvement with business.[17]

The "missing" intervening variable in both sets of findings presumably is that the most successful scholars are the ones called on as consultants, and as indicated by many surveys, academic success—regardless of how measured—is correlated with degree of leftism in political attitudes. The same results should obtain in any estimate of the relationship between involvement in Defense Department research and political liberalism, or even opposition to the Vietnam war and other American foreign policies. Since the Defense Department has been the largest supporter of basic (non-policy-oriented) research in the country, it is likely that its grants have been largely to the most prestigious scholars in various fields, therefore to the most liberal. This presumed relationship may help explain that many of the most prominent faculty radicals and opponents of the Vietnam war have not supported opposition to Defense Department support of basic research when this issue has been raised by student radicals. At Harvard, Berkeley, and MIT, for example, the most radical member of the faculty in terms of public utterances in each case has been a long-term client of the research agencies of the Defense Department.

APPRENTICE SCHOLARS OR PUPILS

These differences between student activists and many of the faculty who stand relatively close to them in general political philosophy or ideology can be conceptualized in another way. Students, including, or especially, the radicals among them, want the university to retain the characteristics of a school and want the faculty to behave like teachers

[17] Noll and Rossi, "General Social and Economic Attitudes of . . . Faculty Members," p. 58; Lazarsfeld and Thielens, *The Academic Mind*, p. 443.

in lower levels of education. Many students seek teachers who will tell them what they think about life generally. They will see professorial claims of seeking objectivity by introducing contradictory material as an evasion of their responsibility to take a stand. Faculty who are themselves committed to a life of productive scholarship—particularly at universities which are major centers of research—see higher education and the role of the professor as highly differentiated, with teaching as only one of the activities. Znaniecki, in his analysis of the role of the intellectual, pointed up the distinctly different functions of the university and the school:

> . . . [T]he school of higher learning performs the specifically social function of an educational institution only because its main activities are not social but scientific, do not aim to contribute to the maintenance of the social order but to the maintenance of knowledge as a super-social domain of culture supremely valuable in itself. . . . The school of general education, on the contrary, as an institution of the modern society serves directly the maintenance of social order—whether it be a traditionally static order or a more or less dynamic new order.[18]

It is important to note in Znaniecki's distinction that he described the institution which advocates radical change and the one which supports the status quo as both being primary schools rather than scientific organizations. Michio Nagai has pointed out that the teacher in nonuniversity education is expected to consider all aspects of the child's life. The school is characterized particularly by the diffused content and method of instruction in it as distinct from the highly specialized university.

Given the assumption that schoolteachers have diffuse authority over pupils and form a particularistic relationship with them, it follows that the method of teaching and the very role of the teacher in the classroom and in personal discussions must be different from that of the university professor who has the authority over the student only in the restricted area of the transmittal of scientific methods and knowledge.

It may be argued that when the activists criticize the educational system today, they seek to retain the status of pupil and to have teachers rather than to be students of university professors. Although their demand is now couched in terms of the faculty taking an activist position in support of radical social change, it is a demand that their professors act like their schoolteachers, that they take part in "bull sessions" in which they discuss the totality of human experience, not simply their subject matter. When the students oppose grades, they are demanding the restoration of a particularistic relationship with their teachers, one in which they are

[18] Florian Znaniecki, *The Social Role of the Man of Knowledge* (New York: Columbia University Press, 1940), p. 155. In the following discussion, I am highly indebted to the brilliant analysis of Michio Nagai, "The Problem of Indoctrination: As Viewed from Sociological and Philosophical Bases" (Ph.D. diss., Dept. of Sociology, Ohio State University, 1952).

not judged objectively according to highly specialized criteria, but rather continue to be treated as total human beings. The available evidence with respect to schoolteachers in the lower schools indicates that such forms of particularistic treatment in the schools facilitate discrimination in favor of those from more privileged backgrounds who conform to middle-class morality.

The argument concerning grades also cuts across the usual left-right dimensions, although in recent years it has been raised largely by student activists. Radicals see the power to grade as an instrument of coercion which prevents free interchange of ideas and opinions between faculty and students. The fact that a meritocratic grading system once was seen as an instrument of freedom which guaranteed equal treatment by those from underprivileged backgrounds is foreign to them.

The general issue is how much and under what conditions institutions of higher learning should reflect in their internal structure the different norms and orientations of the worlds of the school and scholarship. In this respect, we meet again a congruence between the left and the right. The leftist students agree with many conservative critics of the university. Both want the university to be a school. The left, however, wants a school which will favor radical social change, whereas the conservative politicians and alumni want a school that will defend the status quo. Neither wants an institution which is dedicated to subjecting all simple propositions, all explanations, all reforms, to the test of scientific validity. For in essence the university is the enemy of simplification. The norms which must govern a university make of it an environment qualitatively different from that of a high school. In shifting from the status of high school pupil to university student, youth must adjust to a highly specialized and segmented system in which their professors will be men for whom undergraduate teaching is necessarily only one of a number of functions, and not even the most important one in the better institutions.

INFLUENCE OF THE ETHOS OF GRADUATE EDUCATION

It is essential that those concerned with university life recognize that universities are not schools, that the norms which govern scientific activities are quite different from those which characterize schools. The approach of science and of the university has been analyzed in formal analytical terms by Talcott Parsons and Robert K. Merton. The values they specify describe the "role structure of the scientist" (Parsons) and "the cultural values and mores governing the activities termed scientific" (Merton) in terms which are at variance with the involvement of faculty in indoctrination, in preparation for life, and with the total personality and character as found in the school.

Merton emphasizes the neutral, objective, disinterested, and skeptical values inherent in the scientific process. Parsons similarly points out that the ethos of science, which includes functional specificity (professional specialization) and achievement orientation as well as those activities mentioned by Merton, has "above all become embodied in the university as its principal institutionalized frame." These guiding values imply that professors have no general claim to superior knowledge, but must combine and organize skepticism and universality in their application of objectivity to their specific area of expertise, but with an understanding of the boundaries of their professional abilities. Further, both men stress that while scientists must conduct themselves in ways commensurate with these values, nonscientists, including students, must reciprocally respect the scientist's inviolable rights in his own field.[19]

These value orientations which are inherent in the scientific ethos contain liberal-left political implications and call for emphasizing the role of the student as apprentice scholar, not as the pupil of a Mr. Chips, whether radical or conservative. The values of science emphasize the need for a free society operating under the rule of law. State interference to guarantee that science adheres to a party, national, or religious line, that scientists are not free to criticize each other makes for bad science. The stress on universalism, on functional specificity, on achievement orientation, implies opposition to those aspects of stratified societies which limit equality of opportunity. For science, trained intelligence, not family background, race, or wealth, must be the primary quality associated with status and social rewards.

Hence, as noted earlier, the more committed an academic is to scientific research, the more likely he will oppose those aspects of the social system which appear to perpetuate inequality of opportunity.

Some of the same elements of the scientific ethos which press men in a liberal and left direction politically also, of course, include the action imperative to treat students in a highly specific, meritocratic manner. To advance scientific knowledge means that all qualified youth must be encouraged and rewarded, but that little reward (or attention) should be given to the unqualified or to the less able. Science is inherently concerned with locating and rewarding the aristocracy of talent. Anyone familiar with the norms of major centers of graduate study in the liberal arts fields knows that this is the way they operate. The faculty are interested only in graduate students who seem to have the ability to make major contributions to knowledge; the inadequate among them are regarded as out of place in such departments. And such values, which must be present in major graduate and research centers, inevitably inform the treatment of undergraduates in the same institutions. (It may be noted that the lead-

[19] Robert K. Merton, *Social Theory and Social Structure* (Glencoe, Ill.: Free Press, 1949), pp. 308–14; Talcott Parsons, *The Social System* (Glencoe, Ill.: Free Press, 1951), pp. 342–44, 434; Talcott Parsons, *Essays in Sociological Theory, Pure and Applied* (Glencoe, Ill.: Free Press, 1949), p. 189.

ing state universities such as Berkeley and Madison which do not have as highly selective undergraduate admissions policies as the major private institutions, but which maintain an elite research-oriented faculty, have created the optimum condition for fostering neglect of the undergraduates.)

The differences between graduate school faculty and those at four-year colleges are also to be found among the colleges. The ethos of graduate education has affected the entire character of American academe. Reisman and Gusfield have shown how undergraduate schools vary in faculty and student orientation with respect to the different concept of the college they sustain. Much of the consequences of the distinction attempted here between the school and research-institute, graduate-training role of the university, and between the pupil and student roles open to undergraduates, were developed by Reisman and Gusfield in their analysis of the differences in the activities of undergraduate institutions. They distinguish between the "adult-forming" and "youth-prolonging" aspects of higher education in noting that by using adult standards of performance, universities "weed out" the childlike students. In a limited sense, the highly specialized professor also provides a model of one possible adult role. However, the instructor who views himself as a specialist and more as a member of a broad intellectual subculture seeks to preserve the youthful traits of rebelliousness, openness, and noncommitment to specific authoritative roles in both his students and himself.[20]

RESULTING DISSATISFACTIONS

It may be argued that the traits of science enumerated by Parsons and Merton and of "adult-forming" educational functions specified by Reisman and Gusfield are relevant to scientific research and the work of research institutes but not to colleges and universities. The latter are primarily educational, not research organizations. Hence the application of scientific traits to the college properly has made for student dissatisfaction and unrest. This argument, made by both students and politicians in authority over universities, clearly is quite valid. Much of what is done in the American system of higher education is closer in function to the work of high schools than it is to graduate centers of education and research. The courses usually taught in the lower division, in the freshmen and sophomore years, in most colleges and universities are extensions of high school work, if they are not in fact the same as those given in many high schools. The university in much of Europe has ideally at least been closer in requirements to the American graduate school than to the undergraduate college. The *gymnasium, lycée,* and grammar or public school in

[20] David Riesman and Joseph Gusfield, "Styles of Teaching in Two New Public Colleges," in *The Contemporary University: USA,* ed. Robert Morrison (Boston: Houghton Mifflin Co., 1966), pp. 257–58.

Europe cover many of the courses which in this country are included in colleges or universities. The first university degree in Europe is a specialized degree, often in one subject, requiring a thesis. The doctorate is the only degree given in Germany, northern Europe, and many Latin countries, and is more akin to the American master's degree than our Ph.D.

American institutions of higher education today are torn between being schools and graduate research centers. Although relatively few institutions are in the latter category, probably the majority of students attending four-year colleges are in institutions in which faculty are held to the requirement that they engage in productive scholarship, that they be judged for salary, rank, and local prestige by their presumed research rather than teaching merit. A considerable amount of lower-division instruction at major universities is given by graduate students who are devoting most of their energies to getting a doctoral degree.

Students and faculty are properly in a confused state about their respective roles. The increased emphasis on the research function has led the more prestigious professors in the centers of graduate training and research (a relatively small segment of the American professors) to serve as consultants for government, business, and political organizations, and to be increasingly pressured into lecturing, administering large grant funds, and writing. Further, the number of graduate students is rising.

To put the whole matter another way, the leading universities and professors have been accumulating more tasks, while they continue to do their old one, undergraduate teaching, as well. These institutions and faculty are judged for eminence and the rewards which go with high status by their research output. The reports on the relative status of academic departments and universities which have been prepared for the American Council on Education and other bodies, and which are made much of by the press, administrators, and faculty themselves, are ratings of these departments as graduate schools, as centers of research, not of undergraduate teaching. This increased pressure on faculty at such institutions for differentiated involvements and the lesser time given to undergraduate education should make the university world an increasingly less happy place for both faculty and undergraduates.

Governance

The political rebellion stems from factors other than the tensions inherent in institutional and faculty role conflict, but a liberal-radical political ideology and "job dissatisfaction" should reinforce each other. As we have noted, the upshot of many political demonstrations has been an attack on the governance or other aspects of the university as a place in which to work or learn.

The emphasis on the internal governance of the university to which many faculty and student activists have turned as a "solution" to the problems of higher education seems to me to be misplaced. More faculty work, more committees, only makes the situation worse. In previous crises, efforts to democratize university government resulted in involvement in "busy" work (committees) of the less research-involved, also more conservative faculty, once the original crisis which activated the concerns of the younger and more liberal-left faculty ended. The increased "democratization" (more elected faculty committees) thereafter increases the importance of the role of the more conservative and scholarly less prestigious "committeemen" since they can now claim to be the elected "representatives" of the faculty rather than the appointed consultants of the administration. In effect, faculty elections often serve to give populist legitimacy to locally oriented, relatively conservative professional faculty politicians, who rise to the "top" because the "cosmopolitan," more research-involved, liberal faculty see campus politics as a waste of time in normal periods. In a period of renewed crisis, the elected spokesmen of the faculty, chosen before the troubles, usually differ greatly in the political orientations from the dominant faculty mood. William Roth, a leader of the liberal minority on the Board of Regents of the University of California, has noted that the intricate structure of committees and senates which maintain the pretense of a self-governing community of scholars is staffed normally by the academic bureaucrats and politicians. The scholarly professor will rise in a crisis to deal with problems of governance, but he soon lapses again into his own affairs.[21]

Student participation on a representative basis, as a minority of a campuswide faculty-student senate, is not likely to give the majority of the student body any sense of increased participation or involvement. All that they get out of such reforms is the opportunity to vote once a year.

The Need to Separate Functions

There does seem to be a set of problems calling for reform stemming from the multiplication of tasks handled by faculty as individuals and by universities as institutions. Differentiation, separation of functions, has been the pattern of response in all institutional life as tasks have multiplied. In the Soviet Union and other Communist countries, the research-institute—graduate-training set of activities is conducted separately from that of undergraduate teaching. Japan is planning to separate graduate work from other forms of higher education. These alternative systems clearly have liabilities of their own. But if the current wave of politically induced discontent within the American university is to have any useful

---

[21] William M. Roth, "The Dilemmas of Leadership," *Saturday Review,* Jan. 10, 1970, p. 68.

function for the life of the university itself, there is a clear and present need to examine the need for, and the possibilities of, a restructuring of the system into a variety of component parts.

This counsel does not imply the necessity to separate research and teaching. It does suggest, however, the need to recognize and not be afraid to state that a genuine university should not have the attributes of a school in the sense used earlier in this paper. If a university is to educate for adulthood, it cannot be concerned with continuing to be a *gemeinschaft*, a community which resembles an extended family. Students must learn that intellectual life is complicated and difficult, that professors are also scholars who cannot have the time to hold their hands or spoon-feed them with intellectual nourishment. The scholar must share with the student the tentativeness of knowledge, his uncertainties about his conclusions, his self-doubts, and his triumphs. The student must be prepared to challenge the findings of his professors, after he has learned the methodology of the field, as another searcher for truth. To communicate the complexities of knowledge to sharp, questioning minds is essential to the process of intellectual clarification. Scholarship requires dialogue, controversy, not only among established men in the same field, but with students as well. Those who would turn universities into schools or into research institutes are both seeking to escape the intramural conflict by an easy capitulation. The primary function of the university is scholarship, which includes rigorous education. This means, of course, that there can only be a relatively small number of universities which have severe standards for faculty and students, although there will be thousands of accredited institutions of higher education.

JUDSON JEROME

New Attitudes for Faculty

RECENTLY I ADDRESSED the Faculty Council of the Great Lakes College Association meeting at Oberlin. Three representatives from each of twelve colleges attended. There we sat—one of the major problems in American education. A token woman was present; otherwise we were white men in business suits, barbered and collared, cocktailed and beef-fed, ranging in age from about thirty-five to fifty-five, mostly with doctorates in standard disciplines, sitting in a carpeted lounge on velveteen-upholstered chairs, wondering why our campuses were in turmoil and what we could do about it. Though we might have engaged in heated controversy, we shared overwhelmingly uniform viewpoints, vocabularies, assumptions—a thin, dry wafer from the rich feast of human culture. We met to design and set policy for institutions that were struggling to survive in a turbulent world where issues swirl around the counter-culture of youth, endemic violence, racism, the Third World. I was reminded of the Smith Bros. on the cough-drop box. Are we archaic? Is the best we can hope for to be phased out mercifully?

My colleagues tend to feel threatened, defensive, confused, and fearful

» » « «

Judson Jerome writes in the field of educational reform. Professor of English on the faculty of Antioch College, he is currently serving as Director of the Center for Documentary Arts at Antioch's program in Columbia, Maryland.

as the intellectual ground shifts beneath their feet and they hear the legitimacy of their roles questioned. They come wearily home from campus only to have their tensions recreated in confrontations with their own children. When we talk about resolving or avoiding conflict in regard to faculty, we are less concerned with mediating between external forces than with coping with internal conflict and its effects on behavior. There is little we can do by rearranging programs or structures to ease faculty tensions. Those faculty members I know who seem to be making a successful adaptation to the seventies are the ones who have gone through a process of personal change, often motivated by a desperate need to get back in touch with teen-agers at home. Increased ability to listen and respond honestly to the young is a start; but I believe the university will be undergoing a transformation in the next few years in which the qualities by which we measured faculty competence in the past may be largely irrelevant or even dysfunctional. It may be that many present-day faculty will not want or will be unable to continue in the profession under emerging new conditions. We have good reason for being anxious.

Except that we be born again (and I see little likelihood of that), many of us would do well to consider alternate employment. For those seeking rebirth, one might recommend crash courses at Esalen, stints in VISTA and the Peace Corps, summers as migrant workers, joining communes, taking courses in film making, motorcycle trips, marathon dancing to hard rock, peace marching, hair growing, and so on. But most of us are bent beyond unbending. If our colleges provided, and the government subsidized, rehabilitation leaves for professional growth and development, few would undergo such experiences as I have listed. We would read books about them. We would organize seminars.

I am as holy as thou, addicted to security, comfort, and status, to color TV, carpets, cocktails, cars, thruways, Formica, Styrofoam, disposable containers, to the values of suburbia, to the very aspects of American civilization that widen class differences, alienate the young, pollute the environment, overheat the economy, and drain the world's wealth. Day after day I am speckled with inauthenticity as I face my students and children. Traveling the dark segments of our cities, I roll up the car windows in justifiable fear. If they let me live, it is only because my class and race are still temporarily indomitable.

We are the enemy—to the young whom we teach and master, to the blacks, to most foreign nations, to nature itself which, as we indifferently despoil it, brews poisonous revenge. We do not change our values and way of life, perhaps because we despair of doing anything effectively to divert the suicidal course of our civilization. We grab what we can of the overripened fruit. I think most of us know that the necessary reordering of society cannot occur and leave us personally unscathed. But like the dispossessed aristocrats in *The Cherry Orchard,* we drift about muttering such awareness, unable to muster commitment for decisive action.

Why Not . . . ?

If we were to act, what might we do?

Stop doing as much as we can. Cut requirements, hours, assignments, courses, committees—every program element that can be eliminated. Try to create a campus upon which meditation, serenity, reading, thought, and affability are possible. Most of us live in rat races as soul destroying as Wall Street. We need time and security to change. We need the chance to develop programed materials. We need time to get back in touch with one another—our students and ourselves.

Admit everyone we can. If we have a space problem, draw lots. Seek diversity. Try educating those who need it, not those who guarantee us success.

Hire those as unlike ourselves as possible. Hire teen-agers, old people, women, blacks. Hire a Cuban fisherman. Avoid Ph.D.'s. Look for new kinds of credentials. Think whom it would be truly educational for students—and for us—to relate to.

Own the place; use the place. Much of our academic lives we act like French railway clerks, obsessed with the paperwork, following the rules of those above and imposing them upon those below. We ought to get together with the students and buy the college. Run it as a cooperative. Failing that, we might act as though we had done so. Tack up signs. Move chairs. Meet when and for no longer than it makes sense. When we meet, let's remember the hour is ours—and we can't blame anyone else (much less "the system") for what happens.

Get into the field. Seek alternatives to classroom learning, to book learning, in direct experience, in engagement with real issues. Work with students (and others) against poverty, disease, injustice, ignorance, instead of working against students on the battlefield of assignments, papers, and exams.

Open the college to the community. Get youngsters, working adults, dropouts, elderly people actively involved in college programs. Fill in the moat around the campus.

Faculty Renewal

Such program changes might seem designed to increase faculty tensions rather than to diminish them—as they will, if they occur at all, unaccompanied by rather deep attitudinal changes. After twenty years of college teaching, I have very little idea about how to change people's minds, but the most effective format I have seen for renewing professors is that used in Project Changeover in the summers of 1967–69. On the basis of these conferences—sponsored by the Union for Research and Experimentation in Higher Education (a consortium of twelve colleges) and funded by the Esso Foundation—I would recommend a program of faculty retreats of from two to four weeks, mixing about two dozen faculty from various campuses in an isolated setting for mutual and self examination. Visitors (Elizabeth Sewell, Carl Rogers, James Dixon, Goodwin Watson, Jim Nixon, John Holt, Harris Wofford, Eleanor Holmes Norton, James Garrett, Mike Rossman) should be brought in occasionally to hold the mirror up to those assembled. Communication exercises (many nonverbal) and encounter experiences should be available for those who wish to participate. The aim should be, as at revival meetings, conversion. Success could be reckoned by the number who come away with a stronger sense of mission, of urgency, and with a freer, more open life style. Possibly there should be parallel (but separate) retreats for faculty spouses.

Perhaps others can devise ways in addition to, or instead of, retreats to bring such changes about—or at least to get these questions into open discussion. I believe that the more sensitive students, administrators, trustees, and the public become to faculty anxieties, the more help all can be in reinforcing, reassuring, and contributing to fruitful conversion. A pamphlet containing a searching consideration of faculty roles might be useful to generate understanding and discussion. A documentary film contrasting and examining professorial styles might also be useful for this purpose.

I believe the professor of the future will have to cease staking his psychic security on his role as an expert and become more comfortable with himself as a human being—a father, lover, friend, citizen—somehow equal to others when he doffs his academic gown (like Lear, discover self and sanity through nakedness and, perhaps, a period of madness). But, I hear one objecting, "I was hired as a chemist—not a counselor or therapist!" His knowledge was acquired with great expense and difficulty, and now it seems to be disvalued. He is being asked to perform in an area for which he was not prepared. It is possible that the world needs a moratorium on chemistry or, at any rate, may need to emphasize humane uses of the chemistry we have rather than new research and discovery. That consideration aside, the objection disregards the nature of education. The distinction between teaching and therapy is, at best, blurred, and *therapy* itself is a somewhat pretentious term. The educational relationship needs something more like friendship, or, at least, candid two-way communication. Until we can create settings in which that occurs, our special knowledge is wasted anyway.

Joy, I want to say to the nervous professor, is around the corner. If we relax a little and take time to find out who *are* these people storming the citadel and to ask what they want, chemistry may once again become relevant. If it does not, other values may replace it in the professor's life. Our specialties, like coin collecting, are delectable, expensive, rather private pastimes, and occasionally indispensable for social good or the advancement of knowledge. It is not their utility but the inherent reward of knowing that makes us love them. Why can't we so value them in our lives, and not contaminate them by rhetoric which argues they are essential for every undergraduate's education? We ourselves want to be valued for what we are, not for what we have acquired in the way of special knowledge, lest, like the poor little rich girl, we live in perpetual self-doubt, wondering whether we could be loved if our stored wealth were invalidated or exhausted.

Renewal of Learning

Why must we be so preoccupied with "standards," a word implying conformity on the one hand and hierarchy on the other? We should stop thinking our job is to teach people the things we know; rather, we should conceive of it as one of helping them to learn the things they want to learn. Ours is not the job of selecting and training an elite, but of finding applications of knowledge, helping those who need help. Now we are perpetually skimming cream (as we define it) from cream with an intolerable sense of righteousness. We are fearful lest we be found out (for none knows as much as he seems to), tyrannical in our demands on others (implying our infinite superiority), exclusive in our selection of whom we choose to deal with (insecure as we are with those who don't share our values and interests), and effete in our preoccupation with the "forefront of knowledge" (insisting on greater and greater refinement, and further and further separation of education from the issues of ordinary lives).

We are obsessed with evaluation, with defining our objectives and measuring our progress toward them in quantifiable terms. Again and again when I describe experimental programs, my colleagues look at me with honestly puzzled faces, asking, "How do you handle evaluation?" The assumption seems to be that unless there is something to send to the registrar, experience and learning are wasted or invalid. The rewarding experiences of our private lives (a book, lovemaking, a meal, a symphony) are rarely approached with defined objectives, are rarely evaluated. But our academic habit of mind often blinds us to what is actually happening in education, what people are actually learning, so intent are we upon testing what is testable. How can we learn to relax with the fact that we may never know what our students have learned—and that, in a sense, it is no more our business than it is the librarian's business what readers get out of the library's books.

Do we need to revise our sense of priority and proportion in the allocation of time and energy? Should we be draining resources to explore the moon or transplant organs or explicate to the quintessence of nothingness yet another poem by John Donne so long as so many cannot drink water without getting amoebic dysentery; cannot feed their children even grain; cannot overcome the barriers to communication with their families, neighbors, officials, even with themselves?

Until we are more certain that this planet will support a human population after the next decade, some kinds of academic indulgence seem obscene. The whole research orientation of higher education that has developed especially since World War II to promote the acquisition of profits by industry and refine the implements and tactics of warfare for the government, combined with increased social pressure for every young person to go to college, has—as we all know—created an explosive situation. Over seven million young people are trapped in a system that is not basically concerned with their needs or their education at all except insofar as they are potential doctoral candidates who can be absorbed into the research industry. Very little of that research is concerned with the basic problems of human survival. Until professors reorient themselves to the students they are hired to serve and to the manifest needs of the world's population, they will continue to be not only discontented but burdened by a gnawing sense of irrelevance, insincerity, and prostitution.

Finally, in what might be an interminable list of faculty anxieties, I would like to mention the mother hen complex. It is difficult for us as parents not to know where our children are and what they are doing, and it seems almost equally difficult for us as faculty to relinquish control. Often, we hear faculty complaining that students who have been granted a degree of freedom are "doing nothing." This reflects a mother hen's anxiety: we suspect they are doing *something*, but we can only imagine what. Certainly not writing term papers. Some of us in experimental education naïvely imagined that if we removed all constraints, the students would, of their own free will, do all the things the system forced them to do in the past. Generally they do *not* voluntarily come to classes or meetings, read the kinds of books we customarily recommend, or write much of anything at all. They seem to have very little built-in need of taking examinations, testing their knowledge against objective criteria, or even talking over what they have learned with those of us who know more about the subject. All this makes faculty uneasy, not to say cynical. When a chick comes bedraggled back to the coop saying, "I need direction!" we do not look upon that as weakness or immature dependence. Rather, it confirms our deepest conviction of our own indispensability, and we cluck around the faculty lounge saying, "What these kids need is direction!" It is easy to forget that the educator's business is to get rid of his customers, that it is to create independence; we forget that, as older people living off the beautiful young, the greatest danger we have to face is our own dependency on *them*.

In attempting to resolve such tensions, we must create a climate of open discussion on our campuses in which the risks for trying new attitudes are minimized. We must reexamine and revise the reward system that encourages educationally dysfunctional practices such as emphasis on research, exclusiveness, severity of judgment, rigidity of requirements, impersonality, and routine. On our giant campuses, such a climate can be created only by human-sized subdivisions (of no more than about 100 students and faculty per unit) with greatly dispersed authority, budgetary autonomy, architectural settings that encourage informality and intimacy, and as little bureaucratic interference as possible. (Why should students "register" at all? Why "drop" courses? Why not simply assess and record periodically what a student has done in the preceding months —with or without faculty supervision?)

Am I naïve to believe that in every up-tight faculty member is a man who is begging to be liberated? I think we have, in the process of our own education, burdened ourselves with expectations, with ideas of duty, with a sense of guilt that make it impossible for us to approve of ourselves. To hide what we regard as our inadequacies, we cling to a fabric of lies as to a security blanket. Now that blanket is being stripped from us by our rude and candid clientele, by social forces intolerant of our Established premises, by a world responding to domination by our civilization as to the grip of cancer. Those of us who successfully cope with that situation will, I think, emerge as happier and better men.

DOUGLAS F. DOWD

Faculty Contributions to Tensions

By now, it should be unnecessary even to list the numerous issues that underlie the spread and the deepening of campus tensions—a process that saw its clear beginnings no later than 1964. What is necessary for most faculty, administrators, alumni, and trustees, but considerably fewer students (in percentage terms) is to make clear how the kinds of responses to tension have themselves become a source of substantially more tension. If that is a correct judgment, then it is also correct to believe that unless and until the governing bodies of campuses come to grips with their own very serious shortcomings, far from there being any hope of peace and constructive change there is an increasing probability that we have seen nothing yet.

Apart from a few isolated instances of campus unrest in the years before 1964, the real beginnings were in Berkeley in 1964. The specific issue that initiated that process was trivial—indeed, soon forgotten—by comparison with the manner in which the university authorities responded to it. It would be unwise to forget that the university itself created the issue originally by denying permits for legitimate and strongly felt desires on the part of the students. How things begin is usually closely related to how they will continue. The kind of "mistake"—and I believe

» » « «

Douglas F. Dowd, author of Modern Economic Problems in Historical Perspective, *is Professor of Economics at Cornell University.*

that the "mistake" was systemic, not accidental, in its origin—that led to the upheaval and the Free Speech Movement at Berkeley can be viewed in many ways. One way, which must be taken as critical and persisting, was the notion of the authorities that, because the students who began the agitation on the issue were a distinct minority, they could be ignored, isolated, put down. So it has been on other campuses and with other issues. So it is likely to remain until, as I think likely over the next year or so, the combined arrogance, stupidity, smugness, and social insensitivity of governing bodies—by which I mean, in the best universities, principally the faculties—finally produce upheavals that will transform the whole system of governance, inter alia, in many universities.

The kind of transformation I have in mind is not the sort that many universities believe they are promoting; namely, the insertion of students into committees of various sorts or the reconstitution of governing bodies to make students a part of the governance system in all its aspects. That process is self-delusion by those who participate and acquiesce in it, precisely for the reasons that they acquiesce in it: the kinds of changes thereby made possible are peripheral to the concerns of activist students and do not have any success whatsoever in reducing the disaffection of the majority of (nonactivist, but radically conscious) students. It is what the students call it—Mickey Mouse.

Before continuing, I should emphasize what may be otherwise ignored in the preceding sentences. Those who run things make much of the small percentage of students who are activists; they believe they are catching on to how students think and feel. But what is perceived is the number of students who are political in their actions, not those who are radical in their consciousness. The *society* has "radicalized" a very high percentage of the young; Students for a Democratic Society politicized a very small percentage of them. Events politicize, if only momentarily, large numbers of those who are in power, by their stupidity and their arrogance and their insensitivity. That the political movement of radical young people is not larger may be explained by the lack of any sophisticated leadership, strategies, organizing tactics, and the like. SDS failed in all those respects. In its mistaken attempts to radicalize, it failed to learn how to politicize. It will not be long before that failure, already recognized in various quarters, is understood and its lesson acted upon; nor will it be SDS that will lead the way.

Characteristics of Faculty

I should like to dwell on the characteristics I have attributed to faculties: arrogance, stupidity, insensitivity, smugness. Faculties have many characteristics, of course, many of which are in the virtuous part of the spectrum; and faculties, by their very nature and by reason of the great differences among institutions, cannot be expected to behave in patterned ways. But there are similarities that for present purposes are telling. Students perhaps misunderstand who runs what, and how, and why in the universities as much as faculties misunderstand students. (You will think that the prime instance of arrogance in these pages is exemplified by the writer, who apparently believes he understands everyone. Such thoughts would be correct, perhaps, and perhaps not; but they would also be useless diversions.) Students do not understand the arrogance of their professors, nor their fears; but students do comprehend well the insensitivity, which they see as a highly immoral form of selfishness or even greed. But arrogance is a prime part of the problem, and it deserves special attention.

The arrogance of faculties lies precisely in their attitude that they know what is best for the university and, therefore, for the students. It is very much like the arrogance of the administration in Washington and very much like the role the United States plays in the world. What is close to unbelievable about such arrogance is that it can be held in the face of the clear and present dangers of the world in which we all live, where those who have power preside, and where they—if anyone—are responsible. I am still speaking of the university. Faculties cannot, of course, end the war in Vietnam, end racism, end poverty, or construct a new and shining society. Students know that. Faculties can and must change the universities, however. If students are academically disaffected—and who knows whether that percentage is fifty, or seventy-five, or ninety-five— they are disaffected in part because of the academic environment, with what and how they learn. Over that process, faculties have almost total control, regardless of budgets or anything else. Professors are arrogant in many ways, including what and how they teach and how they view students. "Be like us," professors say, implicitly or explicitly, to their students. And what they mean is, "Learn what I learned, the way I learned it, and respect me for it." All this in a world aching for change, screaming with pain—not an insignificant part of which stems from those who say, "Be like us."

More can be said about how faculties think and how they act under pressures for change. Enough should be understood now, however, to show that their thought and action are self-deluding and arrogant, that faculty resist all but peripheral change, and they finally find law and order more attractive than substantive change. Is there any other way of explaining the passive acquiescence to the Henderson law [1] in the colleges and universities of New York State? This law is a clear violation

[1] The New York statute provides that all colleges and universities in the state adopt rules and regulations "for the maintenance of public order on college campuses and other college property used for educational purposes and provide a program for the enforcement thereof."—Ed.

of the independence of the universities, accepted by those who were at the same time resisting students' demands about the war, the draft, racism, social deterioration, etc.—in the name of academic freedom and independence. Thus, to the other qualities of faculties mentioned above, one must add hypocrisy. Students sense this, talk about it, and despise it. They need, and many await, merely the time and the leadership to press against the rotten wall.

From Rhetoric to Reality

What can be done? Not much, I believe. Faculties are quite generally the problem, and where they are not the problem, those "above" them are. In the latter cases, one can scarcely expect faculties, the very antithesis of a group that would promote change, to promote change, except vis-à-vis the administration. And when administrators see the problem, see the need to change, they too much fear the problems they would get from the faculty by promoting change. There is only one thing simple enough to suggest, and even that is unlikely in practice. Top administrators—presidents and deans—must take upon themselves a role of educational leadership, a role in which they explicitly recognize the difference between rhetoric and reality, and face up to the real alternatives between reasonably rapid constructive change or incalculable destructive change. Top administrators cannot force faculties to do much, but they do have the possibility of persuasion, made easier—although still not easy—in that most faculties still acquiesce to authority.

In April 1969 at Cornell, two events alone prevented disaster. On a Monday, the faculty voted, traditionally, for law and order. The first key event happened the next night when thousands of students, in support of the black demands, seized a building (in blatant disrespect for the authorities). Second, the president made it clear the next day that he wished the faculty to change their votes. They did so. There are lessons to be learned there.

SAMUEL D. PROCTOR

The Case of the Faculty

THE SIXTIES PRESENTED to the campuses a new challenge, and the American colleges and universities will never be the same again. Even some of the isolated campuses, securely remote from ghettos and urban unrest, have felt the reverberations within their ivy walls. Voorhees College in Denmark, South Carolina, found itself just as vulnerable as Columbia and Howard. No campus has really escaped the winds of change in academe.

The students have made their case. We have been subjected to the rhetoric and the tactics of revolution. They have gained much more than has been conceded, for the unspoken gains that are now residual in revised faculty attitudes are difficult to articulate. Although some faculty members are more conspicuous than others in verbalizing a new mood, there is much more restiveness than is reported. Prudence and circumspection have delayed the emergence of faculty responsiveness to the turbulence of the sixties. It would be a grave error to confuse the quiet deliberations around the faculty club with phlegmatic detachment.

Time, in early 1970, named a half dozen or so representatives of the new sociology, those who have accepted responsibility for making judgments as well as observations about society. Horowitz of Rutgers, Livingston and Wheatley of Princeton are representative of the young, new

》　》　《　《

Samuel D. Proctor is Professor, Graduate School of Education, Rutgers University, and author of The Young Negro in America.

breed of social scientists who ask for the world as a laboratory. They have abandoned the immunity from activism that sociologists of another day claimed in the name of disinterested objectivity. And it takes no genius to see the connection between this posture for a scientist and the widening acceptance of existentialism. The cool analysis of the Hegelian has given way to the discovery of truth as it unfolds in decisive action. Existentialism has been around for a long time. In fact, all of us are existentialists in one way or another, making the leap before the logic has spun to a dead halt. But in recent times we have seen the apostles of Kierkegaard turn up in some strange places. To be sure, the activist sociologists are by no means the only ones among us who have grown weary of the contradictions, the ironies, and the paradoxes—who are restless, as spectators to the enormous change waiting to be acted out.

The Unfree Professor

Any understanding of faculty restiveness must begin with this growing anxiety about our society and the frustration that accompanies it. It is simply unclear to most adults with moral sensitivity and with shackling financial obligations how to approach glaring social ills to make a difference. Letters to editors and congressmen fall far short of the kinds of confrontations that students have shown do indeed bring results. The black students in 1960 cracked the segregation barrier in restaurants, theaters, and motels with an effectiveness that made their adult contemporaries look like Rip Van Winkles. This contrast between what students —with no mortgages, department store bills, or tuition deadlines to meet —can do and what parents who happen to be college teachers can do is the source of considerable faculty discontent. They may be amused at the president being caught time and time again between a rock and a very hard place, but the faculty is caught in the same way. Their dilemmas are not as visible.

The guilt is burdensome. It creates moral fatigue. Never before have we been so well informed about the inequities at home and abroad. Never have we had to do so much explaining over so long a time to justify a war that burns up so many tax dollars for an end that is so obscure. One finds himself growing more and more tense every day, awaiting some solution that will remove the goad from his conscience. There must be a better way. Meanwhile, we have had just enough success in America in realizing a rising standard of living that we are committed to a policy of a nation without poverty and want. This commitment is implicit, but the poor are holding the leadership to it. Our cities, our schools, our government—all cry for dollars and ideas. But our energy, our creativity, and our money continue to flow into a small, winless war a long way from home.

Faculties are deeply troubled by the discrepancies of what is and what should be. Our campuses, the repositories of the accumulated wisdom of the ages, are in a near-hypnotic state morally because answers are hard to find that will ease the mind about Vietnam. After World War II we watched the U.N. building rise on the edge of the East River and went on about our business. But the entire intellectual community needs to help our government save itself from the Pax Americana syndrome and to work much harder for a viable international peace-keeping organ. What else? Another long spell of hypocrisy such as we are now enduring will make everything done in a library or a laboratory seem like a Disneyland operation. We could not then take ourselves seriously at all.

Add to this nagging moral incongruity another aspect of our life style on campus. For all of the best reasons in the world, business must go on —class cards, drop slips, registration procedures, committee meetings, subcommittee meetings, joint committee meetings, and all the rest that goes with a highly developed democratic system. We like democracy, but somehow things that faculties meet about seem out of place after hearing the news or reading the *Times*. Most faculty members suffer culture shock on returning to the real world after a faculty meeting. The presidents of the Negro colleges in the mid-Atlantic region were in a meeting on football regulations on that Saturday in February 1960 when the sit-in movement began. The presidents of the North Carolina colleges were huddled together to argue over enrollment quotas when President Kennedy was shot.

Simply the amount of business to be attended to harasses those who want time to think, to read, to converse, and to be left alone to follow their interests to whatever corner of the campus, the town, or the state they may lead. And some just don't bother, leaving the tedium and mechanics to those whose nerves can take it. The decision-making process in universities is badly in need of review. It should not require so many meetings to fail as miserably as higher education has in America. This atmosphere, so pervaded with trivia, becomes unbearable when the issues that need the man hours and the brain power drag on unattended. It will not be easy to balance the quest for participation, the distribution of power, and the establishment of priorities. But it must be said that the operation of academic machinery is a time-consuming endeavor. And the imposition discomfits faculty people who are troubled deeply by the affairs of mankind.

The above maladies both have to do with the nature of the society, the limitations that we all suffer, and the timing. One cannot be everywhere and everybody. He has his self-definition and it means something. A college teacher who is a parent of dependent children has a different set of limitations from those of a student; yet he may experience the same moral concerns. This situation generates guilt feelings that are hard to cope with. It also generates impatience with the administration, for the faculty member can easily transfer his guilt feelings to the president's office and expect something to be done in his behalf to ease his conscience.

It behooves the university to encourage dialogue, to keep the issues before the community, and to contribute that flow of facts and ideas that any responsible action requires. If talking and thinking are all that can be done actively, we should then give vigorous sponsorship to the best forum that we can provide.

Curriculum

At this point we are pressed to call into service a much overused and abused concept—relevance. I fear that we are skirting a deeper problem that few want to deal with—curriculum. Printed in expensive catalogs and locked into transcripts, we are stuck with it.

It may be that our discontent should be laid to the curriculum. We are engaged in an exercise of recapitulating man's search for the good, the beautiful, the true, and the ultimate in Western culture while over a half-million American homes are waiting for a father, a brother, or a son to return from Southeast Asia. Two-thirds of the world's people are non-Western. Our time is spent on Anglo-Saxon and Germanic traditions while our world is beset with issues that arise in Eastern Europe, Latin America, the Middle East, Asia, and Africa. Students are learning about those cultures on their own. Their diet in classes is something else. What we do there as standard procedure in the humanities is growing less and less relevant every day. A few courses in non-Western cultures will not suffice. Our curriculum in the humanities must get in step with the world we deal with and liberate us from a narrow provincialism. We are not living in the nineteenth century, safely protected from the "heathen" world by two deep oceans. Wars, television, university exchanges, air travel, the Peace Corps, slavery, revolutions, missionaries, and oil companies have made the oceans into corridors rather than barriers to human intercourse. But our view of man still begins and ends at Western culture, with token exceptions. This esoteric curriculum compels a faculty to feel out of touch and superfluous, ornamental and expensive. Students have constructed their own Third World seminars in the commons, at the bars, in the dorms, and wherever they find time and space.

The social sciences are perhaps the most tenuous of all the disciplines. Their function has been reportorial, describing man's actions and labeling them. Their literature has been pictorial and after the fact. The best social scientists have been those who could trace out hidden correlations and uncover parallel movements missed by the uninitiated. These researches have been useful. Perhaps this is why one of my friends says that history is the *only* social science.

The discontent of the faculty may, however, be related to the irrelevance of this large segment of our endeavor, the social sciences. The crises we face demand more than labels and descriptions. We need prognoses, strategies, techniques, and direction. We need to envision those trajectories that will move us to act and to sustain our hope.

But the move through transition plays havoc with the disciplines as they are now organized. Economics, political science, and sociology will have to abandon their sovereignty in the interest of more direct access to the issues of poverty, urban ecology, environmental sciences, the pre-technological societies, racism in world relations, and social mobility. These topics summon all the social sciences at once, and it is futile to distribute them among the disciplines arbitrarily.

The faculty does indeed experience a discontent that arises out of their inability to relate to the swiftly changing world about them except in the most effete sort of way. A corollary is the spin-off of a few iconoclasts, as long as the total body does not fall apart. Another corollary is a growing distance between radical students who cry for relevance and the faculty who are committed to institutionalism and the traditional inhibitions to change.

Of course, the foregoing is not representative of all faculty. Not all faculty people are discontented. Too many of them are thoroughly accommodated to the anachronisms and the irrelevancies of higher education and are pleased to perpetuate them. They have no interest in things mundane or pedestrian. How long such people can be supported is anybody's guess.

PART FOUR

Administrators
— in the Middle

CLARK KERR

Presidential Discontent

DISCONTENT ON THE CAMPUS and about the campus is one of the dominating themes of contemporary American society. Student discontent, faculty discontent, legislative discontent, public discontent are all well recognized and well documented. But the group almost certainly subject to the most nearly universal discontent—the presidents—has, by comparison, been the most neglected in our obsession with the malaise of others. The discontent of all the other groups piles up on the presidents, and the presidents add their own problems to the mounting totality. They endure all of this discontent largely alone and, with rare exceptions, in silence. Many presidents, for much of the time today, fall into the category of the walking wounded in the continuing wars in the groves of academe. The chief exceptions are the new recruits, and they constitute an increasing proportion.

The president remains the most important single figure in the life of the campus (although he is no longer the central personage he was during most of the history of American higher education). Consequently, his discontent should be of concern to the entire enterprise. Often, it is not. Attention is given to improving the lot of the student and the faculty

» » « «

Clark Kerr is Chairman of the Carnegie Commission on Higher Education and former President of the University of California.

137

member, and to bettering relations with legislators and the public. Yet the lot of the president and better relations with him are largely ignored. Partly this is a matter of numbers. There are 7,000,000 students and 650,000 faculty members, thousands of legislators, and millions of the general public, but only 2,500 presidents. They are comparatively few in number and surrounded by larger masses; the attention goes to the larger groups. The presidents also have no spokesmen, no merchants of their discontent, and, by the nature of their roles, must be largely mute about their own dissatisfactions.

The unhappiness of the president is not a new theme. It goes back to the early days of Harvard. The proof of it is in occasional statements by presidents, in biographies about them, and in the histories of campus controversies which almost always have clustered around the role, the policies, the personality of the president. Campus turmoil for over three centuries has concentrated on or near this one figure.

There are those who say the president deserves this fate: they say that he accepted the job voluntarily, sometimes even avidly; that he has the authority and the perquisites, that he represents the evils of the external world, that he perpetuates the evils of the campus. The theme of the president who must be overthrown—by students or faculty or alumni or trustees or legislators—runs through the literature about the campus, as does the theme of the president who feels himself betrayed by those he sought to serve.

"If a man wishes to be humbled and mortified, let him become President of Harvard College." [1] This was the lament of President Holyoke on his deathbed. He had served as president of Harvard from 1737 to 1769 —longer than anyone else except Charles W. Eliot. He had reformed the curriculum to do away with the system under which one tutor carried a class through all subjects for four years. This development was historic for it began the trend toward greater and greater specialization by faculty members that has continued ever since. He had also been president when Old Harvard Hall, with all the records of the college, was burned, and he had seen many academic and student controversies. His lament has been echoed over the centuries by many others, including two of the college heads who served also as presidents of the United States. "Woodrow Wilson once remarked that he had never learned anything about politics after he left Princeton" [2]—and he did not like politics. Thomas Jefferson encountered severe problems of student and, subsequently, faculty discontent. He wrote that they gave him "a great degree of sufferance." [3] A survey of the history of the University of California leads

[1] Samuel Eliot Morison, *Three Centuries of Harvard* (Cambridge, Mass.: Harvard University Press, 1936), p. 99.

[2] Harold W. Stoke, *The American College President* (New York: Harper & Row, 1959), p. 149.

[3] *The Writings of Thomas Jefferson*, ed. A. E. Bergh (Washington: 1907), 18: 346.

to the conclusion that no president ever left office both happily and voluntarily. The discontented president of today has a long lineage.

The history of the college presidency, however, is not one of unrelieved gloom and doom. Many presidents have apparently been happy in their positions and greatly honored afterward, but this is not the dominant theme.

One test of the mutual contentment of the president and those with whom he works is survival. Presidents are usually appointed to serve until death or retirement. The position is looked upon as "permanent," rather than as for a fixed term. Given the average age at time of appointment, tenure might be expected to last fifteen to twenty years. Legend has it, however, that tenure actually averages four to seven years, or about one-third the normal expectation. If the legend is correct, most presidents leave voluntarily or involuntarily long before they might be logically expected to do so. Seldom is the departure made to take another presidential position, for there is no career line of movement from one presidency to another. Such movement is the exception and occurs in only 10–15 percent of cases. Thus it appears that most presidents leave their positions ahead of the expectation at the time of their appointment, whether by their own free will, under duress, or a combination of both. Turnover is a mark of the discontent of someone or some group or groups. The happy president surrounded by contented admirers does not cut his tenure to one-third the anticipated length of service; nor does he have it cut for him.

The presidents of the most prestigious universities have generally been thought to serve the longest terms. They are the most carefully selected, they are in the institutions that take greatest pride in their stability of leadership, and they are also the most visible symbols of higher education. An examination of tenure of the presidents of the universities included in the membership of the Association of American Universities gives some indication of maximum average length of term and of changes in it. This association is made up of the universities generally accepted as the academic leaders in the United States. Membership now totals forty-eight.[4]

In 1899, the average years in office of this group of presidents was 10.9 years. By 1969, this had dropped to 5.9. The decline has taken place throughout the seventy years, but the big drops came in the 1930s, from 9.5 in 1929 to 7.7 in 1939; and in the 1960s, from 7.4 to 5.9. It appears that the average may still be going down. In 1969, 27.1 percent of the presidents had been in office less than one year, and 52.1 percent less than five years—in each case, the highest percentage in history. The comparable figures in 1964 were 2.4 percent and 38.1 percent; and in

---

[4] I am indebted to Charles P. McCurdy, Jr., executive secretary, for the basic data from which the averages given here have been calculated.

1899 they were 14.3 percent and 21.4 percent. This rapid change is an indication of growing discontent by somebody—often the president himself. It implies that the position of the presidency suddenly has become more difficult. There has been no similar increase in the dropout rates of students and faculty. The new dropouts are the presidents.

Averages are somewhat deceptive, for they include a small number of very long-service individuals. A person halfway up the AAU seniority list in 1929 had served seven years; in 1969, only two years. Thus the median years of experience has been cut by more than two-thirds. Half of the presidents of these leading universities in 1969 were, by comparison, "green hands." The "old hands" in 1969—defined as having ten years of service or more—numbered twelve, or one-quarter of the complement. It has been the "old hands" in particular who have lent wisdom and stability and guidance to all the presidents in the AAU.

The experience of the AAU institutions is that presidents once served one-half to two-thirds of "normal" expectancy, and now serve one-quarter to one-third instead. If comparable figures were available for other institutions of higher learning—and they are not—they would likely show a similar trend.

All of this leads to the observation that a permanent president is more temporary than permanent, and becomes more temporary as time goes on. I shall seek to examine why. First, I shall set forth the major problems now confronting presidents as they see them; second, the nature of the presidency itself and changes in it; and, third, possible solutions to some problems.

It is a sad commentary on American higher education that the central figure—the president—is apparently subject to the greatest discontent and has been so subject for the longest period of time. It could be said today, as it was said in 1940,[5] that "the position has become almost an impossibility"—but the important word is *almost*. It would be a still sadder commentary if that word were omitted; and it should not be.

Contemporary Problems

College presidents have recently set forth the "major problems"[6] that confront them, and the list holds some surprises. The problems they cited

[5] Edgar W. Knight, *What College Presidents Say* (Chapel Hill: University of North Carolina Press, 1940), p. 346.

[6] I am indebted to Harold L. Hodgkinson of the Center for Research and Development in Higher Education, University of California, Berkeley, for access to the answers to a questionnaire filled out by 1,200 college presidents in 1968. This questionnaire was developed in connection with a study of "Institutions in Transition" supported by the Carnegie Commission on Higher Education. The material which follows is drawn largely from answers to a question which read: "What major problems that you are currently facing are of most concern to you?" I shall also draw on my own many conversations with many presidents.

can be summarized under seven general headings in the order of frequency and intensity of mention:

Money
Faculty relations
Control of the institution
Student relations
New directions for programs
Aims and purposes
Personal considerations

Two surprises deserve special attention.

Money stands out as by far the dominant problem, surpassing all others and standing in a class by itself. This seems rather strange since higher education has just completed a decade when funds flowed more readily than ever before. Institutional expenditures rose four times over while student enrollments only doubled. Higher expenditures per student were partly the result of inflation but were caused by a rise in real costs as well. Also, by world standards, American expenditures are substantial. Higher education in the United States never was so rich or seemingly felt so poor.

A second surprise is the comparatively low rating given to student relations. The public conception is that they are the greatest, or even the only, problem. But presidents seem more concerned about the faculty and about external control. They also seem to be quite sympathetic to student complaints. Put another way: behind the public battles involving students lie more serious but also more hidden battles with faculties and with external authorities. The presidents, at the center of the conflicts, see these latter contests as being more currently intense and more fundamental. The more passing and more superficial crisis is the one with the students; the coming and more enduring crises are those with faculty members and with external authorities—according to this set of judgments.

MONEY

The standard presidential answer about "major problems" is "financial" or "money, money, money." Some mention money as the sole problem of importance and most mention it as a major problem. A frequently mentioned problem is how to get the funds for salaries and other benefits to attract and retain qualified faculty members. This difficulty is natural inasmuch as faculty costs are about half of total educational costs and the standing of an institution is largely determined by the quality of its faculty. The other stated major need for money is for capital improvements.

The institutions with the greatest emphasis on finances are the private liberal arts colleges; some of them speak of "threatened survival."

For all colleges, the specific areas that give rise to the greatest complaints are: satisfying faculty demands for research time and facilities, particularly access to computers; and meeting the extra costs for disadvantaged students necessitated by scholarships and remedial work.

I should like to make several comments about the money problem. First, it is not new. A questionnaire at any time in history would probably have yielded the same results. A historical survey of presidential views noted that "Alma Mater" is always seen by presidents as "fast failing under the strain." [7] The president sees the financial problem more completely than anyone else, for this is primarily an area of his responsibility and, by comparison, he sees less of some other aspects of the institution. Also, the demands of the campus for more books, more buildings, more of everything are almost insatiable, and particularly so with the increasingly intense competition for status among campuses that has marked recent years. Additionally, the emphasis on money is partly a tactic. The president, like the minister, pleads poverty—poverty with parents, alumni, legislators, foundation executives. He does not have a standardized product to sell at the least price, but a specialized service to sell at the highest price he can get. His is an enterprise largely judged on its ability to maximize inputs, not outputs. Consequently, Alma Mater is always seen as being on the verge of bankruptcy as a method of raising money. The private goal is constant improvement; the public language is about constant deficits. Alma Mater is Pauline in peril—constantly threatened, always saved.

A case in point is the private colleges. They speak the most about impoverishment. Yet, by objective standards, they have been, by and large, better off during the past decade than public institutions. Their faculty salaries have risen faster, their expenditures per student are greater and have risen more rapidly, and their square footage of space per student is also larger and has increased more rapidly. They have been gaining, in fact, as against the public segment; but they have been fighting a losing battle according to their own rhetoric.

Second, the situation at the moment really may be worse than normal, unlikely as this may seem in light of the great financial gains of the last decade as the horn of plenty of an affluent society was poured onto the welcoming laps of the institutions of higher education. This period of prosperity has raised expectations—of faculty members for ever higher salaries, lower teaching loads, and better equipment; of graduate students for more fellowships for more years; of undergraduates for scholarships and loans more readily available. The curve of expectations is still rising. But the once-rising curve of income is now falling off in its rate of rise—

[7] Knight, *What College Presidents Say*, p. 349.

income from the federal government, the states, the many private sources. A great gap is looming between the aspirations of the 1960s and the harsh realities of the 1970s.

The president is in the middle of this gap, trying unsuccessfully to close it and being pulled at from opposite directions. The institution may survive the process but he fears he may not. He has the hard task of replacing lush anticipations with the new facts of American life. He becomes, even more than normally, the proximate source of disappointed expectations. It is easier to parcel out plenty than scarcity, particularly when scarcity follows plenty. It may be better never to have been rich, than to have been rich and lost.

The institutions which seem, according to their financial accounts, to be in the greatest trouble fall into four categories.

The large research universities are caught with heavy research responsibilities as federal funds stabilize or even decline and as overhead allowances on continuing projects fail to meet overhead costs. They also are incurring the heaviest costs for libraries and computers, and are under the most intense pressures to add ever newer specialties on top of recently new specialties. The knowledge explosion is for them a financial calamity.

The small liberal arts colleges of no national distinction are also under great pressure. Their potential students are attracted to low-tuition community and state colleges. The institutions themselves are often too small for an effective scale of operations and too rural to be attractive to the new generation of students. The same is true of many of the private junior colleges. Catholic and Protestant institutions, of whatever size and wherever located, may also, by their very nature, limit their potential clientele in a less religious age.

The historic Negro colleges constitute a third group. Suddenly they are competing for faculty members in an overactive national market instead of in their formerly depressed and isolated market. They too must expand rapidly and diversify their curricula as they compete for students.

Another group comprises institutions that are engaged in special efforts on behalf of disadvantaged students. This group includes the large research universities, the historic Negro colleges, and, additionally, many of the more famous of the liberal arts colleges. It also includes the public comprehensive colleges—in New York City, New Jersey, and Washington, D.C.—which all of a sudden find themselves committed to "open access."

These institutions, together, number about half of all campuses in the United States. The financial strains within them vary greatly. Thus there is a financial problem, but it is not universal and, where it does exist, it is not uniform. The knowledge explosion, the urban explosion, and the opportunity explosion have varying effects on varying institutions. There are many financial crises on many campuses more than there is *a* financial crisis in all of higher education.

Third, the problem is likely to get worse in the 1970s and perhaps even worse in the 1980s. The nation is shifting its priorities from education after Sputnik to the environment, poverty, and much else. Much of higher education is now politically unpopular—some politicians make a career out of attacking it. Yet costs per student keep rising. This trend is long-term, because higher productivity does not here, as in industry and agriculture, partially offset rising wages and salaries. There is also the short-run factor that many of the new students come from less affluent homes and thus cost more in scholarships and remedial work—cost much more. Also, there are more students in prospect—a 50 percent increase in the next decade.

The 1980s may be even more difficult. Enrollments then will flatten out and, in some years, even decline. Rising costs per student will be recognized as such and will no longer be obscured by rising enrollments. The public may look with even less sympathy on greater demands year by year for more money, when the number of students is stationary or even going down.

The outlook for the next two decades is cloudy. And there is not a great deal that the president can do about it. One helpful factor will be that faculty salaries, under the new supply and demand situation for Ph.D.'s, will not rise so rapidly, but this development will have its debit side in the disgruntlement of faculty members after a long period of rising comparative incomes.

As a further comment, there is a money illusion—the illusion that money can cure all problems, satisfy all faculty and student demands. This illusion assumes that the demands for the things that money can buy are satiable, and they probably are not; it also assumes that all discontent can be bought off, and some of it cannot—some of it has a nonmaterialistic base. Also, while any one president might solve his own problems with more money if he got it and nobody else did, all presidents could not solve all their problems even if they all got more money, for then the competition for comparative advantage would only have been raised to higher levels. Presidents individually often hold to a money illusion—that money is at the root of all their solutions; but money, by itself, cannot solve all the problems of all of higher education.

FACULTY

The presidents see the faculty standing as the next great source of problems after money. The perversity of some of the faculty takes its place next in line after the scarcity of funds. Complaints take four major forms.

The first is that "faculty people are slow to change" in matters of institutional policies and structures, that the imperatives of academic change run up against implacable conservatism. This is an ancient complaint.

The second is that the faculty is too self-serving, too prone to place its interest in research above the students' interest in learning, its interest in external consulting above service on campus committees, its desire for higher salaries over other claims on funds. The more "cosmopolitan" a faculty becomes—and many have recently become much more cosmopolitan and less "home-guard"—the more "self-serving" it also becomes. Many presidents have seen this process at work to their dismay.

The third is that some faculty members are turning to unionization and thus confrontation against, rather than cooperation with, the administration, and turning to militancy on external political issues. As a consequence, a chasm is opening up between faculty and public thinking. This turn is largely new. Traditionally, faculty members have acted more like colleagues than employees, and more like objective observers of society than passionate partisans. The shift to unionization and to militancy, to the extent it occurs, places the president in a far more difficult situation.

A fourth complaint of the responding presidents is that the faculty has deserted the president or even betrayed him, that it does not give him the personal and institutional support he needs. Apparently many presidents entered office with a sense of being part of the faculty and having its friendship only to find, to their horror, that friends deserted them and they were bereft of the enthusiastic support they expected. This again is an ancient complaint; and fortunate are those who do not experience it. New administrative power and old academic friendships do not always go hand in hand; quite the contrary—"a friend in power is a friend lost." [8] The honeymoon is often over as soon as the marriage vows have been taken.

This concern of the presidents for faculty relations bodes ill for the future. Change will always confront academic conservatism, and the need for change continues, perhaps at an increasing level. Cosmopolitanism will grow with the supersonic jets. And the doctrines of the "dissenting academy" can split a faculty as well as create a chasm between the campus and the community. The last great faculty split came a century ago when the proponents of the classical curriculum were defeated by the new specialists and technologists. The ultimate outcome of that battle was inevitable.

The new battle between the supporters of "objectivity" and of "partisanship" has, as yet, no clear result. In this battle, society will stand with the old and not with the new, contrary to the situation a century ago. The presidential giants of a century ago stood with the new and with

[8] Henry Adams, *The Education of Henry Adams* (New York: Random House, 1931), p. 108.

the public. The presidents of today will stand, of necessity, largely with the old and with the public, and yet many of the younger faculty will stand with the newer views of the dissenting academy. It is less certain that any giants will emerge from this historic conflict. Some of the bloodiest confrontations of the future may well occur within faculties, and the presidents will not be able to stand entirely aloof; nor will they be isolated from the public quarrels between organized faculty groups and external bodies. The giants who began rising a century ago rode a great new idea with the support of federal and state agencies and of a growing body of younger and more progressive faculty members. This combination is not repeated in the current situation. The efforts needed will again be herculean but more in guerrilla defense than in frontal advance toward a clear goal.

Gross and Grambsch [9] have noted recently the close similarity of goals between faculty and administrators, but this situation will certainly change as the dissenting academy becomes more influential on campus. It will split the goals of some faculty from those of most administrators in a most fundamental way. The unity of the recent past will dissolve into the partial disunity of the near future. For this reason, in particular, I agree with the presidential view that faculty relations are coming to be among the major problems. A sense of fear more than a conviction of unity marks the attitudes of many presidents today.

CONTROL OF THE INSTITUTION

The presidents are concerned about who controls the institution, but in ways different from those that meet the public eye. The public sees demands for faculty power, or student power, or reassertion of trustee power or even alumni power. But these are not the main directions of presidential concern. Faculties already have a great deal of power in the better institutions and are more often holding onto what they have than they are demanding more. Students have little power and are getting more, and the presidents are generally sympathetic with this trend. Trustees, by and large, are more sophisticated and less interfering than they once were—with notable exceptions. And organized alumni may protest occasionally but they seem to have retired into a sullen silence. Their attachment is to the Alma Mater they once knew and that is fast disappearing. The attachment and the interest, however, continue to endure for the best and the oldest of the private universities and colleges even as they change.

The greater concerns lie elsewhere. They lie with the systemwide administration in the growing number of multicampus units, with the co-

---

[9] Edward Gross and Paul Grambsch, *University Goals and Academic Power* (Washington: American Council on Education, 1968).

ordinating councils and superboards, with the state governors and their administrative assistants, with the legislative committees. They lie also with the closer, less friendly, and more sensational surveillance by the communication media. Particular venom seems to be developing in the relations of campus administrators with the central administrators of systems and with governors and their assistants. The complaint is loss of autonomy, imposition of more and more stringent controls.

The really big power battles are not so much on as off the campus. The old power battles pitted faculties against presidents and trustees in matters of academic freedom. The rules of the American Association of University Professors grew out of these battles. The new power battles increasingly are between the campus led by the president, and external authorities led by the politicians and the bureaucrats, over independence and self-direction for the institution. That is where the hidden knives are really flashing.

In the midst of the remnants of the old and the intricacies of the new power battles, presidents cry for better communications, more of a sense of community, a greater consensus. One president comments about "the lack of a common moral base that permits faculty, administration, trustees, and students to function as a community. The modern university is held together by baling wire and chewing gum, economic advantage and lethargy. The university president presides over spreading chaos." Some of the chaos now comes from the outside as well as from the inside. More people and more agencies with more points of view try to control the campus than ever before. The chaos becomes more highly organized all the time. The old individualistic anarchy of academic life looks peaceful compared with the new administered confusion.

STUDENT RELATIONS

The presidents share the concern of most of the public about student political militancy, student moral standards, the "cultural revolution," black and "Third World" pressures, and student demands for power; but with several important variations.

Student moral standards—excessive use of drugs, anti-intellectualism, intolerance for the opinions of those with whom they disagree, a lowered level of civility—seem to be of greater concern than the more publicized political radicalism. Also, there is a good deal of sympathy with student demands for more power and with the demands of minority students for more consideration, provided solutions can be worked out within reason and through discussions. To the presidents, it is the new moral standards that seem the most troublesome, and some are alarmed at the conformity—"push-button radicalism"—of the growing student "counterculture." As a consequence of these views, presidents and faculties may be parting company about students. Faculty members are willing, even eager, to relinquish control over student conduct, while maintaining essential faculty control over academic matters.[10] Presidents, apparently, would prefer to keep more influence over student life, but give students more authority over academic affairs.

The presidents are almost as much troubled by the reactions to students as by the actions of students—the reactions of alumni and the public at large. A disturbance on a campus is a passing episode soon absorbed within the totality of campus life; but, to the general public, the headlines depict an unending series of episodes at many institutions that conveys a total impression of constant turbulence. Also, the public sees the big political event, and the president sees more of what he considers to be the daily deterioration of student standards of conduct.

NEW DIRECTIONS FOR PROGRAMS

A number of presidents see problems in getting new programs under way. Generally they agree on the need for changes and the general directions of those changes: a better educational opportunity for undergraduates, a better break for minority students, a new emphasis on urban affairs, a general revitalization of the academic enterprise. Here again the faculty and administration may disagree. In a survey of "educational qualities," students ranked "teaching ability" as first and faculty rated it as next to last in a list of ten items; and faculty rated "office space," "sabbatical leave," and "parking" as the three top contenders (out of fourteen) for a claim on "college resources." [11] For the presidents to obtain their new directions, major shifts in faculty interests and institutional resources will be necessary.

A special new direction for the state colleges, as perceived by their presidents, is to achieve "university status."

AIMS AND PURPOSES

A small number of presidents express doubts about the philosophical goals of higher education. They see a loss of "traditional purpose" and a transition into the unknown and, perhaps, the unintended. They mourn the loss of consensus. They call for a "new understanding." They see the old emphasis on truth and individual academic freedom giving way to a new emphasis on societal service under peer group control. They wonder where it all leads. Some of the most thoughtful comments treat these matters.

[10] Robert C. Wilson and Jerry G. Gaff, "Student Voice—Faculty Response," *Research Reporter* (Center for Research and Development in Higher Education, University of California, Berkeley), No. 2, 1969. Two-thirds of faculty members would give students "equal vote" or "entire responsibility" in "social matters," but less than one-tenth would make the same concessions in "academic matters."

[11] Harold L. Hodgkinson, "Governance and Functions—Who Decides, Who Decides," *Research Reporter*, No. 3, 1968.

Until the American Civil War there was a consensus of faculty, administrators, and trustees broken by occasional rebellions by recalcitrant students against the classical college and its social and intellectual straitjacket. A new consensus was formed that ruled the next century—a consensus of faculty and administrators and public leaders about research and service—with the students relatively apathetic onlookers. Now the classicists are rising again on the right, the dissenting academy is being born on the left, and the students want in from all directions.

The schools of theology seem most concerned about aims and purposes. They sound like philosophical disaster areas. They have severe doubts about their place in a secularizing society.

PERSONAL CONSIDERATIONS

A few presidents mention—almost all must experience—personal problems: "lack of sleep," "I have taken to drinking too much," "I am resigning," "My contract has not been renewed."

But the future is not entirely bleak; otherwise many presidents would not seek to continue with their jobs. When people are asked about their problems, they state their problems.

A study of future "events" gives a more optimistic outlook.[12] Institutional (presumably presidential) responses showed five of the most desired events as also among the ten most probable events:

> The great majority of high school graduates will take at least two years of instruction after high school.
>
> Faculty participation in major aspects of academic governance will become a widely accepted practice.
>
> Significantly more Federal and state funds will go directly to students, as scholarships or loans.
>
> Undergraduate curricula will undergo major revisions.
>
> In most undergraduate curricula, the number of required courses will decline to permit more electives and individualized programs.

The five other most probable events, but which were not also most "desirable," were considered to be:

> *In loco parentis* will be much less important than responsibility for self-regulation as a basis for codes of nonacademic student affairs and conduct.
>
> State-wide coordinating councils will have increasing influence over public colleges and universities.

---

[12] John Caffrey, "Predictions for Higher Education in the 1970s," in *The Future Academic Community*, ed. John Caffrey (Washington: American Council on Education, 1969), pp. 261–92.

The proportion of students enrolled in private institutions of higher education will decline at an even faster rate.

Formulas will increasingly be used to determine levels of state and Federal support for various academic programs.

Of all persons receiving earned doctorates in the 1970s, a steadily increasing proportion will be employed by bureaus, industry, and government.

This listing of expectations, both good and not so good, is generally consistent with the presidential views summarized above. It is not the best of all possible worlds, but it is also not the worst.

PROBLEMS OF THE PAST AND THE FUTURE

It may be worth reflecting for a moment on the problems that do *not* now confront the presidents, but have confronted presidents in the past or may do so in the future. Two great issues dominated the period before the Civil War: the dominance of church leaders over the campus, and the enforcement of detailed in loco parentis rules over the unruly students. Only the last vestiges of each of these once-consuming problems any longer remain.

From the Civil War to World War I, the great issues were the complete revision of the classical curriculum and the adding of research and service to the functions of the campus while fighting off the crude attempts of some agricultural and industrial leaders to turn the campus into a trade school dominated by the "interests." The elective system has now replaced the rigid classical curriculum, but new and less crude forms of influence, through money, have allowed the "interests"—by now mainly the federal agencies—to affect the academic enterprise.

From World War I to the end of the Korean War, the major battles were over academic freedom, which reached peaks during the early 1920s and again in the Joe McCarthy period, and over the rise of faculty power through academic senates. The courts and the new sophistication of trustees ended the first series of battles, and faculty dominance over academic affairs is by now well accepted in the leading institutions and is penetrating into all.

In the "apathetic" 1950s, the leading issues degenerated into "sex for the students, athletics for the alumni, and parking for the faculty."

The 1960s saw the great growth of scientific research and of student enrollments, and required an all-out effort at expansion in clear directions. In retrospect, it was a Golden Age. It is notable that, at the end of a decade heavily influenced by the federal interest, almost no presidents complain of undue direct federal control as a major problem.

Certain potential problems have never yet come to plague the campus. Nonacademic employees have been largely quiescent, although there are now problems of minority representation in employment and on construction work. American higher education has never been faced with a lowering of standards across the board, as in India. Generally, standards have risen institution by institution. As new students, with lower academic accomplishments, have come into higher education, they have been absorbed mainly by institutions with lower admission standards within a system characterized by great diversity. There never has been a single "gold standard," as the British put it, to be debased. Were all institutions to be opened to all students, there would then be a crisis of standards. Nor has higher education, as yet, been faced by great technological changes, although TV was once thought by some to be bringing great change. The computer is a much more likely candidate in the future.

Higher education in America has met and surmounted many problems in its three and a third centuries. Many of the past battles were both difficult and important to win. The present age again offers difficult and important battles, but more of them simultaneously and with a shorter period for solutions than ever before. Presidents now, as then, will be in the midst of such solutions as may yet be found.

The Contemporary Presidency

Trouble rises to the level of the presidency and falls to the level of the presidency. The president is the institutional lightning rod. In a time of troubles, the president will be in trouble. Periods of change are periods of trouble, and we are in a period of change. Nothing can alter this fact. We have seen, above, through the eyes of the presidents, the troubles that now cluster around them.

In meeting troubles, the president can work with money and power and policy and persuasion. There is now less money in prospect,[13] and the president has little power. His power was always restricted but has become much more so in recent times, with the rise of faculty and student power and the increased role of external authorities. A recent study concludes that the "most significant change" of the past decade has been the growth in faculty authority and the growth in student authority.[14]

The president must thus work mostly with policy and persuasion, a situation always difficult. The campus is loaded with negative power,

[13] New money is essential to influence. Old money is nearly sacrosanct. And, among new money, much of it—perhaps 50–90 percent—is essentially beyond presidential control. Of 100 percent of old money and 10 percent of new money, a president may himself be able to control only 1–5 percent; with no new money, he can control almost no funds at all.

[14] Harold L. Hodgkinson, "Institutions in Transition" to be published for the Carnegie Commission on Higher Education by McGraw-Hill Book Co., New York, 1970.

with veto groups. William Rainey Harper wrote a memo in 1904 which was found in his files after his death:

> . . . when all has been said, the limitations of the college president, even when he has the greatest freedom of action, are very great. . . . in educational policy he must be in accord with [the faculty]. It is absurd to suppose that any president, however strong or willful he may be, can force a faculty made up of great leaders of thought to do his will. The president, if he has the power of veto, may stand in the way of progress, but he cannot secure forward movement except with the cooperation of those with whom he is associated.[15]

The president can veto; the faculty can veto; so also can the trustees. It takes all three to enter upon a new policy. In more modern times and particularly in state institutions, there are still more veto points. Any really important measure in the University of California must pass at least twelve check points. This means lost time and, sometimes, lost chances. The head of a corporation, by comparison, has great positive power. As the person who most wants things done—to adjust to the market and for many other reasons—he has the most power to do them. No person or group on the campus has similar power to take positive action. The true sign of power on the campus is how much you can stop! Getting things done depends more on persuasion, less on power.

The campus has no clear theory of governance. It is partly collegial, with the president as one of the colleagues, and partly hierarchical, with the president as the chief executive. But it is other things as well. And there are many interest groups both inside and outside the structure of governance. Consequently, decision making can be both confused and cumbersome. This unwieldiness is particularly a handicap in times and situations that call for rapid action. If, for example, the president, acting in his role of chief executive, calls in the police during a disturbance, he will be called to task by his colleagues for lack of consultation and concurrence. If he takes time to consult colleagues, he may fail to fulfill his functions of trust as chief executive. It is a mixed-up form of governance. The collegial approach calls for time and unanimity; hierarchical governance calls for action and personal responsibility.

Also, for the president, there are few clear tests of performance, as the profit-and-loss statement is for the business executive; and some of the imprecise proofs of performance that do exist become evident only over the long run, such as the eventual quality of a new faculty member or of a new endeavor. The president cannot point to one or a few clearly defined, universally accepted, and quickly available demonstrations of his

[15] *The William Rainey Harper Memorial Conference*, ed. Robert N. Montgomery (Chicago: University of Chicago, 1938), pp. 28–29.

stewardship. He does not have available the evidence of a profit earned or an election won to substantiate and authenticate his leadership. Nor has he civil service status or seniority rights. He is more like a minister who cannot prove how many souls he has saved, but nevertheless must satisfy both his parishioners and the hierarchy above him, or like an actor who must please the audience once a night and twice on Saturday—and there are many types of audiences.

The difficulties have been compounded over the past decade. The average campus enrollment has doubled, and in many institutions has increased several times over. Some colleges that once were small communities have become more impersonal environments. The president at such institutions can walk through the campus and meet few people he knows personally, but the academic world prefers personal contact. More people feel he never sees them and does not understand their problems; they may be quite correct. The campus has also become more complex—with a bigger budget, more relations with outside groups and agencies, more varied activities. New service activities, such as those with the local community, add to the burdens on the president's time and to the heterogeneity of his constituencies. The president's attention is both fractionalized internally and drawn externally.

Size and complexity run against the collegial tradition. The collegial president should know all his colleagues and understand their problems. The hierarchical president need not, even should not, know all his employees and understand all their problems. The big and complex campus becomes more hierarchical and less collegial, but collegial expectations still continue.

Further compounding the difficulties is the loss of consensus over powers and goals, already noted, and without consensus on both there is less basis for making decisions and less assurance of their acceptance. Additionally, the students have often become activists. When they were passive, the president, on campus, could be concerned almost exclusively with the faculty. But with students more active and with student and faculty interests diverging, he cannot equally satisfy both. A new and complicating element has entered the situation.

Beyond all these factors lie some personal considerations. Once the president received far more in salary and perquisites than any member of his faculty. Now many faculty members, from all sources available to them, may earn more than the president. He alone on the campus once had a chance to travel widely and participate in public affairs. Now these opportunities are equally open to many faculty members. The comparative rewards to the chief executive have been greatly reduced. Medical deans may have suffered even more in relation to the advantages available to some of their colleagues; and they also have infinitely more complex jobs than they once did.[16] Many presidents and many medical deans reduce their incomes, as well as complicate their lives, when they accept their positions.

And there are other changes. This is not an age of unquestioned loyalty to leaders nor an age of intense school spirit, a change that shows up in faculty and student attitudes toward presidents. On campus, the attitude is generally anti-Establishment. The president no longer has a natural constituency from which he can expect support. Only in such areas as schools of agriculture and football teams is there still some sense of un-questioned institutional and personal loyalty. The president is more alone in the academic world. It is not simply a new age, for the mega-campus and the multiversity are not the types of institutions that in any age could be expected to elicit a spirit of intense loyalty.

We have noted in passing the problems of medical deans. Deans of students and other personnel officers are even less to be envied. The faculty once turned over personal guidance of students to the dean, who with goodwill did his best; but the students no longer want the guidance, even with goodwill. The dean once handled individual discipline, but the students are now turning discipline into a collective problem and placing it directly before the president. The dean once helped the students with their organized activities, but some of their new activities are not so properly subject to the support of the dean. The dean was once helpless in the face of cigarettes and alcohol; he is now also helpless in the face of sex and drugs. I know of no academic administrators today more un-certain about their roles than those in student personnel.

The pressures of the new situation are not uniformly felt in higher education, any more than the financial difficulties are uniformly experi-enced. It is my impression that state colleges, community colleges, and regional universities go along much more as they once did than is true of the national research universities, the historic Negro colleges, the lib-eral arts colleges, and the schools of theology. The greater troubles now seem to center on the presidents in this second set of institutions. This may not be true indefinitely. In the next decade the state colleges and the community colleges will experience the greatest growth among insti-tutions. Thus they will recruit more of the new generation of college teachers, many of whom are already disenchanted with the world and will be particularly disenchanted about teaching at a community college or state college instead of at a great university like the one where they got their Ph.D. Supporters of the New University Conference, with its dissenting academy approach, may end up having their greatest employ-ment in and greatest impact on the nonuniversities. But at the moment,

---

[16] Their average length of tenure has also been reduced, from seven to four years in the short period from 1962 to 1969. (Robert J. Glaser, *Journal of Medical Educa-tion,* December 1969, p. 1124.)

the problems are concentrated elsewhere and, particularly, on the great university campuses. The "large university" has undergone "the most far-reaching changes," [17] and the greatest problems are centered on its president. Solutions, such as there may be, are particularly needed where the problems are the greatest.

Directions for Solutions

There are no panaceas for presidential discontent. The position is inherently a difficult one. In seeking remedies, it is the beginning but not the end of wisdom to know what is given, what cannot be changed. The president will never have enough money to solve all his problems and particularly not over the next two decades; nor is his power likely to be much increased. Society will continue to be in trouble and the campus in need of reform. The ordeal of change through which the United States and higher education are going will continue to disrupt the campus. The faculty will become even more cosmopolitan; the students will continue their experiments with new styles of life; a new age of loyalty is not on the immediate horizon; and the public will be disturbed by what it sees and hears. These are among the largely fixed attributes defining the situation within which solutions must be sought.

The task is to find out what both can and should be changed. Since the president is at the center of the administrative processes, his lot can be improved only in smaller part by direct attention to the office he holds. The larger part of any improvements lie in the general environment, the system of governance, and the general atmosphere of understanding. Additionally, the characteristics of the president himself need to be re-examined.

THE GENERAL ENVIRONMENT

Size of campus should be subject to direct policy consideration and not allowed to increase indefinitely. The tests of appropriate size are effective use of resources and quality of program. The burden of proof should be on those who want to increase the size of an institution beyond the requirements of these two tests. I should like to suggest that resources can be well used and a quality program developed certainly at the level of 15,000–20,000 students per campus for the national research universities, 7,500–10,000 for the regional universities and comprehensive colleges, 2,000–5,000 for the community colleges, and 1,000–2,000 for the liberal arts colleges.

Rate of growth should be modest and as regular as possible. Unduly rapid growth brings problems of building faculty attachment, administra-

---

[17] Hodgkinson, "Institutions in Transition."

tive competence, and new policies; and sudden starts and stops are up-setting.

The academic enterprise works best if the decision-making units are kept as small as possible and if decisions are made as close to the point of origin of the problems as successfully can be done. Thus, in multicampus systems, the move would be toward maximum effective decentralization to individual campuses and the breaking-up of monolithic and huge colleges of letters and science into smaller multidisciplinary schools or into cluster colleges. Decisions, again as many as possible, should be made before the level of the president, and the responsibility for decisions should be spread widely over deans and provosts. But the solution of Paul Goodman of tiny self-governing communities of students and resource leaders is not generally feasible.

Partial and selective disaggregation of the more complex institutions is desirable, and in two directions. First, many campuses are still "company towns," and company towns are notoriously filled with tension as the employer seeks to serve also as landlord, grocer, police chief, and judge. The campus should, as far as possible, seek to turn over residence halls, eating facilities, and bookstores to private contractors or consumer cooperatives; and violations of general laws on interference with persons, property, and programs, to external police and external courts.[18] Second, many campuses have taken on activities that are not central to their academic functions, including some external service and developmental research. Many of these could either be made completely independent or at least semiautonomous, with their own governing boards and budgets. Some of these nonacademic activities have accumulated like barnacles.

There are those who favor more complete disaggregation than outlined above. Flexner would have stopped all service and all semiprofessional activities; Hutchins and Barzun would also stop most of the research as well; and many radicals join in the opposition to traditional service and research functions. Others, who have no philosophical antagonism to any of the current functions, still feel that the multifunction campus is no longer viable, is too subject to disintegration; and they would split off research in one direction, graduate training in another, undergraduate instruction in another, and so forth, for the sake of survival. I reject the philosophical arguments on the grounds that the complex environment is a highly stimulating and productive one and should be preserved, and the realistic arguments on the grounds that reality is not all that desperate and that we need not turn to tactics of last resort.

In general, the fewer the rules and the more the options for free choice

---

[18] Thomas Jefferson reached this latter conclusion in 1826: "But the most effectual instrument we have found to be the civil authority" (*The Writings of Thomas Jefferson*, p. 356). He had started out as a strong supporter of "self-government" on campus.

offered to individuals, the less the burden on both central and local administration.

The campus can be made a more manageable community if size and rate of growth are controlled, if reasonable decentralization is undertaken, if there is selective disaggregation of unwise or unnecessary functions, and if rules are minimized and options maximized. A central strategy should be to disperse discontent over as many separate units and as much time as possible, rather than allow it to be concentrated at one place and at one time. More of the community more of the time should be given the responsibility for the reconciliation of differing points of view and for decisions made. Not just the president.

THE SYSTEM OF GOVERNANCE

Faculty and students must be associated appropriately with the process of governance to make policies more effective and the process more legitimate. One way is to give each a standard percentage of membership in each governing body, as is now being done in France and Germany. A more satisfactory way, in the American context, is to award authority on a pragmatic basis in accordance with the specific functions performed: faculty and students would be assigned—depending on the function— anywhere from no authority to all authority in accordance with their interest, their competence, and their responsibility. This division of labor approach is not as elegant as an overall precentage formula, but it is better adapted to getting good decisions area by area. The sorting-out process to make the governance fit the functions involves much detail and, in the end, there will be overlapping responsibilities. One task is to sort out collegial and hierarchical situations, and to apply collegial decision-making to collegial situations, and hierarchical decision-making to hierarchical situations, and not unduly mix the two. There are other types of situations—for example, inherently democratic or inherently master-apprentice—requiring still other types of relationships.

The whole community, however, must be held together. Historically, this has been the function of the president, who has gone from committee to committee and group to group and person to person. This process has caused much loss of time in going from one checkpoint to another, and has led to the dictatorship of veto groups. It can be greatly simplified by the creation of a central advisory council where representatives of all groups can be met by the president, and where responsibility for getting a consensus is borne by the council as a whole. In such a council, forces that now meet only through their mutual contact with the president can meet directly and, if necessary, confront each other face to face. Within such a council, the more progressive forces in relation to change (trustees, administrators, students) can bring their efforts to bear more directly on the more conservative forces (mainly the faculty). Such a council should concern itself only with broad policies that affect the entire community. It would not replace more specialized consultative instrumentalities.

There are dangers in this approach. Direct confrontation may agitate antagonisms that are now muted through the president as intermediary, and the whole process can be highly politicized according to external political orientations. Consequently the selection of members, the appropriate items for the agenda, and the parliamentary arrangements are of utmost importance.

Such a council, through an executive committee, can provide the president with a quick avenue for consultation and action.

At its best, such a council can provide the president with a better mechanism for his persuasive efforts, and the community a better opportunity to develop a consensus on matters of fundamental importance.

The president lives most intimately with the trustees. They select him, they continue him in office, they make some of the most essential decisions. The composition of the board, consequently, is of great importance. Membership by public officials, in an ex officio capacity, brings in the possibility of an unfortunate element of external politics and of conflict of interest (of governmental policies as against campus welfare). Faculty and students should be associated in the process of selecting at least some of the members to assure understanding of their points of view and their acceptance of the ultimate decisions.

New layers of authority are being added outside the campus and complicating academic life. External planning, coordination, and surveillance should be kept to a minimum. We need a set of principles (as has been worked out to protect academic freedom), an evaluative body (the equivalent in this area to the American Association of University Professors), appropriate mechanisms for giving money (general formulas, applications judged on individual merit by impartial panels, and disbursement through the many hands of the students), and a sense of restraint (as in Great Britain). Otherwise the higher layers of authority will become unduly burdensome.

Additionally, we need agreed-upon rules controlling the forms of expression of dissent to avoid violence and the suppression of points of view by peer groups. Historically, the American Association of University Professors and the American Civil Liberties Union have worked out rules to protect individual faculty members and students from undue control by administrators, trustees, and public authorities. The attacks on free expression of opinion then came from the right and the outside. Attacks now come from the left and from within as well. A new set of rules is equally necessary here to protect free expression of opinion and the uncoerced search for truth. The American Association of University Professors and the American Civil Liberties Union have both special competence and a special obligation. The dissenting academy should not be allowed to suppress the dissent of others on the basis of its own intolerance.

The purposes of governance are to obtain effective actions and to achieve essential consent; these are also the basic responsibilities of the president. These purposes can be furthered as governance is related to functions, as the will of the whole community finds better means of expression, as trustees are better selected, as external authority is minimized, and as rules of conduct inhibit attacks on academic freedom from right and left and outside and inside alike. Under these circumstances, the role of the president as chief persuader or constructive mediator or community leader can best be enhanced.

THE PRESIDENCY

Within the modest limits possible, the power of the president should be preserved and even enhanced in a period when it takes leadership to move in new directions. In any event, he should take and keep the initiative in making proposals. His chief influence is as initiator. Most academic reforms, most new programs come about through his efforts.

It has been suggested that the presidency be divided into two parts: an external-affairs president and an internal-affairs president. Except under unusual circumstances this would, I believe, prove unworkable. External and internal affairs are too intertwined. One person must coordinate them. Otherwise there could develop a two-headed monster. Rather, the president should have adequate assistance at the vice-presidential level, particularly in external affairs, now that much more of his time is taken up with internal affairs.[19] Instead of an academic provost, he now needs more a provost for external affairs. Also, where this is not already the case, the president should have all administrative and staff officers, including the legal staff, reporting to him and not directly to the board. Additionally, he needs the highest quality of technical staff. In the new situation he does not have the time for detailed supervision and review of staff work, and yet he is absolutely dependent upon the competence of the staff endeavor.

Most important, I believe, among changes is to place the president on a term appointment of reasonable length. This will give him, except under exceptional circumstances, a fixed period on which he can plan. At the end of the term, he will have an easy opportunity to review his own desires and for others to review his conduct. If he is reappointed, he will have received a reaffirmation of his authority as he meets new crises. In any event, opponents will not feel that they must wait forever for a change unless they mount massive opposition. A term of office could re-

---

[19] The president of Columbia was out raising a huge endowment when trouble broke out at Columbia in 1968. His successor stayed home and helped reduce the trouble, but did less toward raising the endowment. This illustrates the dilemma.

lax their opposition. This is not to suggest, however, that under exceptional circumstances a president may not be terminated at any time.

The term of office should, I think, be made not less than five and not more than ten years. My preference is for six, partly on the grounds that this is now the actual average term of office at the leading universities.

Exits should be made easier; reaffirmations should be more clear cut. However long the term, the president should have available and should take substantial vacations and periodic leaves, much as do faculty members.

THE GENERAL ATMOSPHERE

An understanding of the limited and complex role of the president by faculty, students, trustees, and the public is of great importance: an understanding that his powers are not unlimited and that his responsibility for both good and evil is not total. He should not be held fully responsible for the conduct of people and the nature of developments over which he has little or no influence, let alone control. Too often his role is that of Mr. Lazarus in the firm of Undershaft and Lazarus as depicted by George Bernard Shaw in *Major Barbara:* to serve as the convenient personage who is consistently "blamed" for the faults of others. But it is too extreme to say that all the president does is preside over a "tangle" that "is.full of queer animals, old, young, and middle-aged" with the sole ability "to stand on a height above it and squirt perfume on the ensemble." [20] It is more accurate to say that the latter is the essence of some of his more ceremonial speeches and statements.

Beyond this understanding of the presidency should lie an appreciation of and tolerance for the manifold problems that beset the modern campus, a realization that it cannot and should not be entirely quiescent, a perception that it cannot and even should not meet the ideals of all groups. Political leaders and the mass media have a central position in the spread of both understanding and misunderstanding in the public mind, and thus a very special responsibility. The American public has come to accept strikes of workers without fearing revolution. It must also come to accept campus unrest without fearing the end of all it holds dear. Violence, however, is quite another matter—it neither should be nor will be accepted.

THE STYLE OF THE PRESIDENT

Most of the presidents before the Civil War were clergymen. They now appear, in retrospect, as stern figures standing for morality and character. After the Civil War, the great leaders and models were the academic en-

[20] Somnia Vana, "College Education: An Inquest," *The Freeman,* March 1, 1922. (I am indebted to Professor Seymour Martin Lipset, of Harvard University, for calling this article to my attention.)

trepreneurs who were building research programs and new professional schools and recruiting scholarly faculties. They were great public figures, highly visible and even flamboyant. They ruled in a very personal way, often as academic autocrats, usually but not always benevolent. The style changed after the initial period of university building. There were more checks and balances, bigger budgets, more diversified interests. By the end of World War II, the preferred style was that of the competent academic executive handling resources, personnel, policies, and public relations in a quietly effective manner. The method was the small and private discussion with representatives of all the interest groups concerned and the working-out of satisfactory solutions to be promulgated without fanfare. The executive sought to maximize, from a long-term point of view, the facilities available and their effective utilization. He was custodian of a permanent trust making long-range plans. Reforms were undertaken and new endeavors started when appropriate and when possible without unduly disturbing consequences. He dealt with interest groups and appealed to rationality, to goodwill, to concern for the general welfare, to tolerance.

Now new styles are being born. Some presidents, in a more polarized situation, are appealing to one pole as demagogues crying for law and order; others, to the opposite pole as the new sycophants seeking to flatter every whim of radical students and professors, and to embrace every idea provided it appears sufficiently new.[21] Many are seeking a low profile by serving, so to speak, as staff officers without opinions of their own, as reticent civil service officials. Still others turn to an emphasis on current tactics like politicians facing a hotly contested and proximate election, cautiously balancing actions and words, tiptoeing on the high wire—surviving but not advancing.

The dominant new style will come to be, I think, that of academic statesman. The academic statesman will seek the same goals as the academic executive—of resources well used, effective policies, reform, quality, consent—but with new methods. Generally his conduct will be less in the committee room and more in the open. He will appeal more to mass groups and less to representatives. Thus he will be more attentive to sentiments and attitudes, even when irrational. He will speak more in terms of principles and less in terms of interests; but he will not ignore interests. Public relations, on campus and off, will be a greater concern. He will be more visible, more accessible, more of a public personality. Thus he will be more like the mayor of a big city walking in the streets, meeting the people, wrestling in public with the great issues of the day

[21] None yet have fully accepted, however, the view of some radicals that the campus should become a "center of disloyalty" and the president should serve as "chairman" of the center.

and less the executive with his experts working in comparative silence with other elites.

The academic statesman will be more the political leader dealing with large publics, with his own image, with the image of his institution, with the image of his programs, with the organization of mass political support. His obvious concerns will be more short-term; his expenditures of funds more for their immediate and noticeable effects. He will continue to be the chief persuader, the mediator, the community leader, the "unifying force"[22] holding the campus together; the initiator, the policy-maker seeking to move it ahead to meet its problems; and the defender, the gladiator seeking to protect it from internal and external attack; but he will also be the image-maker and the political leader and the public relations expert trying to turn mass sentiment on campus and off in the directions he wishes to go. He will be in the plaza and on TV, as well as in the office and in the faculty club. The new leaders will be seen more directly and less indirectly, will marshal mass support more than just leadership support, will appeal more publicly to principle than privately to interests, will win and lose battles more openly. Popularity in the short run will be more of a test; quiet effectiveness in the long run, less.

Good men keep coming along to be presidents, although more reluctantly and in lesser numbers than a decade ago. Some respond to duty; others to the honor and recognition; others to the challenge and the chance to test their leadership abilities; others to the call to an exciting life including social and public affairs; but most to the opportunity for public service, for helping to solve some of the pressing issues of the age. The availability of good men to be presidents is the ultimate test of the viability of the college and university system. The faith of these men and their willingness to try is now the key resource of higher education.

Solutions to grave problems of higher education have been found in the past and the presidents were central to their implementation. Graver problems exist today. Their solutions will depend more on the quality of the presidents than on any one other factor—on the quality of the new academic statesmen. They will need the best of environments, the most effective of governing arrangements, the greatest of understanding, and the most appropriate of styles. They will be in the midst of the trouble and the midst of the changes and the midst of the new advances for higher education and for society.

[22] Stoke, *The American College President*, p. 171.

LANDRUM R. BOLLING

Communicating with the Young

CAMPUS CONFLICTS in recent years have been defined repeatedly in terms of struggles for power to govern the educational institution. Student power versus administration power, or student power versus faculty power, or the power of the more alienated undergraduates and their young instructor and graduate student allies against the institutional Establishment—these sets of adversaries and their disputed causes seem often to symbolize and define the college conflicts. At some point in the process of turning tension into a confrontation, polarization over power is almost certain to occur. In a showdown, each side's decision-making authority or will is bound to be tested against the other's. Indeed, often, the substantive issues in dispute have been lost in the struggle over who has the final authority, the power, the superior will, and force to make and impose a decision.

Inevitably, an outcome of many campus conflicts has been a review and restructuring of campus governance. Given the arbitrary, archaic, and at times whimsical uses of power in some American educational institutions, the wonder is not that trouble over rules, policies, and administrative procedures has come with recent and present generations of students

» » « «

Landrum R. Bolling is President, Earlham College. He has served as Chairman of the Board of the Great Lakes Colleges Association.

163

but that such trouble didn't come earlier. The clarification of rules and procedures is, thus, undoubtedly a necessary approach to the reduction and containment of conflict. Likewise, at most institutions the introduction of a greater measure of student participation in decision making should reduce the incidence and intensity of conflict and help create a healthier and more humane academic community life. It may well be argued, however, that campus tensions really have far less to do with issues of ultimate decision-making power than with the endless human problems of communication.

Even though the rhetoric of student protest is often couched as demands for student power, what most of them really want, many times, is simply (*a*) to know what is going on and (*b*) to be consulted. As in all human associations, one must never underestimate an individual's, or a group's, desire to know about those things that affect its interests; and one should never overestimate how much people know, understand, or remember of what has already been said. As institutions have ballooned in size, as academic bureaucracies have expanded, the problem of communicating effectively with students has grown increasingly complex and difficult. Even if there were no faction of institution wreckers bent on promoting suspicion and hostility and creating confrontations over nonnegotiable demands, there would still be today serious problems of interpretation and communication between students and the older members of the academic community. It is to the task of improving intrainstitutional communication, on a comprehensive and sustained basis, that we should be giving major attention—with at least as great a sense of urgent concern as we have for the task of rearranging administrative structures and procedures and reshuffling the processes of decision making.

As with "talkin' 'bout Heaven" in the Negro spiritual, everybody talking about improved communications "ain't goin' there," either—at least not to the degree necessary to bring about a real reduction in campus tensions. Some approaches to the problem may be counterproductive or at least of marginal value. For example: *More written reports:* Most educational institutions are already drowning in a sea of mimeographed paper; longer and more frequent memos will not necessarily bring about more effective communication, even if all students were put on all of the interoffice mailing lists. *More presidential speeches:* This student generation is increasingly allergic to formal lectures; most don't attend convocations anyway; and administrators' pronouncements on controversial issues are, standing alone, likely to be suspect. *Special campus "town meetings":* In some crisis situations these are essential, or at least inescapable, and can have desperate usefulness. If, however, they are held only to announce the already hardened lines of division, or to proclaim administrative capitulation, then such meetings may be exercises in communicating too little (or too much) too late. On the other hand, campus town meetings on a more-or-less regular basis, over a long period of time, may be of substantial importance in providing for the sharing of information, and some institutions have used them effectively.

Crises of Beliefs

To get at the problems of communicating with students, efforts to improve the mechanics for reporting and for exchanging views about issues of conflict have to take second place to things more fundamental and more difficult to bring off. By now it should be clear that the central reality about student unrest is a widespread crisis of belief. More precisely, there are interlocking crises of belief—in the goals and methods of education, in the quality and direction of the whole society, and in the traditional values and standards of personal conduct. With obvious variations in feelings and tactics, students are today attacking the social environment with a determination, even a kind of fury which, on this scale, has never been known before. Large numbers of students are rejecting the society which they are being trained to serve and are rejecting much of the education which is designed to provide that training. Corollary to that rejection is often a retreat into a privatism in which young people affirm a new life style, with overtones of humorless moral snobbery—a sort of new puritanism, which is itself a repudiation of the moral and social code that parents, school, and the adult society have tried to impose on them.

If we are to avoid destructive conflict and ease tensions on the campus, we must reestablish much more comprehensive, honest, and searching communication between the generations. To get anywhere with such an enterprise, we must go far beyond bargaining and debate (however necessary these may be) over campus rules and regulations and the mechanics of power. What we really need is sustained, in-depth communication between old and young over survival questions:

1. How do we reconstruct our society to make it serve truly human purposes?
2. How do we provide the best education for preparing people to bring about that more humane society?
3. How does an individual search out and affirm personal values and purposes to guide him in acquiring his education and in taking up a creative and constructive role in society?

The first question about the building of a more humane society is one on which the older generation has been communicating with younger people, in a certain sense, more effectively than it realizes. It is from adults, chiefly parents and teachers (and from adult-run television), that young people have learned that war is horrible, that environmental pollution is destroying our air and water, that racial discrimination is evil, that hunger could be abolished. Young people, even in their wildest protests, are acting out what they intend to be a positive response to the social concerns they acquired from their elders. What they have not learned from their elders is how to be patient, or resigned, or apathetic in the face of continued injustice. What, sadly, many of them may never learn is how to master the skills, the knowledge, and the understanding necessary to cope with complex human problems. Hence, the great danger is that student social concern will be perverted into impotent withdrawal or destructive rage or simplistic new forms of discredited obsolete revolutions.

To communicate with young people today, certainly with the brightest and the most alive, we must involve ourselves with them in a sustained wrestling with the urgent social problems of our time. For this wrestling to have real significance to them, it must go far beyond historical or statistical analysis. They are not to be put off with assignments for memorizing more facts about the past or the present—nor even with the often exciting tasks of discovering new facts, however relevant such information may be to an understanding of contemporary issues. They want to feel that what they learn and what they do can contribute directly to the solution of problems mankind has already endured, and studied, too long.

What this mood means, in whatever wrong-headed ways it may be expressed, is that teachers and counselors can no longer count on the intrinsic worth of a given academic study or of the whole educational experience to engage the real interests of students, even the brightest ones. What we have to do is devise new strategies for linking together the widespread interest in social issues with rigorous intellectual study of those issues and with some kind of experiential involvement in significant work directed toward dealing with those problems. Field work has a long-established validity in many areas of academic study. That field experience concept has to be built into far more courses of study than we have yet considered possible to treat in this way. Out of such experiments with experiential learning—foreign and other off-campus study terms, broadly conceived internships, field work, and independent research projects—we can establish more generally the kind of context in which sensible and meaningful dialogue can take place between faculty and students about broad social issues. From such experiences, students will, on their own, discover much more about the complexity of these problems than they would likely learn from conventional classroom lectures and discussions. Further, these experiences can help to shrink the distance between the student's life and subculture and the adult world. Only as they can come to feel genuinely related to and involved in that adult world are students likely to be able to communicate in real openness with their elders about social issues. Out of such communication, there is reason to hope, young people will be significantly helped to establish solid beliefs in the possibility of building a just society and to commit themselves to work toward that goal.

All of this may seem a long way around to get at the problems of discontent and of faculty-student communication on the campus. However, we delude ourselves if we think we can divorce the problems of the campus from the malaise of the broader society. Students and their teachers won't solve those great problems in their educational programs, on or off the campus, but they can relate their studies to the real world in such a way as to assist young people to escape from the curse of smug but powerless academic criticism and analysis removed from hopes for solution or responsible efforts to find solutions. Part of the obligation of the educational institution in this turbulent period—in any period—is to assist the younger generation not only in learning how the system works and in analyzing the system's faults, but also in exploring a variety of ways in which those faults might be corrected and in discovering what the alternative costs would likely be. If the colleges and universities did better on this whole job, they would have less difficulty in engaging young people's interests, energies, and loyalties, and in communicating with them about anything; they would almost certainly reduce the amount of empty chatter about "relevance" in education.

Search for Meaning and Values

One major concern among young people about which there is urgent need for better and more extensive communication is the basic purposes and methods of education. Here again, what has worked in the past can no longer be taken for granted. The young person's innate sense of general curiosity may be as great as that of his parents or of his older brother, but it is not so easily aroused for all or most of the traditional academic disciplines. Many bright young people come to college these days with the quite clearly defiant attitude of "show me why I should be interested in or spend any of my time on this subject." Indeed, a not uncommon attitude is, "All right, so I'm here; now show me why I should get a college education." For many young people today, the driving force of the old climb-the-ladder-of-success, Protestant ethic no longer has any really compelling power. Since economic motives and the shared family dream of upward social movement through education have lost much of their motivating influence, it becomes urgently important to lead young people into a candid examination of what the ongoing purposes of college and university education may be and of how those purposes may be best achieved. Although many campus protests have centered on objections to

particular campus rules or administrative actions, these surface manifesta-
tions have masked deeper discontent about the perceived purposes of
education and the uninspired, impersonal ways in which the tasks of
education are pursued. Put simply, a large percentage of students in
colleges and universities today are seriously confused about why they
should be in school and are bored with what they are doing. There are
at least two keys here. One is that many of them should not be in school—
at least not until they have sorted out the reasons for getting a college
education and have made a personal commitment to some kind of education. The other is that the older members of the academic community
have, as a major teaching responsibilities, the task of undertaking with
students an open examination of the purposes of education, an honest
evaluation of how the educational programs are working out, and a comprehensive continuing study of how the educational experience can be
improved. Student-faculty-administration committees to work on these
matters are essential for maintaining the vigor of any academic community, whether any kind of crisis over campus governance ever arises.
More and better communication about the goals and the results of
education is a major essential if we are to handle the problems of campus
unrest.

Finally, there is the question of the search for personal purpose, meaning, and value, the relations of that search to student discontent, and the
problem of communication in any meaningful way between teachers and
students about these matters. Although there are dangers of falling into
pietistic or psychologizing pontification, it is right to point out that many
of the activist dissidents and many of the passively discontented share
an overpowering sense of purposelessness, a rootlessness with respect to
values, and, in varying degrees, a kind of existential despair. Here again
the student culture mirrors some of the spirit and mood of the general
society.

As organized religion has lost much of its power over young people,
as home life has for many become raveled, as the restless mobility of
millions of families has destroyed neighborhood and community ties,
many students come to college very much at sea about the meaning of
their own lives and about the values by which they can guide their
search for meaning. Colleges and universities are not ideally suited to
deal with these ultimate issues of life. The positivist tradition in the
educational world, the preoccupation with quantifiable data, the habit
of objective observation and analyses tend to make academics embar-
rassed when confronted with issues of ultimate meaning and value. It
would be a relief to be able to say that these questions are for the
church, or for parents, or for private speculation. Such an answer is no
longer good enough. Much of the discontent on college campuses, much
of the aberrant behavior with respect to drugs, sex, and occultism

among students is related to their groping struggles to come to terms with questions of feeling, of being, of purpose, of value. Such searchings cannot be ignored or passed along to external agencies. While shunning all orthodoxies and pieties, the academic communities of America have got to find ways of bringing members of the older and the younger generations into frank encounter over these fundamental questions. Perhaps, the beginning point has to be engagement with "the material," the appropriate literature, in courses in literature, religion, philosophy, and psychology. But if this approach is to be fruitful, it cannot be on the basis of business-as-usual in courses-as-usual in a curriculum-as-usual. Here is an important segment of the educational experience where creative innovation will be required, using the best powers of informed and rational minds.

Today large numbers of our best students at even our most prestigious institutions are caught up in such phenomena as pot parties, hippy communes, psychedelic light-and-music shows, astrology, witchcraft, the use of Tarot cards and the I-Ching book, Zen Buddhism, and Indian transcendental meditation—often to the neglect of their academic work—these must tell us something. I believe we are being told that increasing numbers of our young people are marching to different drums than the ones that ordinarily sound on the traditional campus. Those drums, however incomprehensible they may be to the older generation, are perceived by the young as speaking somehow to their need to make a search for meaning and value, for a way of reconciling the feelings and the intellect, the mystical and the rational. Such searchings the academic community can no longer ignore.

In the classroom and outside the classroom we must find ways to promote more open and continuing communication between young and old over questions that really matter concerning society, concerning education, and concerning the personal search for value and meaning. If we can really find the right ways—appropriate to each institution and its resources and life style—for promoting and sustaining significant communication on these fundamental issues, of concern to both young and old, we will have done a great deal to remove the provocations for expressions of destructive discontent.

STEVEN MULLER

Preventing or Resolving Conflicts

THIS BRIEF ATTEMPT to make recommendations for preventing or resolving conflicts among members of the various constituencies on a campus will focus on only two major points: better communications and improved undergraduate teaching. It is based entirely on personal experience and involvement in central administration on a major university campus, and this experience, though intensive, is surely not equally applicable on all other campuses, particularly as it derives from a university rather than a college context.

My single greatest lesson from past conflicts at my institution is the crucial role that better communications can play in preventing and allaying tensions and disturbances. A point of departure is the recognition that most universities, until now, have put greater effort into external communication than has been devoted to on-campus communication.

Communication on the Campus

Specifically, four aspects of improved internal communication appear to be of importance. The first concerns the ability of the central administration, speaking for the whole institution, to address its own community

» » « «

Steven Muller is Vice-President for Public Affairs and Associate Professor of Government at Cornell University.

on a regular basis. Most campuses in the past have lacked a vehicle for expression of administrative opinion and—even more significant—for putting on record before the whole community the full texts of crucial reports, recommendations, addresses, and so on.

On almost every campus, there are one or more student-produced newspapers, but these devote little space and show little inclination to publish essential material in full. There is normally extensive communication with the faculty through mimeographed and like materials. The nonacademic staff and students, however, do not normally share in the vital communications addressed only to a faculty audience, and, further, genuine faculty attention to bulky, periodic mimeographed distribution is, on the whole, minimal. It may be useful to make the point that internal communication within the echelons of a large university administration is usually severely neglected. As an example, recent campus disturbances have produced low morale and great confusion in the vital lower echelons of the administration, where staff rightly regard themselves as neglected and ill-informed in comparsion to faculty and, increasingly, also in comparison to students.

To resolve the problem of communication, Cornell University, in the academic year 1969–70, began publishing a weekly official newspaper of record called the *Cornell Chronicle,* available free of charge to all members of the campus community. This newspaper contains no original writing but is, instead, a vehicle for the dissemination of official information and for the regular publication in full of all significant reports, studies, and evaluations. The publication of the *Cornell Chronicle* has had a marked and beneficial impact on the campus. For the first time, students, faculty, and nonadministrative staff feel they are being given the benefit of complete access to everyone else's thinking about major issues, and also for the first time people are talking on the ground of common information, which is now being provided.

A second move to improved communications involves face-to-face discussions between central administrators and key elements among both students and faculty. This process is time consuming and difficult, but it does produce results. In the first part of 1969, for example, key administrators and potentially disruptive black students were dealing with each other primarily in infrequent, formal, stiff, and increasingly hostile confrontations, between which administrators would ask themselves what the black students were really thinking, what they were going to do next, and how deeply they felt their grievances. To a substantial degree, a parallel situation existed with respect to radical students, roughly encompassed by the SDS label. This year an enormous amount of time is being invested in a continuing set of administration-student dialogues involving both individuals and groups, so far with excellent results.

Communication between administration and faculty in earlier 1969 tended to be equally anomic. Most frequent were meetings with a small group of faculty, constituted as the Faculty Council, who, as a result, acquired a reputation of being brainwashed by the administration, if they were not actually called tools of the administration. Less frequent were meetings with the entire university faculty, which are always likely to be so large and confused that they prove minimally productive. Changes made later included direct communication with other key faculty groups, sometimes with the separate faculties of individual schools and colleges, sometimes with department chairmen from the entire university, sometimes with academic deans who have now been given full access to central administration policy discussions and who can, therefore, report back to their own faculties with full knowledge and involvement.

Continuing face-to-face communication with disaffected students on the part of administrators is anything but easy, but it has a second fundamental reward beyond preventing disruptive activity. To me, it seems to involve a crucial teaching function on the part of administrators, who have the opportunity to persuade students of the uses of reason rather than disruption and coercion in resolving matters at issue.

A third key to improved communications requires visible personal leadership on the part of the president, particularly at moments of the greatest tension. There is a natural tendency either to hold the president in reserve or to protect him from too much public exposure during a crisis because there are, necessarily, so many other vital things for him to do or because public appearances are for him somewhat risky and almost always uncomfortable. Nevertheless, when moments of great stress arise, people, given the opportunity, do seem to respond to effective personal leadership.

For certain, much has already been lost on a campus when a major disruption occurs. The institution has a better chance of coming out of it well and recovering itself quickly if the president is willing to stake his future on a highly active and visible role in attempting to resolve the situation.

Finally, any sizable university is, inevitably, a multifaceted, confusing, and at times disorienting entity to come to grips with when an individual or a group of individuals have an urgent sense of grievance and either are not acquainted with the appropriate channels through which to proceed or find those channels confused and clogged. To meet this problem, Cornell University has established a campus ombudsman, in the form of an office directed by an experienced and respected senior member of the faculty on a full-time basis. The office of the ombudsman serves three crucial and related functions. It is, in part, a traffic cop, simply directing individuals and problems to the appropriate address; it is, in part, a source of information, because in a number of instances a grievance can be resolved almost immediately by providing basic information; and, in part, the office sees that valid problems hung up in the administrative machinery are at least promptly and efficiently dealt with. There was skepticism about the need for the ombudsman function when the office was created in September 1969. In the weeks that followed, however, this office did business at veritable flood tide, and the conviction is growing not only that it is necessary but also that it has prevented some rather serious matters from escalating into sources of protracted tension and potential disruption.

Undergraduate Teaching

The second major point to be made involves better undergraduate teaching. Undoubtedly, a substantial amount of current student disaffection can be directly traced to large and deep social problems, such as the war in Vietnam and this country's racial crisis. I would argue, however, that student disaffection is at least aggravated by valid student discontent in a general sense with undergraduate teaching and that, in some cases, it is primarily caused by this academic discontent rather than off-campus factors.

While it must always be noted that there are many widely recognized exceptions to this generalization, it nevertheless appears that most students are very plainly bored with a substantial amount, if not the bulk, of their classroom experience. They can be persuaded that learning is hard work, but they find difficulty in accepting that it must also be dull. A generation reared on television entertainment in a society that has virtually canonized an enormous entertainment industry and its leading personalities is not prepared to suffer through an endless succession of dull and large-scale classroom presentations. I believe the basic point to be made is that by no means all, but still far too many, members of the faculty really prefer passivity in the classroom, at the very time when a TV-reared student generation is satiated with passive and vicarious experience and has a great need for creative involvement. The lecture system, admittedly, has some built-in efficiency, but, in my view, in the age of television and a glut of paperback reading, it is an academic anachronism and its impersonality and passivity actively breed student discontent.

I would, therefore, argue that what I mean primarily by improved undergraduate teaching is a renewed basic commitment to the teaching function, which involves much more than better or small lectures, or lectures with discussion, or lectures supported by audiovisual materials. Real teaching is a highly personal activity for both students and professors. The tutorial process or the personal evaluation of essay or laboratory work appears to me indispensable. I am fully aware that I am talking about something that is enormously expensive and that requires a basic reorientation, but I am, in fact, talking about an absolutely basic new commitment of this character. Furthermore, I am in disagreement with some of my colleagues who are prepared to deal only with already self-motivated students and who find it beneath their dignity to make the crucial effort to motivate their students and actively to engage their interest.

The greatest danger in the American effort to provide mass education for everyone up to the limits of individual abilities is that it will produce mass boredom with higher education. I am convinced that the most needed and effective step to end student alienation and disaffection is to provide better teaching, which will restore the learning process to the center of the student's attention and will make it an exhaustively challenging and interest-consuming core of his campus experience. There have been many studies and reports articulating the need for better undergraduate teaching, and every college and university pays lip service to this idea. At most universities, there is more rhetoric than performance in this respect. To reverse this situation on a large scale is perhaps the greatest challenge the American university has ever faced. I sincerely believe that it also represents the price of its survival.

HARRIS WOFFORD, JR.

The Search
for Liberal Education

IF THERE WERE no tensions on campus, a Special Committee on Campus Tensions should be asking why not. More than seven million Americans are enrolled in colleges and universities, double the number a decade ago. Nearly half of all young people go on to higher education, and the promise of universal higher education is being made in state after state. Blacks and the poor are demanding an education that will make up for years of discrimination and poverty, and enable them to catch up and get ahead. The expansion of knowledge outdistances academia's ability to assimilate and teach it, and the increasing complexity of society is requiring a much higher intellectual level among the people. The big, buzzing confusion of the world reaches almost everyone through the mass media, and almost no one sees the world steady and whole.

If there were no discontent, it would be an educator's duty to create some.

The present crisis of tension and discontent within higher education is therefore inevitable, and we should want the tension to continue until we are sufficiently educated by it. With distance, one might be tempted to relax and enjoy the situation, seeing the disarray of academia as an early stage of a continuing crisis of quantity and quality in our

» » « «

Harris Wofford, Jr., President, Bryn Mawr College, was formerly President, State University of New York College at Old Westbury.

society, a necessary consequence of universal education, and a precondition for a renewal of liberal education. But we in higher education do not have that distance. We are parties to the discontent. We are blamed for it and we share in it, for it is remarkably reciprocal. Students complain that teachers don't want to teach, and teachers lose their verve because students don't seem to want teachers; both accuse administrators of being mere technicians and seek to reduce the administrators' power to just that. The mutual frustration and incrimination is becoming debilitating. Fortunately, the discontent seems strong and ubiquitous enough to force some of the issues to a crisis. Time will bring some resolution; yet we know it is not time alone that will help, but the constructive use of time. Our duty as educators is to do our best to turn the tensions into an intelligible dialogue, to help people see this season of discontent as being round one of a large Socratic dialogue on the education needed for our Republic.

What have we learned so far? By now, I hope we have a better idea of how little we know—of how inadequate most of our education is and most of our proposed reforms are, even all added together—of how far we are from the liberal education the people of a republic need in the late twentieth century. Never have so many been so thirsty for the clean water of liberal education, or so lost in finding it. Never has the search for such an education been more important or more urgent or more difficult. The liberal arts appropriate to an age, the arts by which people can learn to be free in a particular time and place, have always been elusive, but never more so than now.

At the beginning of this first dialectical round, the student rebels seemed to be coming like a giant Socrates, beard and all, to stir us from our pragmatic slumbers. As gadflies they sting rather well, in places where it hurts, puncturing some inflated pretensions. Seeing quantity expand, the rebels ask questions of quality; seeing means increase, they ask questions of ends; seeing the technological society take over more and more of life, they ask questions of freedom and purpose.

The Un-Socratic Beard

In specific academic terms they have registered their negative insights. Lectures are too large and too frequent and should not be the main form of learning. Too little good teaching takes place, and too little attention is paid to the quality of teaching. Too much attention is paid to exams, grades, and credits; there is not enough joy in learning or adventure in ideas. Students are too often treated as subjects, not citizens, with neither their consent sought nor dissent heard. The body of knowledge is divided among too many compartments, and the lines between them are too rigid. The structure of special departments leaves too little room in the curriculum for the study of critical general problems such as racial injustice, urban chaos, and war, or the perennial personal problems of sex, politics, and religion.

But it takes more than a beard to make Socrates and more than negative insights to create a good curriculum of liberal arts. If the bright vision of an aroused Socratic generation held simply true, the discontent of administrators, faculty, and public could be discounted and the crisis of student discontent welcomed as an antidote to mass education and the technological society. Student power would indeed be the answer— or at least the next step. But from the vantage point of one who welcomed student discontent as a major force for reform and who has been wrestling rather intensively with the spirit of the student generation, there is also the dark side that needs to be seen and stated.

Students can smell sophistry, hypocrisy, and irrelevance—especially in others—but with their resistance or hostility to teachers, books, courses, history, laws, hard work, and most of the other traditional sources of education, they are not likely to get much of a liberal education on their own. Nor is the self-indulgence that so often goes by the name "identity search" an adequate equivalent. Power to control the curriculum, faculty, or administration is no solution. Even the sharing of power, if it becomes too absorbing, can be as misleading an escape from education as the prevailing student notion of relevance. Never having tasted the clean water of liberal education, most students assume there can be no such thing, or that it is irrelevant. Knowing only dirty water, they are in no mood to search for springs where clean water might be found. Thus for all their signs of great thirst, students tend to settle for academia's dirtiest water, the ultimate irrelevance—an undisciplined and unintellectual curriculum in an unlimited version of the elective system, with no educational principle other than the anarchic slogan, "Let everyone do his thing."

If the search for the clean water of liberal education is the most important and most relevant thing—if, as I believe, it is the common thing that we, the people of the Republic, most need—we should face the fact that the present round of protest and reform has not taken us very far. At least it should have taught us some humility, for in expressing disappointment with the students, I am not suggesting that faculties or college presidents can be relied on either. Even if more of us agreed with Rosemary Park that the chief task of a college administrator is to be Socratic and go around campus asking upsetting questions, such questioners are in very short supply. It takes no great wisdom or Socratic skill to puncture the pretensions of the students' platform of academic reform and show that it does not add up to a good liberal education, any more than it took great ability on the students' part to expose the most glaring faults of conventional academia. But this negative round will be worthwhile if we recognize our ignorance, take what we do not know as a statement of what we need to know, and join together for the next stage of the search—and give that search much greater priority.

Some Options

Out of the experience of college-making in this time of trouble, I do have a few clues for the direction the search should now take, including the formation of small experimental colleges or curricula within existing colleges or universities, the granting to students of well-defined areas of real responsibility in independent study and student-initiated programs, and the common reading and discussion of the classic books that offer contrasting views of the world. But before any affirmative steps can be taken with much success, some obstacles must be cleared away.

First, the academic water is badly muddied by the presence in colleges and universities of millions of young people who think they do not want to be there. Whatever the other ingredients of clean educational water are, there must be a high proportion of genuine intellectual curiosity and very little coercion. Teaching and learning the liberal arts required to master the knowledge of this complex age while at the same time searching for better ways of teaching and learning them is difficult enough. The large numbers of students who complain that they are captives and refuse to cooperate compound all the difficulties. The draft puts heavy pressure on young men to stay in school in order to avoid an ugly war, and parents in particular and society in general put other pressures on young people to stay in school through a college degree, if not through an advanced degree. The consequent sixteen to twenty years of constant classroom education is too much for many people, and the element of coercion is corrupting for all.

The new draft lottery will provide a partial remedy, and an end to the war in Vietnam would help in academia, as in most other areas of our public life; but the coercion toward college will continue until either the draft itself or all student deferments are ended. American higher education should insist that one or the other of these steps be taken.

Another direct way the federal government can foster the educational autonomy of young people is to end their financial dependence on parents for support in higher education. The Zacharias Committee's proposal for an Educational Opportunity Loan Fund, with very favorable long-term loans, would do this. The committee's proposal or some equivalent program should be adopted to enable students to finance the full cost in a college of their choice.

Relieving the coercion toward college that parents and society at large exert will be complicated, for it reflects a certain realism. Another good step would be to develop and make legitimate more opportunities for full-time work and service between high school and college, or for a year or more in the midst of college. The Peace Corps and VISTA are largely designed for college graduates or specially skilled technicians, but they point the way to equivalent programs for younger people. The Student Teacher Corps legislation, proposed by Senators Nelson, Javits, and Kennedy, would enable high school and college students to be employed as teacher's aides, working with older teams of the Teacher Corps in disadvantaged elementary or secondary schools.[1] These programs and others should be supported to encourage young people to serve in public schools, community action or public health projects, hospitals, prisons, or other institutions in need of volunteer manpower. A federally financed National Volunteer Service Foundation could be created to offer living-allowance fellowships to young people working in such programs.

Another helpful step would be to increase opportunities for older students—including women who have raised children—to resume their studies at later points in their lives and careers. We need to demonstrate that liberal education is not something to be sought solely in the years immediately following high school. Business and other institutions might give leadership by providing sabbaticals to enable employees to go back to school, just as colleges give sabbatical terms to enable faculty to get away from school.

Colleges and universities could similarly encourage students by advising those who want to take a break from school to do so and make it clear to them that they will be treated favorably when they apply for admission later: by reserving places for older students; by granting some academic credit for off-campus work under appropriate conditions; and in some cases even by organizing off-campus service programs. In these or in other ways, it should be made clear to students that they should not be in colleges or universities unless they want to be there and that other reasonable alternatives are available.

These steps will not cure the alienation of students or the ills of society that they see, but it may reduce some of the symptoms of alienation to the point where education and the search for better education can go on without almost insuperable obstacles. It would take away from students, faculty, and administration some of their present excuses for not proceeding with that study and search.

No academic reforms will end tensions or discontent on campus or make life easy for teachers or administrators. The liberal education of any person inherently creates something of a crisis of discontent, within himself if not within his family or community.

---

[1] The Student Teacher Corps was incorporated as Section 804 of the omnibus Elementary and Secondary Education Act enacted by the Ninety-first Congress (Public Law 91–230).

PART FIVE

A New Role for Trustees?

J. L. ZWINGLE

The Lay Governing Board

To WHAT EXTENT are governing boards responsible for the campus tensions that now disturb the academic scene from coast to coast and around the world? To what extent do their members feel this discontent with the academy? To what extent can the cure be found by modifying the composition of governing boards or changing the style of governance? To proceed directly from such questions to recommended actions would oversimplify a complicated issue. Hence the need to examine certain assumptions and certain historical aspects of governance.

Prior to the present crisis, now half a decade old, changes had occurred that foreshadowed present conditions. On one campus, the master of a residential unit (a professor of philosophy) recalled a time, some years earlier, when a campus disturbance was quickly suppressed by other students. A few telephone calls produced a quick gathering of campus leaders who then formed a silent procession across the area of the disturbance. The sight of these students in slow and silent march, arms folded and raised, so cowed the other students that order was immediately restored.

Even at the time of the retelling (1960), that campus would no longer

》　》　《　《

J. L. Zwingle is President, Association of Governing Boards of Universities and Colleges. He is a former Vice-President of Cornell University.

have yielded to such a counterdemonstration, and probably that procession could not have been assembled. Implied in the episode are precisely those elements now missing in the academic world: consensus among campus leaders (young and old), loyalty to the institution, an overriding sense of tradition. Everywhere these stabilizing elements have been eroded, and nothing has replaced them. Indeed, throughout society, a shift in mood has lessened respect for tradition and for established authority, with the campus being the most extreme example of the shift.

As for the governing board, its classic position is fairly clear: it was the legal repository of the charter, employer of the chief executive, validator of recommendations, putative protector of the institution, representative of the public interest. As the final legal authority, owner-in-fact, the governing board is logically the ultimate target for exponents of radical change. To what extent, then, is the nature of the governing board a partial cause of the campus tensions? Does it have the capability for resolving the conflict? Or must the board itself be changed before the conflict can be resolved?

In all institutions, the tendency prevails to take established programs for granted, and failure to reexamine basic assumptions underlying programs ultimately leads to difficulties, if not disaster. It is not a matter simply of mounting defenses against the most radical or most nihilistic minority of students in contest for the uncommitted majority. If defense is the major concern, disorder can be put down. In some instances maintenance of order may indeed be the prime need. In the long run, however, it is more important to win the collaboration of all elements of the institution, to mount programs which command the interest and win the support of the faculty, students, alumni, and the public.

Aside from the legal requirements of trusteeship, the one term encompassing the general function of governing boards is: the formulation of policy. In practice, however, they have been validators, not formulators, of policy. In fact, most institutions operate by habits, by assumptions, by accumulated decisions—all acquiring over time the force of common law. But the vulnerability of institutions to attacks by radical minorities has been dramatized by an awareness that boards have given inadequate attention to the review and refinement of policies and to the effective communication of policy.

The present crisis, it can be said, results in part from the lack of policy, or at least from the failure to examine the presuppositions that control the operations of the institution. An analogy can be drawn from the Second World War: The British sea base at Singapore fell to the Japanese because false assumptions by the British had dictated the construction of defenses directed toward the sea. But the enemy attacked by land at the tip of the peninsula, coming in by the back door, where no defenses had been thought necessary.

Forces of Change

What is the nature of the current problem? How can a structure of authority be found once again? To answer these questions, one must recognize some background elements: the development of an international youth culture which discards the doctrines and structures of Western society; the vast changes in Western society which appear to call for new institutions; the consequences of the American venture in mass education; the psychological consequences of technology.

Jousselin has written an extraordinary analysis of the international aspects of these forces: He cites the loss of the folk hero, and the substitution of contemporary star-performers, those who, at the moment, can do whatever they do in a spectacular and overpowering fashion (the singularity of the star contrasted with folk-identification with a hero who symbolizes the ideals of the society). To this change in tradition, he adds the rapid obsolescence of knowledge, of skills; hence, a future with small reference to or dependence on the past; hence, freedom to discard the older generation as irrelevant to an unpredictable future.[1] For the trustee in America, special factors must be added: a general frustration over the breakdown of organizations and procedures heretofore considered reliable.

This society has always put great faith in education, however the term may have been understood from era to era. Within the past century this reliance on education and faith in its consequences have been increasingly dramatic. The development of the public school system (itself the great bonding element for the growing community and nation), the concurrent development of the land-grant university, the later development of the community college, the expansion of enrollments, the rise in percentage of population enrolled—all these are part of the drama. Further, federal involvement with higher education rose during the depression years, a more important involvement came with the recruitment of talent from the campus for federal programs, a still more important involvement of talent from the campus as the nation moved toward the Second World War, and, finally, the carry-over of defense-related research and consultation that outlasted the cold war and became a major point of attack for the militant students of today.

Meanwhile, the ascendancy of the United States as the dominant world power, with the attendant problems of international engagement, further involved the academy in all aspects of public policy. In short, *in everything American, too much has happened too fast.*

---

[1] Jean Jousselin, "Today's New Adolescents," reprinted from *Student World* in *AGB Reports*, January 1966. The close analysis of these and related points makes his essay worth careful reading.

Drucker comments that we have come to the end of an era, that everything requires a new set of assumptions.[2] In Walter Lippmann's view:

> This is the most revolutionary period that has occurred for centuries. . . . We know . . . that when you have a revolution by the invention of steam engines or the invention of printing, social developments follow from their application. The absolutely revolutionary invention of our time is the invention of invention itself. When Charles Snow wrote that lecture about the two cultures, he didn't say then, as we would say in America, that we have a large generation now that doesn't understand science and it doesn't understand the old humanist tradition. They understand only their own personal appetites, prejudices, ambitions and hates.[3]

And Paul Goodman—no particular hero of mine—had this to say:

> Dissident young people are saying that science is anti-life, it is a Calvinist obsession, it has been a weapon of white Europe to subjugate colored races, and scientific technology has manifestly become diabolical. Along with science, the young discredit the professions in general, and the whole notion of "disciplines" and academic learning. If these views take hold, it adds up to a crisis of belief, and the effects are incalculable. Every status and institution would be affected. Present political troubles could become endless religious wars. Here again, as in politics and morals, the worldwide youth disturbance may indicate a turning point in history.[4]

These vast differences in values have led to a change in mood within the country, a new sense of impotence and confusion, the first serious doubts whether the American way can prevail. Accompanying this shift of mood is the overcommitment in every American enterprise, including education. Result: a nation that allowed itself to assume it could do virtually everything now wonders whether it can indeed do one major thing well aside from the purely technological.

While all these forces and events were having their run, the colleges and universities were changing as never before in any society: a tripling of enrollments within a decade, a rush of construction, a new mobility within a onetime stable, quiet, even somnolent profession. In higher education, the former dominance of the private sector gave way to the public sector; relatively small governing boards have found themselves responsible for multiple-unit systems that count enrollments by the tens of thousands, whereas relatively large boards have become responsible for a shrinking part of the total enrollments and for institutions which

---

[2] Peter Drucker, *The Age of Discontinuity* (New York: Harper & Row, 1968).

[3] "Walk with Walter Lippmann, at Eighty, about This Minor Dark Age," an interview, ed. Henry Brandon, *New York Times Magazine*, Sept. 14, 1969.

[4] Goodman, "The New Reformation," *New York Times Magazine*, Sept. 14, 1969.

individually face a doubtful future. Higher education thus has become a subject of great debate, of recrimination, of attack and defense on both good grounds and bad.

Trustees share a typical American characteristic in being management-minded; they are prone, as are students, to overemphasize managerial as against substantive problems of education. For example, the conflict in Vietnam: while it has had certain consequences on campus, both in dramatizing the moral dilemmas of American foreign policy and the inequities of the draft, failure to dispose of the problem is itself a source of frustration. Probably neither the issue of the draft nor the demonstrations against the war would have erupted with such force had American policy succeeded and the Southeast Asia problem been contained. The American intervention in the Dominican Republic also caused a flurry of distress, but the "success" of that venture is all that is remembered by most people. We appear to value success, even in dubious ventures. Unaccustomed to failure in a national enterprise, we resent the appearance of failure.

The agenda of the nation today is a long list of major issues, all seemingly beyond the reach of successful management. Hence the fear grows that the country is overcommitted, even in education; here is a direct reversal in fundamental American ideas, which, for education, is a signal of grave danger.

Influences of Mass and Technology

Among the many comments about our difficulties in higher education, two points have been inadequately recognized: the first, a matter of mass; the second, the side effects of technology.

Never before has a major nation undertaken advanced formal education on so great a scale. This undertaking involves far more than the increase of numbers; stability in formal education has rested upon acceptance of certain ideas about the nature of education and of society. More than doubling enrollments in higher education within ten years is different from doubling industrial output in the same period.

Education is more complex than most laymen and even some educators have understood. Well-founded criticisms of higher education today and the enumeration of its shortcomings are not necessarily erroneous, but they are often naïve. Most theories of education have been inadequate (at least for mass education), and, in practice, they have suffered from lack of personnel to carry them out.

Formal education has never been scientific in the sense of producing uniform and predictable results. Even today, for all our command of scientific information, we know too little about the nurture of the young and about effective education. What little we do know is violated by most of the conditions under which education today takes place. It is generally true that systems of education have always been approximate and designed to serve only one of three types of students: a group comprising the roughly 70 percent of students who can cope with the curriculum and the going level of instruction but may not be particularly creative or imaginative. The other two types have never been well served by educational systems: the underendowed or the disadvantaged, and, at the other extreme, those who are highly intelligent and creative.

Furthermore, effective teaching is a rare skill—so rare that the supply is unlikely ever to equal the demand. When one reckons the problem of mass now confronting the leaders of education and the general imperfections of formal education, one would do well to rejoice that things work at all. Training is, of course, another thing. It is still astonishing to me that the Air Force can take an eighteen-year-old and quickly train him to be a competent operator of military aircraft. Yet that difficult task is incomparably simpler than, for others of his age group, inducing and cultivating competence to deal with concepts and value systems, self-discipline in dealing with knowledge, development of attitudes of social responsibility, and recognition of the delicate balance between objectivity and subjectivity, between advocacy and criticism.

Combined with sheer mass and the sudden urbanization of our society is still another factor, the psychological consequences of advanced technology. On this much-discussed topic, two points: first, the abolition of a sense of time, of the natural periodicity in developing persons or systems or organizations; and second, the notion that any problem should yield to immediate solution if only enough effort is made or enough money spent. Here arises the incongruous linking of technological competence (successes) and failures in managing domestic problems. Thus the normal impatience of the young with their elders is heightened.

In the destruction of the small unit—the family, the neighborhood, the small town—we have destroyed the element that made possible the absorption of youth more steadily and systematically into the adult culture. Hence, we find not only youth against age, but also youth culture against the adult culture; and we have the lack of concern among youth for the time-consuming, piecemeal, bit-by-bit assemblage of "the system" that many of them would so happily demolish with no thought of the future.

To repeat, coupled with the vast increase of population in higher education, we have lost those structures which might make possible the absorption of these new masses.

Education as an Institution—Governance

These forces in turn have affected the academy: foremost, uncertainty and conflict over the role of the institution. So popular has become the idea of education—particularly higher education—that it is conceived by some as a direct instrument of society, by others to be free-standing, autonomous, unrelated to contemporary events. Involved here is an old quarrel over the relative importance of teaching versus research versus public service and a quarrel over whose rights are foremost in benefits to be expected from the institution: faculty, student, government, industry, or something vaguely known as the "public interest." In consequence, we have debates over the legitimacy of authority vested in governing boards and administrators, and, worst of all, we have a perversion of the hard-won principle of academic freedom, evidenced in the irresponsibility among activists and nonactivists alike.

Now for issues in governance. Campus unrest in the recent past has dramatized the problem of academic governance, but it is not the central issue. Governance is overdiscussed and overemphasized and beclouds the real issue, one that has never been resolved: Under what circumstances, with what kind of program, is it possible to produce good education for the largest number of people?

This question calls up conflicting concepts of the college that need fresh examination, though they are all familiar:

The college as a community of scholars.

The campus as a business operation, legally incorporated, functioning under a charter, responsible to a governing board whose chief executive is the president.

The campus as an agency of the state, operating with public funds, with personnel paid out of the public treasury, subject to the same procedures as other state agencies.

The campus as a community of students for whose benefit all other groups in the university are organized and who should, therefore, be immediately responsive to student interests.

The campus as a public agency, operating for the public good, which should be responsive to the interests of the society which provides the funds.

Each of these concepts has a degree of validity. If taken as a signpost pointing toward a larger truth, each is useful, none encompasses the total meaning of academic enterprise. Therein lies the difficulty in governance.

From another point of view, one purpose of the campus is to modify human behavior. There are relatively few means of accomplishing this outcome, though all of society is organized with this purpose. Society is entitled to self-defense; therefore the military in one form or another has always been with us. Human beings have spiritual aspirations; therefore the religious institutions in one form or another have always been with us. Society requires government; therefore political organization has always been with us. Society requires the means of sustenance; therefore commercial organizations have always been with us.

As opposites stand the military and the church. Though the military has its critics, its structure of authority stands firm; except in cases of utter demoralization, the military has ample means of enforcing its will internally. The church has relatively few available sanctions, and these appear to be diminishing. Moral suasion and personal leadership have been the reliance of the church, though of course in certain circumstances witchcraft or power have lent additional force. In politics and commerce, the sanctions are largely economic and are usually effective.

The complexity of academic governance is to be seen in the light that the college encompasses some aspect of every other form of organization, though for its principal objectives (the education of the young, the establishment of the intellectual community, the service of the public) it may, as an administrative phenomenon, be more like the church than any other social entity.[5]

Now let us move by stages toward recommendations. Surely the need for a legal entity requires no comment. Organized group activity requires legal status, definition of role, allocation of responsibility for its fiscal and programmatic elements. All social institutions experience a familiar cycle: early pioneering activity, later settling into routine, still later a stage of self-justification when the institution takes itself for granted and becomes the central concern rather than a means to an end. The staff of the institution slowly changes roles; "maintenance" rather than "leadership" sets the mood. Then institutions cease to be objects of concern while the segments of administration and program within them become more and more self-serving. Innovation and flexibility are reduced, and rigidity increases. Finally innovation seems to require new institutions, the reform of the old being too difficult. But such new efforts again require organization and status. So the cycle starts again.

In another sense, however, the educational institution is not the corporation. As a functioning unit, it has a certain quasi-political style of existence. This comment does not apply to relationships to state or federal governments but to something more subtle and pervasive—an inescapable element of "political" flavor in its own way of meeting problems,

---

[5] For more on this subject, see Charles H. Monson, Jr., "Metaphors for the University," *Educational Record*, Winter 1967, pp. 22–29. Monson, of the University of Utah, skillfully elaborates the problems of the university that grow from the varieties of analogies underlying the conflicting roles the university is expected to fulfill.

even in maintaining internal tone. In a state of high morale, all sectors of an enterprise are conscious of mutual aspirations and institutional goals, each element making its contribution. In this very condition, administration requires a political art little considered or practiced. Note, for example, the objections to bureaucratic behavior within an institution. While bureaucracy is always necessary, as explained in a recent volume,[6] bureaucratic behavior is always a liability (procedure first, substance second). The new popularity of the campus ombudsman illustrates a rejection of bureaucracy: the demand for an honest broker to circumvent standard administrators, whose procedures are often objectionable.

Note further the seeming invisibility of administrators and governing boards. Even though a president may have superior knowledge about the state of his campus and its components, his constituents among the faculty and students are not likely to think so. They view him as almost exclusively concerned with outside affairs, mostly absent from the campus, and, when present, inaccessible. As for the highest authority, the governing board is almost invisible except perhaps in times of crisis; then it is likely to be assigned the role of villain or scapegoat.

We have learned the hard way that institutions do not sufficiently bring their fundamental policies to public attention. Though presidents and board members may be zealous in their devotion to duty and though the policies of the institution may be updated and clear, if the political art has not been exercised and the central leadership and policies (goals) of the university are not visible and generally acknowledged, these assets become frozen. In a broad sense, the president is essentially a political figure. Regardless of his authority or that of the board, he must exercise certain political skills if leadership is to be effective.

Successful academic governance also requires *a developmental outlook*. Students, faculty, and the public must be convinced that the institution is pursuing goals to which the majority can respond: the development of individual students, the development of faculty competence, the development of both social stability and social change. Institutions tend to measure and proclaim their success in the wrong terms (competitive ranking of departments and faculties, growth in budget, physical plant, and financial support), not in truly developmental terms, that is, an overriding concern for the large goals of an open society. Hence the charge of irrelevance.

Trusteeship in higher education is more demanding than would be granted by those who have not probed the responsibility. The corporate, legalistic requirements are perhaps the least important, though essen-

---

[6] Herbert Stroup, *Bureaucracy in Higher Education* (New York: Free Press, 1966).

tial. It is the political and developmental aspects which test the quality of leadership.

CRITICISMS OF GOVERNING BOARDS

What are the complaints against governing boards today? That the average age is too high; that the members are from the same mold; that they are disengaged from the campus; that they are passive in their concerns for the institution; that they exploit the institution (conflict of interest); that they act in secret and arbitrarily; in sum, that the administration and the board are in compact against the welfare of students and presumably of faculty and perhaps of society itself. But the cure is hard to find when so many view the institution as a massive vending machine, expected to provide one or another kind of benefit for various types of customers.

A new style of leadership and spokesmanship must be devised to focus the nation's attention on some coherent exposition of the problems in education, from functional illiteracy to needed improvements in professional and technical manpower. More cooperation and support for education might be achieved if better means were used to make clear to every sector of the population what the dimensions of the problem are and the proportion of the gross national product required for what period of time if we are to begin to catch up with critical shortages.

If the present national situation bears comparison with the domestic crisis of 1930–35 or the wartime crisis of 1940–45, it should follow that the population could be rallied to a full-scale national effort in which various segments could participate meaningfully. Such an effort could be more effective than proceeding from year to year, or from legislature to legislature, or from congressional session to congressional session, on the assumption that a little more of this or that will, by accumulation and the passage of time, resolve the problem. The passing efforts made (the most recent, the White House Conference on Education) have produced mostly reiteration of well-worn assumptions and formulae.

Finally, I would suggest a reemphasis on a work-study program, including the much discussed but never authorized National Service Program for Youth. If the current crisis is owed partly to the disengagement of youth from the functions of society, no amount of additional concentration on formal education can produce anything but more frustration. Yet a national work-study (or a national service) program will help enlist the energies of young and old alike and make the activities of formal education more meaningful and inviting to many people. Such a program, however, calls for a commitment from industry and from government on a larger scale than heretofore contemplated—a scale perhaps beyond achievement unless there is a dramatic rallying of all resources to

new effort and a new sense of realism. The memory of the Civilian Con-
servation Corps is perhaps out of scale, but despite its many defects, it
was a significant effort.

At a time when every thoughtful commentator is pondering the future
of this nation, there is obvious need for a fresh assembly of a grand design
and a new vigor in spokesmanship on its behalf. In education, there might
well be a new distribution of responsibilities for each of the major components, to reverse the present folly of encouraging every institution to do
something of everything.

RESPONSES FROM TRUSTEES AND PRESIDENTS

Before this paper was completed, a brief inquiry went to a number of
members of governing boards and some presidents. The question was:
"At the moment, what are the one or two concerns uppermost in your
mind about higher education?"

The majority of respondents did not put problems of governance in
first place. First place went to finance, an emphasis that appears to support the critics of governing boards, that finances always come first. But
a close second was governance. Several respondents considered the faculty a more serious problem in governance than were students, particularly because faculty have been slow to take responsibility for change.
(Here it is timely to observe the prediction that the faculty would become the next target of attack by students.)

The next most notable point was the underlying complaint that both
board members and presidents have too little "time to think."

Obviously, financial problems of colleges and universities will grow; yet
in this brief correspondence—involving about half of the states and representative trustees and presidents—strikingly few spoke of the more fun-
damentally important issues of the allocation of resources and the rede-
sign of education. There was no notable difference between responses
from the public and the private sectors on this particular issue nor, for
that matter, on the issue of governance and student-faculty activism.

It appears that, until recently, if the campus was orderly and the books
balanced, trustees were unlikely to feel any great concern. This situation
resulted partly from the administrative practice of limiting the purview
of trustees to funds and property. Today, however, the heat of conflict
is felt in every part of the country and in virtually every type of institution, and the need for serious reconsideration is no longer debatable.
Hence the frequent assertion that the lay governing board is an anachronism. Hence the comment of Galbraith that boards which are supposed
to protect institutions from public pressures instead have become typically the conduits of these very pressures. Hence the growing notion that
the welfare of the institutions is understood and can be protected only
by a combination of students and faculty.

Should governing boards, then, become in effect chambers of deputies or constituent assemblies or some other type of representative body? Who should decide upon membership? How should the process of selection be revised? Whose is the paramount interest? That of current students? Current faculty? The public? And if the public interest is paramount, how should it be defined? By prospective employers? By donors? By legislative bodies?

AUTONOMY AND CONTINUITY

In the answer to the above questions, a prior decision must be made about the autonomy of the institution. Granted that every institution of learning had its beginnings in some form of special interest; yet every lasting and significant institution of learning has outgrown special interests, including those of the founders. True, institutions of learning must be responsive to contemporary needs and must not be self-serving; yet they cannot thrive if their autonomy is threatened or weakened. A balance between the two necessities is hard to maintain or even define, but the institution should make the decision.

Threats to autonomy arise from many sources. For the public group, legislative restrictions are threatened as regularly as the calendar turns. (This despite the prominence of alumni in the legislatures.) On the private side, donors, prospective donors, and the relatives of donors are ever present. And both sectors share pressures from dissident alumni, the press and other news media, professional organizations, patriotic groups, parents, commercial interests, and so on. Many of these pressures tend to balance out, but the administration and trustees are often exhausted by their dealings with those who press for attention while the institution's other constituents—faculty and students—go on their way, unregarding and perhaps unaware of the hazards to the institution.

There must also be concern about continuity, though no institutions should be continued simply for the sake of tradition. Institutional vitality and stability depend in large measure on a sense of continuity and a perspective beyond the immediate past or the immediate future. Since all social institutions, including those of higher learning, are structures of the society itself, there must be a demonstrable prudence in the management of their affairs.

As in other important enterprises, the long-range public interest should be represented by nonprofessionals. Professional groups have a poor record of self-correction—the clergy, the military, the physician-surgeons, and so on. (Note, for example, that hospital management has improved only as medical practitioners have given way to nonmedical hospital managers. A brief examination of this phenomenon alone sheds light on the comparable problem within the academy. Now hospital administrators themselves constitute a new force, and so it goes.)

Can, then, governing boards be designed to meet these apparently self-contradictory requirements? If the final voice in academic governance is to rest with representatives of the current students or the current faculty, how shall we deal with this conflict of interest? Governing boards should not represent special interests of any sort, student or faculty. Boards that carry provision for ex officio membership for the governors of the states and their principal cabinet members violate this principle. Alumni representation has a certain sentimental acceptance, but the rationale is not at all clear. The fact of election to a board by alumni per se guarantees perhaps a special interest and willingness to work, but the elective procedure does not guarantee good selection.

CAMPUS TENSIONS AND GOVERNING BOARDS: WHAT NOW?

Diagnosis, predictions, and recommendations for campus reforms have come in a mounting flood from every possible source in the last five years. The literature of higher education, general publications and the public press, radio and television, and the public platform have produced a glut of advice. Firm up the administration . . . Call the police . . . Crack down on the agitators . . . Screen out the visiting radicals . . . Shape up the faculty . . . Junk the governing boards . . .

Acknowledging the many comments already recorded about the special vulnerability of colleges and universities, where do we stand on the vexing question of the governing board?

First, the governing board must not meddle in the administration and must not assume the initiative unless every other alternative has been exhausted. What options remain open to governing boards to deal with the continuing problem of campus tensions and the continuing contest for control over institutional policy? At this point, one should shift attention from conflict on the campus back to the fundamentals of academic trusteeship, though this may be tantamount to saying that if a person stays in good health, he will not get sick.

Campus tensions, it now seems obvious, arose from one shortcoming among governing boards (with more than equal share among administrators): *failure to understand what was developing on the campus* (California and Columbia). These were *not failures of intelligence but failures of attention.*

Assuming that the presidents (and chief associates) and the governing boards should form a well-connected working unit, it appears that, in the rush of events, both governing boards and administrators have been diverted from their joint first duty—*to understand their situation.* Here is a serious test of the lay governing board: Should not trustees, or some of the trustees, show greater foresight and broader understanding than do the professionals? Inside this puzzle lies the key to the greater issue.

The new priority for governing boards is the question: Do we *understand* the current issues of the academy?

Next we ask, "How can anybody know?" True, nobody can certify to his complete understanding of any complicated matter. But one can certainly answer the corollary question: "Have we put our minds to the task?" Hindsight gives a negative.

Requisites of Educational Trusteeship

To improve performance of trustees in their functions, two new components must be added to the accepted functions: *more time and better judgment*. The recommendation that more time be spent on trusteeship is easy enough. But how much more? The amount of time required for educational trusteeship these days is related to other factors: reform of the agenda; improved staff for board functions; and the kinds of judgments expected.

Reform of the agenda has been long recommended. The requirement for board action to validate many detailed recommendations produces a cumbersome, sometimes overwhelming agenda, made up of matters of detail that lay trustees cannot be expected to judge. They rest on staff work, which can be tested in various ways but which must be trusted. If the board of trustees were to make serious business of such matters, the institution would grind to a halt. This condition, however, can certainly be corrected. The "rubber stamp" notion arises from the failure to construct an agenda suitable for the attention of a lay board. A considerable part of the typical agenda could be disposed of by a blanket motion covering a variety of subjects, provided work had been done beforehand by staff and board committees. The time thus saved could be turned to the consideration of major issues of policy which deserve the time and the judgment of governing boards.

Judgment is, of course, not related to mere intelligence or the expenditure of great amounts of time in preparation for board meetings. Like other such imponderables, good judgment is more easily recognized than described, and is certainly not available on requisition. Judgment on many issues of academic governance, moreover, is not related to the abstract "correctness" of a matter. Refer again to the "quasi-political" aspect of academic government. Acute judgment involves a sense of timeliness, the financial consequence, a refined sense of relationship between one new decision and a complex of other matters. Not least important, if the judgment proves wrong, is there the capacity to withdraw or change direction without too much loss? At this point we face another imponderable, the power of the board and administration (as a composite) to withstand adverse reactions or, on the contrary, to press successfully for carefully considered policies and practices sure to meet various levels of opposition, internally and externally.

Governing boards cannot, of course, exemplify the virtues of all the great men. What is suggested, however, is an essential to the welfare of any enterprise, most especially the academic venture, that is, a certain largeness of mind and of outlook. Here we come close to what is commonly understood by "statesmanship." This quality cannot be achieved by the simple decision that it should be so.

If it be agreed that time, the capacity to understand the basic issues, the capacity for good judgment, and a certain largeness of mind and outlook are essential, we not only must hope for a reform of the agenda and for improvement in staff work, but we must also ask how to find such a board.

First, no one should accept trusteeship unless he has confronted the requirement of time and has pledged himself to devote the necessary time.[7] Thus the board member must place academic trusteeship in the front rank of his commitments, to be grouped with very few others. Even so, no amount of knowledge of the institution and no volume of time on the job can compensate for poor judgment, a meddlesome spirit, a lack of experience, or a point of view restricted either by parochial interest or professional specialization. Be he ever so loyal, interested, dedicated, a person with those qualities will be a liability, a troublemaker.

Should the chairmanship of the board become a full-time, salaried position? These comments might seem to point that way, but the result would be only an inflation of titles. There can be but one chief executive. When the chief executive becomes the chairman, the lay trustee may become even less effective. Seeming parallels in business are deceptive. Adequate staffing for board work is another matter, noted earlier.

Now to the question of diversity of membership. Diversity should be simply a guarantee against the parochial or the specialized point of view. The diversity of professions represented will provide some variety in judgment and experience, but should not be confused with the notion that voluntary professional services should be sought by placing specialists on governing boards. Quite the contrary. Not merely to avoid scandal or exploitation but also to guarantee competent judgment, no trustee should gain professionally or financially from trusteeship.

The need for diversity among members of governing boards has recently been used as an argument in favor of younger trustees, in favor of faculty representation, in favor of student representation. This argu-

---

[7] One institution makes a practice of laying before the prospective trustee the time requirement and asks for a straightforward commitment. Fortunately, that institution can command the best talent among national leaders and can procure commitments of time not to be exceeded by commitments to any other voluntary activity.

ment overlaps another: that the governed (students and faculty) should have a voice in their government. The argument may have some validity in minor aspects of campus regulation but has small validity when applied to the ultimate function and purpose of the governing board: the exercise of final voice in determining institutional policy.

If the educational function should be the standard for judging all other institutional matters, the participation of students in institutional affairs should be judged primarily on the educational effect to be achieved. Potentially, student participation enhances the educational process by enlivenment of students themselves and, in consequence, by enlivenment of faculty, administration, and perhaps others. While it has become popular to talk about student and faculty participation on boards of trustees, such participation is both more useful and more important at other levels of campus operation. All important recommendations reaching the board result from considerable staff and committee work before presentation to the board. Adequate faculty and student involvement can be provided in a variety of ways without affecting the composition of the board: students and faculty can be granted representation on board committees; they can be involved in administrative and board committees; and committees of the faculty, the administration, and the board can be open to accredited observers, advisers, or consultants from a variety of sources.

What seems to be required is a dramatic move toward participation without a dangerous altering of the legal structure of the institution. While the present trend toward the inclusion of students on boards may have a generally good effect, it may also lead to a certain disenchantment with governance.[8]

Conclusions and Recommendations

With specific reference to current campus tensions, certain interim recommendations can be separated from others that are more fundamental. First, it is urgently suggested that boards of trustees and administrators agree upon interim devices for more openness and an improved sense of participation.

> Currently, if decision-making and policy-determination processes are characterized by openness and accountability, excessive concern for structure and process is reduced. To the extent student participation has been realized or that institutions have become responsive to the original student power concern, there is frequently a shift of emphasis

[8] "Student Power Revisited," a revision of the June 1968 Statement on Student Power prepared by the Ad Hoc Committee on Student Power, National Association of Student Personnel Administrators, *NASPA Journal,* January 1970, p. 127.

away from the procedural-structural matters toward the central issue of improving the quality of the learning process.[9]

This step requires no legal revisions but does call for ingenuity and the establishment of short-term committees on whatever topics of immediate concern may affect the peace of the campus. The conclusions and recommendations of such committees should be well publicized, and the final disposition of the recommendations by administration or board should also be publicized and thoroughly explained. Or, without commitments to permanency, committees of the board and of the administration can be periodically and systematically opened to groups having special interests at stake.

Further, the blight of "invisibility" so often attributed to both board and administration should be removed; for this purpose there are available the most elementary techniques of public relations, provided they are not patently used as mere techniques.

Growth in numbers of students and consequently in numbers of administrators has tended to separate the upper reaches of administration and policy making from faculty and students and helps stimulate the complaints about depersonalization. A good deal of campus unrest may mask that students (intellectually advanced as they are, but emotionally immature as they inevitably are) suffer from the lack of simple human contact with the center of the authority that controls a good part of their lives. Not at issue here are parietal rules or even the tradition of in loco parentis; these problems would require attention in any case. What is meant results from the sheer invisibility of those who bear the greatest responsibility, perhaps the greatest authority, perhaps the greatest power. Frivolous though it may seem, improvement could well be achieved by a systematic program for greater visibility of the president and at least members of the executive committee of governing boards among students and faculty.

Token appearances here and there are not sufficient—the typical meetings of committees and of student representatives in the office of the president or the social engagement with its pleasantries (often superficial and strained). Rather, a well-planned program must provide brief, informal exposures of the president, other administrative officers, and key members of the board in various places and under various circumstances, week by week, month by month, throughout the college year,

---

[9] A student board member at one of the large state universities is quoted as being worried about "getting removed from the students." Other young trustees are reported as concluding that membership on the board may not be the most effective way to influence university policy, less effective than membership on committees of the faculty or administrations whose proposals are presented to the trustees for ratification. One young student trustee held the view: "Actually the board is sort of superfluous. But I don't think it is necessarily bad. Policy making is left up to those who have closer contact to students and faculty." *Washington Star*, Dec. 28, 1969.

at events on the campus. Most of these should involve reasonably serious discussions of campus affairs. Such a plan is not easily carried out; the president and others will have to forgo something else in favor of this activity.

All these suggestions are superficial aspects of more fundamental reforms in governance. If constructive and fundamental reforms can be made, there is reasonable prospect that campus tensions can be lowered and the educational process can be invigorated. Among the recommendations below, some concern governing boards; others deal with a wider range of academic governance.

1. *Nominations for trusteeship.* In both public and private institutions, evidence points to serious faults in the process for recruiting members of governing boards. In public institutions, the selection process is largely controlled by the office of the governor, with a few exceptions where trustees for higher education are chosen in the regular election processes of the states. (Many governors find competition for membership on boards of higher education keener than for other appointments, even though they are the only distinctly unpaid public appointments available through the governor.) Many excellent trustees have come into volunteer public service by this route, though nothing in the system itself encourages favorable results. Suggestions for improvement have been offered over the years, but legislatures are slow to revise procedures. In any event, it should be possible for governors to authorize a process that would involve at least the equivalent of a public panel on nominations, the panel being guided by published criteria. Governors with foresight and courage might take the initiative to remove the virus of ex officio membership of state officials (including the governor) on governing boards. And much could be done by abandoning political payoff at the expense of education.

As a step toward improving recruitment for both public and private institutions, a standing committee on nominations (or its equivalent) should maintain a list of potential trustees. A fairly long-term screening process should then be applied, which, over time, would include some involvement in higher education through such activities as service on various commissions appointed by the officials of the university.

To bring afresh to a board of trustees or regents a substantial minority or, worse, a majority of persons utterly new to the task creates hazards and difficulties that institutions should be spared.

The suggestions about public institutions have even greater applicability to the private sector, where wide discretion prevails in the selection of trustees. The casual, fortuitous, sometimes perverse selection of trustees for colleges and universities is an easy target for critics. It is not statistically true that all trustees are wealthy or occupy positions of great personal influence. The appearance, however, is that trustees are recruited with other objectives in view than the potential capacity of the persons chosen to exert long-term leadership. Thus, increased cynicism about boards.

2. *Limitation of term.* Just as youth is no guarantee of special virtue, age is no guarantee of special wisdom, and age itself should not be a dominant factor in eligibility. Age spread may be good simply for its own sake. It is doubtful that any trustee, young or old, should serve longer than about ten years, and it seems almost axiomatic that turnover be required at some point between eight and twelve years of service, with at least a year's lapse for reappointment.

3. *Evaluation.* This analysis has been directed to the complexities and importance of education in American society. It follows, then, that those upon whom rests the legal responsibility for the conduct of higher education should themselves invite periodic evaluation. Although self-evaluation is part of this process, outside consultants should be retained to report to the board on its own performance. Such a periodic inside-outside audit of performance could tone up the effectiveness of the central governing board.

4. *Statement of mission.* A great weakness throughout higher education is probably the lack of clear statements of institutional purpose. Everyone is so preoccupied with a particular aspect of the institution that few have a useful concept of the whole. Whatever guiding concepts may operate are therefore largely not discussed and may be ascertained only by inference. Certainly, the usual catalog statement is inapplicable.

I have long favored a plan that could provide maximum flexibility and minimum tampering with the structure of authority. Without reference to charter or bylaws, let the administration report in the spring of each year, both to the board and to the campus community, a plan of operation for the ensuing year. This plan should give first priority to those matters requiring the most urgent attention, as seen by the president and his chief associates, including trustees. The topmost matters could be given projections of time, manpower, and budget required for study and report, varying from three months to three years. This announced plan of operation would include special provision for the study and resolution of matters of uppermost concern to the particular institution, *without immediately changing the normal operations.*

Such a plan does not require changes in fixed structures; it does permit periodic revision of program priorities, budget allocations, and planning priorities. It also provides opportunity for the widest participation horizontally and vertically within the institution and invites serious, productive participation by those competent to participate. At the same time, it has the advantage of not freezing the administration into some pattern later to be regarded as either sacred or offensive. In short, impulsive changes in the legal structure of authority can promise little improvement and a great deal of instability. But an open and orderly approach to important issues of the moment makes possible a certain flexibility, participation, and foresightedness, while maintaining the regular structure of authority.

This suggestion for preparing, making, and announcing policy will not satisfy those who yearn for legal standing in "the system." To them I can say that no form of representation has risen above the quality of the persons involved or their devotion to duty. And the more complex the system of representation, the less promise of success. The suggestion is offered not as a panacea, but as a prototype. It has some elements of program budgeting, some elements of long-range planning, but most of all it involves open disclosure and constructive involvement of able participants. The details of identifying and selecting appropriate participants have been purposely omitted.

In student-faculty relations the goal is to win the commitment of the uncommitted majority, not to forfeit them to the radical, nihilistic, anarchistic minority. The route to this achievement is not through concessions under confrontation, but is the enlistment of students and faculty in a total program formulated by and acceptable to the principal parties. Such a goal does not necessitate politicizing the campus or wrongfully changing the locus of authority. It does require leadership that will heighten common aspirations for a freshly vigorous intellectual community.

Inasmuch as students and members of governing boards are both novices in the field of education, but since both bear responsibility for the success of the enterprise, there would be value in some means whereby both could acquaint themselves with the fundamentals of the history and the philosophies of education, at least in a semiformal fashion. At the moment the two parties are standing at a distance apart, the one tending to hurl insults and recriminations, the other tending to defend something that is but dimly grasped. A prerequisite to the annual report of priorities and scheduling would be, of course, a moratorium on confrontation, demands, disturbances, and seizures. Although experience is somewhat limited in these unusual undertakings, enough is available to lend encouragement. Progress depends upon the kind of questions governing boards will choose to raise. And raising the right questions may be their most important function.

RALPH D. HETZEL, JR.

A Constitutional Review
of Role

TRUSTEES OF universities and colleges suffer great frustration and discontent because they do not know clearly what their responsibilities are and how to do whatever it is they should be doing. The peculiarly American device of the governance of universities and colleges by boards of trustees requires a reexamination, a kind of constitutional review of the role of the trustees in the governance of their institutions. This review should include not only the internal constituency—students, faculty, and administration—but also external relations with alumni, legislatures, governments, money givers, and many other groups. Much of the existing potential of campus tensions, so far as it relates to things the university can or cannot do, arises from a constitutional confusion of responsibility.

Sorely needed also is a new constitutional structure within the university that reflects today's conditions. The board of trustees has the primary responsibility of initiating fundamental constitutional reexaminations in each university. Though frequently ill-equipped to do so because of a shortage of time, experience, ability, and youthful energy, the board cannot evade this obligation.

The first question it might honestly ask is, Does the university need a

» » « «

Ralph D. Hetzel, Jr., Executive Vice-President, Motion Picture Association of America, is a Trustee of the Pennsylvania State University.

board of trustees? There might somewhere be a board ready to say no and thus hasten an earnest self-examination in many other places.

It is clear that trustees are expected to choose presidents with appropriate advice and consent and help raise money, privately or politically. But beyond these boundaries lie disagreement and uncertainty, and the tensions inherent in a situation in which trustees are uncertain about whether or not they should take *or accept* responsibility are obvious.

The tripartite statement of 1966 [1] launched a move to find consensus on appropriate responsibilities and powers in the government of universities and colleges. A few institutions have since then made or considered making changes in their trustee structure, largely under the stimulus of student turmoil. An honest judgment of today's situation, however, must admit that few institutions have yet made a searching basic reassessment of the appropriate functions of their boards and their relationship, in a constitutional sense, to other constituents of the university.

Efforts to set up guidelines of trustees' functions specific enough to be useful must be approached gingerly, with due deference to the diversity of American higher education and to its traditional independence. Great value could come from a national constitutional convention for universities, which would devise concrete guidelines to be used by the institutions. Such a convention would have to be followed by a series of constitutional reviews in each institution, each measuring its own situation against the guidelines and against its own needs. The differences between trustee tasks in publicly supported and private universities are great and must be recognized.

Some propositions I would want considered in an examination of trustee function are:

1. The trustee function (if there is one at all) should be restricted to few and fundamental matters.

2. The trustees should accept the fact that, although they are the nominal source of constitutional power in universities, they are not organized or equipped to deal with the complexity of educational administration. They should reject the temptation to evade their basic responsibilities by being drawn into the details of building construction and fiscal management, among other things.

3. The trustees must organize themselves soundly. Boards usually suffer from an extraordinary looseness in operating structure—both a constitutional and political problem, involving structure and the role of the leadership.

4. Each board should have a clear, carefully written constitution or by-

---

[1] *Statement on Government of Colleges and Universities,* by American Association of University Professors, American Council on Education, Association of Governing Boards of Universities and Colleges.

laws, to be reexamined periodically. These should define the board's function, the functions of its committees, and the nature of its actions.

5. Terms of trustees should be arranged so that there could be a reasonable turnover without destroying continuity. So-called life-time trustees do not seem to be justified. If a restriction on the number of terms served does not deal with superannuation, some upper limit should be put on age.

6. How trustees should be chosen is another urgent issue. Clearly alumni, especially recent alumni, should be effectively represented.

In public universities the appointment of trustees by the state governor with a proper judicial aura is preferable to a public election. But the inclusion of governors on boards of trustees is usually not helpful. The governor himself is put in an untenable position. He must make fiscal and policy decisions involving many other public institutions, often with conflicting interests. If he is on a board and does not participate, he may have to accept responsibility for matters he did not act on or consider. From the institution's point of view, the governor's role is either one of too great influence or, more usually, of no participation at all. For the well-being of everybody, governors, or their surrogates, should not be on university boards.

7. In my view, students should not be placed on the board. The student viewpoint and interests are much better handled, in relation to the board, by effective liaison with student leaders in association with the administration, and by arranging for the election of recent graduates to the board. One attractive possibility is to include certain elected student leaders automatically as members of the board upon their graduation. In this way the student experience and knowledge are made available without bringing to the board a student leader with a political responsibility to represent his constituency.

8. Similarly, there are persuasive reasons not to include faculty representatives on the board of trustees. If they are put on the board, they will be under great temptation to bring the board matters that should be handled by the faculty alone or by the administration and the faculty.

9. The absence of students and faculty from the board of trustees requires, however, that special efforts be made to keep an active liaison between the trustees and these groups for the purpose of information and understanding. Some form of all-university council may be helpful in this regard.

10. A constitutional decision of the first urgency is the broadening and sharpening of definitions of the powers and responsibilities that should be given to students and their organizations. The new significance of university education in students' lives and the time that many students spend in higher education compel the universities to give the students both greater authority and greater freedom. On the other hand, there is

a need to define afresh the areas appropriate for the exercise of authority, discipline, and order between the universities and the civil authorities and between university custom and civil law.

11. More important than the student's voice in discipline and order is his voice in determining the quality and freedom of his education. But to say that the intelligence and commitment of American students qualify them for a greater voice, determining individually as well as collectively what their educational needs may be, is not to say that the faculty should abdicate its responsibilities for educational content, quality, and discipline.

12. Meetings of boards should be planned with great care. If possible, most meetings should be full meetings of the board even at the expense of dropping or restricting the use of an executive committee. It would be better to have smaller boards that could meet frequently in full than to have large boards that meet, almost uselessly, once or twice a year. Certainly most boards should meet at least six times a year. Trustees should be relieved of membership if they cannot attend a reasonable number of meetings.

13. The most crucial function of the board must be to make sure that the president selected is the best who could be obtained. Much of the effectiveness of the board will depend upon the president and the relationship he builds with the board.

14. Aside from choosing the president, it is most necessary for the board to make certain that the top administrative structure of the university is adequate to the enormously complex responsibilities involved. The board should be well equipped to apply modern management techniques in devising a sound administrative structure. Sound administration means not only central structure but, most important, effective decentralization of university functions, to re-create under modern conditions close relations between students and faculty, the loss of which has fanned student discontent.

15. Trustees should consider whether a full-time chairman of the board might be employed to handle, say, external relations and financial matters, leaving academic and internal affairs to the president. Most presidents are far too overburdened by fund raising, political pursuit of appropriations, and public relations.

16. The president and other top executives should be given full trust and support by the trustees, who have the right to expect it to be reciprocated. The trustees also should expect the president to make the decisions he should make and not use the board as a scapegoat. Nor should he flood it with a mass of detail, distracting it from essentials.

17. Asking the right question until it gets satisfactorily answered is perhaps the most effective board function on major policy. It should expect the administration to be scrupulous in providing it with full reports

on what is happening at the university, good or bad. These reports should be devised, not to justify the administration's course, but to make an honest appraisal.

18. The trustees of a contemporary university must be most insistent that the university have a soundly based, long-range plan, constantly revised and encompassing not only fiscal and physical projections but also the best possible thinking about the changing education to be offered.

MORTON A. RAUH

Toward Improving Trusteeship

THE HYPOTHESIS from which I write is that trustees are not a primary factor in creating campus tensions;[1] rather, by doing certain things and failing to do others, they do not exert their full potential to alleviate or forestall tensions. The specifics I propose here, however, would improve campus governance even in the absence of the current tensions.

Most boards, it seems to me, tend to react passively, aggressively, petulantly, cooperatively, but almost never constructively, imaginatively, or sensitively. To attribute these failures solely to the board of trustees is a gross oversimplification, for it is properly the role of the president to be a party to determining the board's style. He must share responsibility for shortcomings of the trustees. The specifics which follow, therefore, are descriptive of institutional change, although they focus on a distinctive part of the structure—the board of trustees.

Diversity: There is something almost pathetic in the current rush toward opening board membership to the youngest available person—some-

---

[1] The notable exceptions to this statement tend to lie in atypical board intrusions or in situations involving conflict of political and academic interests.

» » « «

Morton A. Rauh, Vice-President, Antioch College, is author of The Trusteeship of Colleges and Universities.

one either in school or newly out. It should not have taken our survey,[2] which showed that there are almost twice as many trustees over seventy as there are under forty, to establish the skewed character of the age distribution. To redress this situation by picking one or two trustees in, or just out of, school is tokenism in its most foolish form. About all such a move can accomplish is to lower the average age; it will do precious little for the median.

A more significant flaw in this move to youth is that it obscures the major problem of board composition, which is the lack of diversity. Age is but one measure of diversity. I propose, therefore, that boards break with the stereotype that trustees must have (*a*) money, (*b*) experience in business, and (*c*) wide participation in community enterprises. Diversity can best be measured by attitude, sensitivity, and background. With these kinds of criteria, diversity of age will almost certainly follow.

Enlarged franchise: There is a great deal of interest in the issue of seating faculty and students on the board of trustees, a practice that would introduce the element of conflict of interest. Further, the debate diverts attention from the need for a much more fundamental change: the need to replace the widespread practice in private institutions of giving to the board itself the right to fill all its vacancies except those assigned to alumni.

The franchise should be enlarged, but more to the point would be the right for students and faculty to choose some number of trustees, even though candidates were required to come from outside the institutional community. The extension of this right states the essential interest of the students and faculty in the board proceedings. A revised method of selection involving an enlarged franchise would enhance the stature of the board in the eyes of the academic community which it heads and at the same time the new selecting constituencies would diversify the membership.

Open meetings: In a community which holds so fiercely the concept of open inquiry, the practice of most boards to meet in closed sessions is strangely alien. If the purpose of a board is to deal with substantive issues, it is indeed odd that the very segments of the educational community most immediately affected by the outcome of these deliberations are barred from attendance. The "board room" concept—in many cases taken from the corporate model—is singularly inappropriate to the educational institution. Assuming the right of executive session for privileged matters, it is hard to see why fully open discussions can be anything but helpful. A more broadly constituted board could function with greater impact in open meetings.

---

[2] Rauh, *The Trusteeship of Colleges and Universities* (New York: McGraw-Hill Book Co., 1969).

The open agenda: The corollary of the open meeting is the open agenda. Typical agenda, carefully machined by the president and the board chairman, offer little assurance that the major concerns of the campus will receive a proper airing. I speculate with some interest on what board meetings might be like if at least some portions of meetings covered topics selected by the entire academic community. Certainly, meetings could be much more significant if the agenda were formed with some input from the campus community.

Involvement and evaluation: Midst the uncertainties about what trustees should and should not do, there is one fixed point of agreement: trustees are responsible for the selection of the president and, if need be, for firing him. What is much less well understood, and all too frequently ignored, is the function that lies between hiring and firing—the function of evaluation.

Evaluation, properly performed, constitutes continuous criticism of the institution's management. When sensitively and sensibly performed, it is both constructive and supportive. Unfortunately, in far too many cases trustees have such a mortal horror of searching for a new president that they tend to back the incumbent with a blind faith that serves neither the president nor the institution.

Most boards are not in the position to perform qualitative evaluation because they are too little involved in the affairs of the institution. The typical trustee, who spends about eighty hours per year on college business, largely in formal board and committee meetings, is hardly in the position to judge the quality of stewardship of the president and his staff. A different kind of involvement is clearly indicated—one that will call for more time for some and different activities for others. The need for more sophisticated evaluation is more likely to be met with greater involvement. This goal has a better chance to be achieved if at least some of the membership is drawn from outside the small circle of "eligibles" as presently defined by wealth and position.

Self-study: Many trustees are frustrated in their roles, and many are complacent. Neither attitude is likely to be based on a critical examination. A real need in our institutions is to devise means that will permit trustees to consider from time to time what their function is and how it relates to the total governance structure. When only 2 percent of the trustees think that students should have a major role in selecting the speaker at their own commencement while 29 percent would give that power to the administration, I suggest that some reexamination of the decision-making process is in order. What better place to start that examination than at the board level itself?

Whatever may be accomplished by changes of the kind outlined above and other changes as well, the board's operation must be scrutinized by periodic evaluation and self-study.

E. WILLIAM ZIEBARTH

Trustees in the
Academic Revolution

A Board of Regents, representative of the university constituency, is more important now than at any time in the history of higher education.

A business executive

Boards of trustees and regents are an anachronism, and should be abolished, if not immediately, certainly over the next five years!

A graduate student

It's about time regents helped constituencies understand the revolutionary changes taking place in academic life and not simply interpret what they think are our wishes to the academic community.

An attorney

Students and faculties are now so irresponsible and militant that trustees have an obligation to demonstrate who holds the actual power. We hold it, not the faculty, not the president, not the students, and it is time we started making that clear!

Trustee of an Eastern college

The Trustees demand that the president expel the student editor and assistant editors [of the student daily newspaper] and place the remainder of the

» » « «

E. William Ziebarth is Dean, College of Liberal Arts, University of Minnesota, and a Trustee of Macalester College.

211

staff on probation for publishing an obscene, tasteless, offensive, and un-Christian paper.

Chairman, board of trustees, a private college

THESE QUOTATIONS document the often sharp and growing conflict between trustees and students, trustees and faculty, and occasionally trustees and institutional administrators. An informal and limited study made by the author could supply other querulous, truculent, puzzled, or totally disenchanted reactions from all factions involved.

Regents and trustees are understandably puzzled by criticism from both their constituencies and the academic communities they believe themselves to be serving. Boards are mostly made up of able, intelligent, and dedicated men and women who recognize the importance of higher education and earnestly wish to improve its quality. They are, overall, sensitive to the wishes of their constituencies as they interpret them, whether the institution is public or private, and many have made personal and often heavy sacrifices for the institutions on whose boards they serve. They wish to maintain high quality in teaching and research.

Recent studies confirm some common assumptions about trustees. They are distinguished and "successful" people, usually more than fifty years old, who tend to be wealthy and are disproportionately likely to be alumni. Such characteristics suggest one source of the current abrasions. The trustees respect and wish to preserve the system that produced them —the social, economic, and academic system. In response to this assertion, one regent said, "Does that mean that success should be penalized? Ought we carefully to select a few failures who therefore resent the system and want to use the universities to change it?" The answer of course is no. But there are many kinds of success, and boards of regents or trustees should hardly be so constituted that one requirement for service is to profess inexperience or ignorance about what one is to "govern."

This oversimplification points to the desirability of the increasingly common practice of including on the board a distinguished and thoughtful educational leader from another institution. This member can, within the structure of the board itself, interpret the academic community and its incredibly rapid changes to other board members as an equal, examining issues without the hazards faced by the institution's president. It might also prove useful to appoint men and women from other professions that are related to the academic world at least as closely as is business. All this suggests that across the nation we have not looked carefully at other sources of wisdom and experience in academic governance.

Sources of Tension

Both administrators and board members still subscribe generally to the view that major functions of a board are to act somehow as protector of the academic community against the pressures of the marketplace and to persuade legislators, foundations, and private donors to provide support for the institution. Ingraham's study, for example, shows that presidents tend to view the functions of trustees as somewhat limited and concentrated on protection, fund-raising activities, campus planning, and the selection of the president.[1] Some presidents also point to the desirability of trustees bringing to institutions an externally generated viewpoint, but, somewhat surprisingly, relatively few presidents in my sample argue that trustees must also translate an internally generated set of views to the external constituency.

Structure is of course essential to survival of the institution. Yet there may be basic—though often unrecognized—conflicts between the academic community's assumptions about the nature of a free community of scholars and the assumption of trustees, outside constituencies, and sometimes administrations that the source of power and order actually resides in an identifiable body, usually the regents or trustees.

Another source of tension between trustees and elements of the academic community lies in a natural but relatively new development of a loose coalition of students, teaching assistants and associates, and junior faculty, against what seems to them to be the Establishment—senior faculty, administration, and trustees. If, further, junior faculty in some of the major academic institutions are "softer" in the basic disciplines and are using the disciplines and the institutions as instruments of social change, the conflict will inevitably grow unless, at the very least, trustees and constituencies approve what is happening. Similarly, if one of the frequently unarticulated objectives of the university is that of critic of society, perhaps the basic conflict was made explicit recently by the New York state official who, believing he understood the nature of the conflict more clearly than most, argued publicly that trustees and regents must serve the function of protecting society *from* the university, not the other way around.

In the context of tensions among young faculty, it is significant, as Hodgkinson has pointed out, that faculty tenure is now going to much younger men. If a man, for example, receives tenure as an associate professor at thirty-three, he can look forward to only one more major reward from ages thirty-three to sixty-five, that is, promotion to full profes-

---

[1] Mark H. Ingraham, *The Mirror of Brass: The Compensation and Working Conditions of College and University Administrations* (Madison: University of Wisconsin Press, 1960).

sorial rank. If professorship comes at thirty-eight, there may still be a chance of a regents' professorship or a distinguished professorship, but there is no immediate, visible, and attainable goal in terms of reward other than the annual salary increment. That this hiatus in rewards contributes to faculty restlessness in the middle years is not to suggest that trustees must drastically alter the reward system, but it does suggest that it be examined.[2]

Perhaps the most frequent negative generalization about boards of regents and trustees is that they try to impose business management procedures on the academic community, a move that inevitably causes resistance when it fails to take account of the differences between the two kinds of social institutions. The implications of the experience for trustee–academic community relationship are obvious.

Thus far, the seating of students with regents or trustees seems to have caused as much tension as it has eliminated. Presidents tend to feel threatened by having students sit with trustees, both because they are less free to communicate confidentially and candidly and because administrators cannot rationalize refusals to respond to student demands by implying that, while *they* would be willing to act, the trustees would never approve. The administrator is in a difficult position, as Hodgkinson has said, when a student making a request can say, "But I talked with the chairman of the board yesterday, and he said the board will be willing, if the administration and faculty would support the idea." Recently, one articulate regent of a state university argued publicly that faculty and students are already adequately represented in academic governance and should therefore not serve on boards which "control" their own institutions.

Academic communities seem increasingly to believe that the trustee power should derive from the population being governed. Seeley has pointed to this factor in the conflict without at the same time suggesting that *all* such powers should derive from the "governed" population,[3] perhaps because such segmentation of clearly affected populations is impossible.

Spencer has differentiated between the regent and the trustee by pointing out that the regent is usually the watchdog of the public, especially the taxpayer, whereas the trustee is the watchdog of the university facing outward toward the world and presumably protecting the institution by trying to interpret it to the larger community.[4] Many would be reluctant to agree to the first definition, however, if it implies that the regent

---

[2] Harold Hodgkinson, "Alternatives and Campus Governance," unpublished list and verbal report to the Council of Colleges of Arts and Sciences (Berkeley: Center for Research and Development in Higher Education).

[3] John R. Seeley, "The Trustees/Regents," *The University in America*, report of a convocation (Santa Barbara: Center for the Study of Democratic Institutions, 1967).

[4] Lyle Spencer, in "The Trustees/Regents," *The University in America*.

has no outward responsibility. In the same panel discussion Parten reviews the legal powers of governing boards of state universities in such a way that it seems clear that typically boards cannot fulfill their legal obligations or act to the limits of their legal authority.[5] For example, the standard legal function of selecting and appointing the president is no longer regarded in any major American university to be exclusively a regent or trustee matter. Student and faculty committees almost everywhere work with regents in this increasingly awesome task.

The Hartnett study points out that more than two-thirds of the trustees studied favor a screening process for all campus speakers and that about half believe that students punished by local authorities off campus should be further disciplined by the college.[6] The 1968 example of the Regents of the University of California who voted to withhold certain college credits and the reaction of the academic senate at Berkeley are too familiar to be detailed here. Such cases make regent-community tensions inevitable.

The finding that trustees generally favor a hierarchical system in which decisions are made at the top and passed down will surprise no observer of the academic scene. It is somewhat more revealing, however, that more than 50 percent of a large sample of trustees believe that faculty and students should not have authority to make decisions about a list of issues which are largely academic, and that 63 percent feel that the faculty should not have major authority in the appointment of their dean. (Being dean or president is tough enough *with* support from both faculty and trustees.)

Efforts to Reduce Tensions

Because an increasing number of trustees and a significant segment of academic communities recognize the nature and perhaps even the cause of conflicts mentioned here, significant steps are being taken to reduce tensions. The efforts of Chancellor Roger Heyns, for example, to put members of the Board of Regents through cram sessions to acquaint them with student, faculty, and administrative problems, as well as with institutional objectives as viewed internally, are widely believed to have been helpful in preventing even more serious conflict at Berkeley.

Presidents, chancellors, academic vice-presidents, and deans have, during the very recent past, been meeting with trustees in information sessions in public and private institutions, often at the request of trustees themselves. Efforts to have trustee committees work with faculty committees in two dozen or more private colleges studied resulted in signif-

[5] Jubal Parten, in "The Trustees/Regents."
[6] Rodney T. Hartnett, *College and University Trustees: Their Backgrounds, Roles, and Educational Attitudes* (Princeton, N.J.: Educational Testing Service, 1969).

icant trustee recognition of the complex nature of academic problems not previously faced.

Davis argues that trustees have an obligation to set a new tempo and a new tone in colleges and universities and to establish policies which will, step by step, lead to measurable performance achievements. He refers indirectly to the administrative accountability principle recently emphasized by Roger Heyns and Kingman Brewster and provides illustrations of trustee leadership in setting new academic patterns. One of these illustrations, although it involves the familiar theme of significant institutional giving, deals with a trustee at Rensselaer Polytechnic Institute who proposed and financed a "project reward" system for testing and demonstrating innovations in the teaching-learning process. The president of Rensselaer reports that it not only improved the teaching-learning process but also saved at least a million dollars a year.

Davis urges each trustee to visit a neighboring institution or two, spend time discussing innovative ideas in depth, and use these experiences as springboards for trustee discussion and analysis, presumably leading to greater trustee understanding of methods of innovation and procedures for improved trustee–academic community relations.[7]

There are serious dangers in direct trustee participation in educational innovation. The writer, while serving on a trustee committee of a college of which he was not at that time actually a trustee but in effect a consultant, was told at his first meeting: "We believe that individual members of the board should visit classes in the college and do so on a regular schedule in order to learn what is going on and to demonstrate our interest in the improvement of instruction." When I suggested that this might be viewed as a form of implied supervision and would not be popular with certain faculty members, a few trustees agreed; others were astonished. They pointed out that their motive was to understand the educational problems facing the institution and to get to know the faculty better. They felt that the visits would be regarded as an expression of support. But trustee participation in faculty discussions, community council meetings, joint sessions with students, and planned meetings with faculty are one thing; a series of unannounced (or even announced) classroom visitations is quite another.

Since virtually all recent studies show that the trustee is typically almost completely unfamiliar with the literature of higher education, the planned distribution of materials to board members with scheduled brief discussions and evaluations of the materials distributed has begun to have impact in scattered situations. In some cases, administrations have assigned a research assistant to make summaries available to board mem-

---

[7] Paul H. Davis, *A Trustee Speaks on Innovation,* Philanthropic Paper, No. 15 (New York: John Price Jones Co., 1969).

bers, who are understandably too busy to do much homework. At the very least, memoranda and recommendations should flow regularly from administrations to trustees and regents and copies of materials or summaries should be sent when possible.

Some Examples

A few attempts at solutions to the "trustee problem" are drastic. Hodgkinson illustrates the extreme by citing the suggestion made that the office of president be eliminated entirely and a full-time chairman of the board, who becomes the chief executive officer of the institution, be substituted.[8] This, some argue, eliminates the concept of the chairman of the board as an "absentee landlord" and reduces the conflict concerning who actually runs the institution. (Incidentially, the number of boards having student representatives at meetings is reported by Hodgkinson to number 184, and 13 actually have student representatives on the board. The Board of Education for the State of California now has a student member, although, as this paper is written, he is without vote.)

Since some of the suspicion between legislators and university administrations (and, occasionally, between trustees and presidents) may be based on presidential inexperience with financial matters, experiments in reordering administration are also being tried, although somewhat cautiously. At one university, for example, the board voted to appoint a chief financial officer, who does not report to the president at all, but rather communicates directly with the board. Part of his function is apparently to interpret the financial problems to the constituency of the university, and presumably he is chosen with these skills in mind. So open an invitation to divisiveness must have been decided upon only after the most careful consideration and will seem to many observers of doubtful wisdom.

At Antioch, the trustees have given the community council the legal power to govern the institution. The trustees have therefore made themselves virtually powerless, although what would happen in case of flagrant misuses of what the trustees regard as the functions of the community council is still unclear. Many colleges are attempting an extraordinarily detailed and careful codification of function, power, and authority of boards of trustees as well as of academic administrators. While this would appear to fill a significant need, some experience suggests to those who have been studying it that careful codification does not necessarily result in mutual trust or high morale, although it may eliminate some of the misperceptions about where and when decisions are actually made. At Waterloo in Ontario, a single governing board, with student, faculty, ad-

---

[8] "Alternatives and Campus Governance."

ministrative, and lay membership, has been established as the ultimate governing authority. A study of faculty membership on boards shows that representation from the institution is still relatively rare, though it is no longer uncommon to see an eminent person from one institution serving another.

The establishment of trustee committees to interact with students and faculty is, in many places, meeting with some success. Faculty, especially, often express genuine surprise at the interest and concern of trustees not only for the institution but also for students and faculty and their welfare. More astonishing to students particularly is the evidence that trustees do not expect to manage the academic or personal lives of either faculty or students.

The Regents of the University of Minnesota in 1963 issued what has become a widely known and respected formal statement on academic freedom. It has, in the intervening years, been reproduced and widely distributed to alumni, faculty, students, and others and has been reassuring because it is a clear and meaningful document. The academic community is assured of the support of the Regents on issues of academic freedom; the larger community understands the Regents' definitions of such freedoms and the reasons for the definition.

One more example may be worth mentioning: Laird Bell, a lawyer and businessman, as chairman of the Board of Trustees of the University of Chicago (he also served on the boards of Carleton and Harvard), made public on behalf of the Chicago board statements differentiating the academic from the business community and helping each understand the other. The statements were also published and widely distributed. He said, for example:

> A university is, unlike a business, not an organization of employees responsible to a hierarchy of bosses, but merely a loose collection of individual scholars. This is and always has been the essence of a university. It is a community of scholars. . . . A man enters university life because he wants to teach or to do research or both. To do a good job he must have freedom to go his own way. . . . The head of a university cannot give orders. A scholar must be free to think and to say what he thinks. . . . This nation was founded by dissenters. If the voices of dissent are hushed the life of democracy is crushed. Freedom of thought is not just an indulgence of a few professors. If freedom is extinguished in universities it is on its way out everywhere.[9]

Long-range planning committees, growing out of central planning, are being set up in many colleges to include trustee, administrative, faculty, and student membership, and the resulting discussions of objectives and directions appear, if nothing more, to demonstrate to each of these groups

---

[9] Laird Bell, address before the Citizens Board of the University of Chicago, 1958.

the enormous complexity of the academic world in which and for which they are doing the planning. Relatively few states, however, have gone as far as Kentucky, which now requires by law, according to Hodgkinson's study, that student and faculty representation on the governing policy boards of all state institutions is required (it is not required that they have a vote). The resistance to the inclusion of alumni representatives as such on boards of trustees and regents continues, but this seems insignificant from the alumni point of view since many boards tend to be self-selecting and include a disproportionate number of alumni. The criticism is likely to be of too much alumni representation rather than too little.

The institutional loyalty that once was a part of collegiate life has been eroded not only by the new mobility but also by noninstitutional grant systems and the incredibly rapid and revolutionary changes of the past five years. The trustee who holds strong feelings of institutional loyalty, particularly if he is also an alumnus, understandably finds both student and faculty attitudes on this matter a source of alienation. Efforts to share with trustees the history and reasons for the change have, in at least a half dozen instances, reassured concerned trustees.

Definitional disputes about what constitutes an academic and what a nonacademic matter are inevitable. A regent of a major state university, presenting a paper to a group of academic deans, pointed out that the regents of his institution regarded the decision to change the normal teaching load from 9 to 7.1 hours without direct consultation with the regents a violation of the principle that major fiscal decisions were not to be made without such consultation. He pointed out that it may or may not have been a proper decision, but that its fiscal implications were obvious, and that the issue should have been cleared with the board of regents rather than presumed by administration and faculty to be an academic matter only and therefore in the hands of the academic senate.

Nothing has been included here about improper use of the trustee role to influence individual student admissions, building decisions, and the like. Flagrant misuse of regents' power is rare, and student-faculty suspicion seldom grows from this source.

In summary, no simple redefinition of the role of the trustee or regent seems likely to reduce significantly the abrasions that are almost certain to increase during the next decade. Perhaps no judicious local application of the mixtures suggested here can do much to reduce them. Failure to consider changes in the system of representation underlying the selection of boards of regents and trustees is, however, certain to lead to a conflict of unmeasured dimensions.

AMERICAN COUNCIL ON EDUCATION

LOGAN WILSON, *President*

The American Council on Education, founded in 1918, is a *council* of educational organizations and institutions. Its purpose is to advance education and educational methods through comprehensive voluntary and cooperative action on the part of American educational associations, organizations, and institutions.

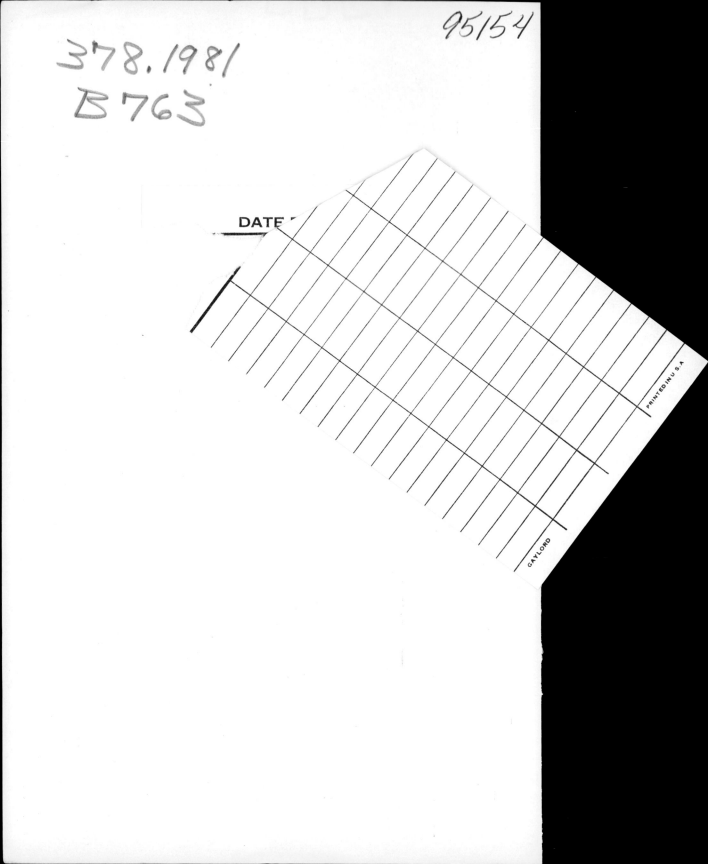

DATE

GAYLORD

PRINTED IN U.S.A